Ottoman Culture and the Project of Modernity

Ottoman Culture and the Project of Modernity

Reform and Translation in the Tanzimat Novel

Edited by Monica M. Ringer and Etienne E. Charrière

I.B. TAURIS
LONDON • NEW YORK • OXFORD • NEW DELHI • SYDNEY

I.B. TAURIS
Bloomsbury Publishing Plc
50 Bedford Square, London, WC1B 3DP, UK
1385 Broadway, New York, NY 10018, USA
29 Earlsfort Terrace, Dublin 2, Ireland

BLOOMSBURY, I.B. TAURIS and the I.B. Tauris logo are trademarks of Bloomsbury Publishing Plc

First published in Great Britain 2020
This paperback edition published in 2021

Copyright © Monica M. Ringer, Etienne E. Charrière and contributors 2020

Monica M. Ringer, Etienne E. Charrière and contributors have asserted their right under the Copyright, Designs and Patents Act, 1988, to be identified as Editors of this work.

Copyright Individual Chapters © 2020 Monica M. Ringer, Etienne E. Charrière, Zeynep Seviner, Melih Levi, Owen Green, A. Holly Shissler, Ercüment Asil, Benjamin C. Fortna, Neveser Köker, Ayşe Polat, Ali Bolcakan, Özen Nergis Dolcerocca

Series design by Adriana Brioso
Cover image: Street in Istanbul, Turkey. (© Keystone-France/Gamma-Keystone via Getty Images)

All rights reserved. No part of this publication may be reproduced or transmitted in any form or by any means, electronic or mechanical, including photocopying, recording, or any information storage or retrieval system, without prior permission in writing from the publishers.

Bloomsbury Publishing Plc does not have any control over, or responsibility for, any third-party websites referred to or in this book. All internet addresses given in this book were correct at the time of going to press. The author and publisher regret any inconvenience caused if addresses have changed or sites have ceased to exist, but can accept no responsibility for any such changes.

A catalogue record for this book is available from the British Library.

A catalog record for this book is available from the Library of Congress.

ISBN: HB: 978-1-7883-1452-7
       PB: 978-0-7556-4624-1
       ePDF: 978-0-7556-1666-4
       eBook: 978-0-7556-1668-8

Typeset by RefineCatch Limited, Bungay, Suffolk

To find out more about our authors and books visit www.bloomsbury.com and sign up for our newsletters.

Contents

Notes on Contributors   vii

Introduction   *Monica M. Ringer* and *Etienne E. Charrière*   1

1   Thinking in French, writing in Persian: Aesthetics, intelligibility and the literary Turkish of the 1890s   *Zeynep Seviner*   19

2   How not to translate: Cultural authenticity and translatability in Recaizade Mahmut Ekrem's *Araba Sevdası* and Ahmet Midhat Efendi's *Felatun Bey ile Rakım Efendi*   *Melih Levi*   37

3   Beyond binaries: Ahmet Midhat Efendi's prescriptive modern   *Monica M. Ringer*   53

4   Cultivating Ottoman citizens: Reading Ahmet Midhat Efendi's *Felatun Bey ile Rakım Efendi* with Ali Pasha's political testament   *Owen Green*   65

5   Perils of the french maiden: Women, work, virtue and the public space in some french tales by Ahmet Midhat Efendi   *A. Holly Shissler*   85

6   The Tanzimat novel in the service of science: On Ahmet Midhat Efendi's *American Doctors*   *Ercüment Asil*   103

7   Mizancı Murad's *Turfanda mı yoksa Turfa mı?* as historical novel   *Benjamin C. Fortna*   117

8   Inconvertible romance: Piety, community and the politically disruptive force of love in *Akabi Hikayesi*   *Neveser Köker*   133

9   The late Ottoman novel as social laboratory: Celal Nuri and the 'woman question'   *Ayşe Polat*   147

10 Ottoman Babel: Language, cosmopolitanism and the novel in
   the long Tanzimat period   *Ali Bolcakan*   161

11 Translating communities: Reading foreign fiction across communal
   boundaries in the Tanzimat period   *Etienne E. Charrière*   177

12 The Tanzimat period and its diverse cultures of translation:
   Towards new thinking in comparative literature
   Özen Nergis Dolcerocca   193

Bibliography   209
Index   219

Notes on Contributors

Ercüment Asil currently teaches courses on Islamic and Ottoman History in the History Department at Ibn Haldun University. He received a BA in Political Science and an MA in Modern Turkish History from Boğaziçi University, and a PhD from the University of Chicago with a dissertation entitled 'The Pursuit of the Modern Mind: Popularization of Science, the Development of the Middle Classes, and Religious Transformation in the Ottoman Empire, 1860–1880'.

Ali Bolcakan received a BA in Cultural Studies from Sabancı University. He is currently a PhD student in Comparative Literature at the University of Michigan, working primarily on language debates and linguistic reforms in the late Ottoman Empire and early Turkish Republic.

Etienne E. Charrière is Assistant Professor in the Department of Turkish Literature at Bilkent University in Ankara. He received a BA in Modern Greek Studies from the University of Geneva and a PhD in Comparative Literature from the University of Michigan. His research focuses on the literary production of non-Muslims in the late Ottoman Empire and, in particular, on the rise of novel writing during the Tanzimat Era.

Özen Nergis Dolcerocca is Assistant Professor in the Department of English and Comparative Literature at Koç University in Istanbul. She received a BA in English Literature from Boğaziçi University, an MA in Cultural Studies from Sabancı University, and an MA and a PhD in Comparative Literature from New York University. She is the author of *Self and Desire in the Modern Turkish Novel: A Study on Non-Western Literary Modernities* (2012). In 2017, she guest edited a special issue of *Middle Eastern Literatures* entitled 'Beyond World Literature: Reading Ahmet H. Tanpınar Today'.

Benjamin C. Fortna is Professor and Director of the School of Middle Eastern and North African Studies at the University of Arizona and formerly Professor of the History of the Middle East, SOAS, University of London. He received a

BA from Yale, an MA from Columbia and a PhD from the University of Chicago. His research focuses on the late Ottoman Empire and the early Turkish Republic. His books include *The Circassian: A Life of Eşref Bey, Late Ottoman Insurgent and Special Agent* (2016), *Learning to Read in the Late Ottoman Empire and the Early Turkish Republic* (2010), and *Imperial Classroom: Islam, Education and the State in the Late Ottoman Empire* (2002).

Owen Green received a BA in History from Amherst College. He is currently a PhD student in the Department of Near Eastern Languages and Civilizations at the University of Chicago. His research interests include nationalism, identity and reform in the Ottoman long nineteenth century.

Neveser Köker is an Honors Faculty Fellow at Barrett, the Honors College at Arizona State University. She received a BA in Political Science from Galatasaray University, an MA in Social Sciences from the University of Chicago and a PhD in Political Science from the University of Michigan. Her research examines political membership and belonging through the rich history of transnational interaction and exchange between Europe and the Middle East.

Melih Levi received a BA in English Literature from Amherst College. He is currently a PhD student in Comparative Literature at Stanford University, working primarily on twentieth-century Modernist poetry and on post-war responses to Modernism in English, German and Turkish literatures. He co-translated Ahmet Midhat Efendi's *Felatun Bey and Rakım Efendi* (2016) with Monica M. Ringer.

Ayşe Polat is Assistant Professor of Sociology at Istanbul Medeniyet University. She received a BA in Political Science and Sociology from Boğaziçi University and a PhD from the University of Chicago. Her dissertation, 'Subject to Approval: Sanction and Censure in Ottoman Istanbul, 1889–1923', examines the Ottoman imperial governance of Islamic publications, and public conduct and morality during the Empire's last decades. She is currently revising her PhD thesis as a book manuscript and expanding on her examination of the late Ottoman religious bureaucracy. She has published articles on secularism, Ottoman press, Ottoman censorship and late Ottoman intellectual thought.

Monica M. Ringer is Professor of Middle Eastern History at Amherst College. She received an MA in Islamic Studies and a PhD in Modern Middle Eastern History (1998) from UCLA. She is the author of numerous articles, and two books, *Education, Religion and the Discourse of Cultural Reform in Qajar Iran* (2001), and *Pious Citizens, Reforming Zoroastrianism in India and Iran* (2011). Together with Melih Levi, Ringer provided the first English translation of Ahmet Midhat Efendi's *Felatun Bey and Rakım Efendi: An Ottoman Novel* (2016). She is currently working on a book exploring the theological foundations of nineteenth-century Islamic Modernism.

Zeynep Seviner is Assistant Professor in the Department of Turkish Literature at Bilkent University in Ankara. She received a BA in Cultural Studies from Sabancı University, an MA in Comparative Literature and a PhD in Near and Middle Eastern Studies from the University of Washington. Her dissertation, 'Blue Dreams, Black Disillusions: Literary Market and Modern Authorship in the Late Ottoman Empire', explores the ways in which a set of contextual factors, such as the proliferation of printing technologies, the rise in literacy, standardization of education and the emergence of journalism as a professional field, impacted perceptions of authorship in the Ottoman imperial capital during the 1890s. She has also published articles on the late Ottoman novel, translation and digitization of Ottoman texts.

A. Holly Shissler is Associate Professor of Modern Middle Eastern History in the Department of Near Eastern Languages and Civilizations at the University of Chicago. Her research focuses on the late Ottoman Empire and the early years of the Turkish Republic. She is the author of *Between Two Empires: Ahmet Ağaoğlu and the New Turkey* (I.B. Tauris, 2003).

Introduction

Monica M. Ringer and Etienne E. Charrière

The nineteenth century as the Age of Reform

The nineteenth-century Middle East was defined by modernizing reform programmes, ranging spatially from Egypt to the Ottoman Empire, Iran, and Central Asia, and temporally from the defensive military reform programmes implemented by Ottoman, Egyptian and shortly thereafter, Iranian reformers in the early part of the century, to the more robust Ottoman *Tanzimat*, Arab *Nahda*, Iranian and Central Asian *Jadid* movements that characterized the latter half of the century. While not uniform, all of these reform programmes, and the reformers who articulated and implemented them, grappled with two principle challenges: the rise of European Great Powers, and industrialization and the increasing interdependency of European and Middle Eastern economies. The impact of growing Western expansionist and imperialist powers posed very real dangers to the sovereignty of Middle Eastern countries. Middle Eastern leaders were concerned to fend off rising European military capacities, commercial pressures, and diplomatic aggressions, and to integrate into and thus benefit from opportunities afforded by new commercial and political systems. Reformers believed that success would result in economic development and increased international power and stature; failure would lead to political and economic domination by European Great Powers.

The Ottoman Empire was the first Middle Eastern power to take up the mantle of reform, in large measure because it was the closest, both physically and economically, to Europe, and was thus the first to experience the military, political and economic effects of industrializing, expansionist and colonialist European powers. Ottoman reforms, and both the 'problems' and 'solutions' that they articulated, had precedents stretching back into the late eighteenth century and early nineteenth century, notably in the form of the important military and administrative *Nizam-i Cedid* reforms implemented during the reign of Selim III (1789–1808). Over the course of the nineteenth century, reforms grew in both substance and scope. The more comprehensive reforms later in the century, collectively known as the 'Tanzimat' (literally, 'reordering'), were largely inspired and implemented by a series of prime ministers who enjoyed the sultan's support. Tanzimat reforms attempted a re-formation of Ottoman administrative, financial, military, as well as legal, educational, social and intellectual institutions. Tanzimat reformers recognized the importance of citizenship, national solidarity, public accountability, and transparency as prerequisites for a modern state. The survival of the Ottoman Empire, many reformers believed, hinged on the development of citizens able to sustain, and participate in, a constitutional state. As Ali Pasha (d. 1870), prime minister under Sultan Abdülaziz (r. 1861–1876) and one of the principle architects of the Tanzimat reforms, explained: 'It was imperative for the Empire to hold its ground, maintain its position and not to be intimidated or dismembered. The country needed to be revitalized gradually within available means ... We were lagging behind the intellectual and material progress achieved by our neighbors ...'[1]

The Tanzimat period is usually considered to begin with the proclamation by Ottoman Sultan Abdülmecid I of the Imperial Decree of Gülhane (*Gülhane Hatt-ı Hümayun*) in 1839 and to conclude either with the promulgation of the first Ottoman Constitution in 1876, or with its suspension by Sultan Abdülhamid II in 1878 in the wake of the Russo-Turkish War – an event that marked a return to a period of stronger absolutist power lasting until the Young Turk Revolution of 1908 and the revision and re-promulgation of the Constitution a year later. Instead of restricting the Tanzimat to the traditional 1839–1876 period, one might instead define the Tanzimat period more broadly as the period of self-consciously 'modernizing' reforms that characterized the nineteenth- and early twentieth-century Ottoman Empire up until First World War. This longer time frame problematizes the implicit 'rupture' of the constitution of 1876, suggesting instead that we include the last quarter of the nineteenth century and the first two decades of the twentieth century up until First World War, not as a separate period, but as a contiguous chapter in the complex story of modernizing reform. In the present volume, recourse to this more capacious conception of the 'long Tanzimat' allows us to consider the period as a continuum – one defined, politically, intellectually and culturally as one when reformers and intellectuals of various ilk grappled with competing and evolving concepts of modernity, as well as with the challenges associated with the practical implementation of modernizing programmes.

Tanzimat as translation

The Tanzimat was a response to an existential crisis. In seeking to recalibrate political, economic, military, commercial and financial systems within the contours of a shifting international landscape, reformers initiated substantive changes. Some of these changes were inspired by similar solutions to similar problems implemented in Europe; others grew out of the common conviction that to respond to new needs, administrative and bureaucratic rationalism, centralization and the concomitant harmonization, homogenization and integration into trans-national networks were necessary prerequisites. Modernity, therefore, was not a process of the dissemination of institutions and ideas *from* Europe *to* the rest of the world, but rather a more complex and interactive process of different actors in different societies responding to similar challenges, in sometimes similar, but often different ways.

In other words, the dynamism and demonstrative power of European Great Powers served as empirical evidence of the utility of some European institutions – particularly standing militaries, medical, scientific, and educational advances, and ultimately, accountable government enabled by a participatory citizenship. At the same time, Ottoman Tanzimat reforms were not merely a process of adopting and adapting European examples. Reformers also implemented strategies in response to the internal dynamics of the reforms themselves. The reform process was complex. Reformers sought to identify prerequisites of reform and to implement changes in concert with local needs, conditions and commitments. They also understood that reforms, while urgent, were complex and deeply interconnected. Reformers recognized that top-down government initiatives needed to be buttressed by transformations at the social and cultural levels. Prime Minister Ali Pasha appreciated the necessity of integrating top-down with bottom-up reforms, and cautioned against a simple 'importation' of European-inspired institutions. In a letter to the sultan, he warned that 'when a civilization is imported and does not evolve gradually from within, people usually acquire more of its vices than of its virtues.'[2]

The context of European relationships with the Middle East as experienced and perceived differently in different contexts complicates any attempt to generalize the mechanics of interaction between the Middle East and 'the West.' It is also the case that these complex interactions did not take place in a political vacuum. The economic and political power disparity between Europe and other societies effected realms of cultural and intellectual interaction. European countries were aggressive, threatening, and dominating, even as their societies offered attractive models and ideas for thought. The conversation thus was effected by these relationships of power. Any discussion of the dynamics of these relationships must take this into consideration, and avoid pitfalls of 'orientalism' or 'nativism' – both of which distort the complexity of these processes.

Traditional scholarship on this period of profound mutations has tended to focus on political reforms framed as attempts to remedy the perceived weakness of the Ottoman Empire vis-à-vis European imperial powers. The image of an ailing body, most notably in the well-known expression of 'Sick Man of Europe' that became commonplace in Western discourses in the second half of the nineteenth century, was frequently mobilized to describe an imperial polity plagued by recurrent economic turmoil since at least the end of the seventeenth century and increasingly faced with the reality of irretrievable territorial losses to European powers. More recent scholarly endeavours have sought to redress and complicate various sets of entrenched binaries ('modern' versus 'traditional', 'European' versus 'Ottoman'), whose pervasiveness and actual validity had seldom been challenged or questioned in conventional accounts of the Ottoman age of reforms. Scholars have notably sought ways to understand the period not primarily – if at all – driven by imperatives of imitation and civilizational mimicry, or by the uncritical adoption of European institutions and mores, but rather as one of complex social and cultural experimentation, during which reformers drew upon both existing local traditions and innovations imported from outside of the Empire, repurposing, reinterpreting and reformulating both 'native' and 'foreign' elements as part of a profoundly creative process of transformation. Ottoman intellectuals explored ideas of modernity, citizenship and subjectivity in dialogue with European ideas, but equally, if not more importantly, in dialogue with ideas and cultural forms both local and emanating from the broader Middle Eastern region. Recent scholarship has also sought to emancipate the narrative of Ottoman modernization from the various incarnations of traditional 'top-down' historiography on the period that had remained largely focused on elite and state actors, and has begun to address questions of intellectual, cultural, and artistic change involving broader strata of late-Ottoman society.

The Tanzimat, and other reform processes more generally, were not hybrid adaptations of Western forms to local conditions. The impetus for reform was, ultimately, domestic; Western ideas and forms were inspirational, but the process itself was much more than a simple importation and adaptation. The ongoing challenge for scholars of the Tanzimat period broadly conceived is to move away from distortive binaries and the organizational epistemologies of unquestioned definitions and categories. We need to more accurately articulate the ways in which reformists engaged and reshaped both existing traditions and new ideas, in both local and trans-local contexts. Rather than positioning reform along a linear spectrum from imitative to rejectionist, we should turn instead to conceptualizing reforms as products of complex, intersecting intellectual networks – networks which operated in local, and trans-local contexts, as well as across time. Reformers were engaged not only with ideas from other traditions and contexts, but with ideas from their own. Reforms were as much a product of selection from a local menu of options as they were from other, newly available menus. The choice between one or the other is a false one – the project of reform is more accurately characterized by the profound interaction between them.

Ahmet Midhat Efendi, a leading Tanzimat reformer, explained: 'If we try to Europeanize only for the sake of becoming European, we shall lose our own character. If we, on the other hand, add the European civilization to our own character, we shall not only preserve, perpetuate and maintain our character but also fortify and refine it.'[3] Locating reforms in their various contexts and embedded meanings, rather than assuming they were pale approximations of Western reforms, allows us to recalibrate questions of causality, European influence, argumentation and intent. It also allows us to emphasize the variety of sources of models, possibilities and discourses available to reformers, rather than focusing solely on the European. In addition to Europe, reform programmes in other Middle Eastern societies, together with intellectually rich indigenous traditions, provided many sources and models of reform.

Reform as translation

Ottoman Culture and the Project of Modernity frames the complex dynamic of conceptualizing modernity as one of 'translation.' While the term 'translation' typically implies a particular linear directionality, the present volume investigates the various modes in which translation operates not simply between cultures or languages, but also within them. Conceiving of the Tanzimat period as one of translation as opposed to mere appropriation allows the discussion to move from a linear one of non-Western 'response' to the West, to a three-dimensional set of contemporaneous, multi-directional conversations. Such an approach foregrounds the dynamics internal to the debates themselves as well as the connections between different nexuses of conversations, as 'connected histories.' Reformers, in other words, in their engagement with the 'modern', were in dialogue with each other, even as they interacted with ideas, ideals, models and institutions both from their own, local and trans-local traditions, as well as from Europe, the Middle East, South Asia and, to a lesser extent, East Asia.

Tracing the complex genealogies that structured knowledge production during the Tanzimat, this volume explores the various ways in which Ottoman literati of the period mobilized translation to allow for the emergence of new patterns of thought, of new epistemologies and new methodologies. Collectively, contributors to this volume frame translation as a force that unsettles the relationship between sign and structure, as the interaction of various scripts making demands on new modes of textual production and reading, as well as a methodological tool that undermines the conception of cultural contact as an encounter between binaries. By foregrounding translational acts, this volume highlights a conception of late Ottoman culture as an assemblage, shifting the focus from notions of ownership to notions of agency. In addition, using the notion of translation broadly defined as an entry point into a larger discussion of late Ottoman modernity, this volume recasts concepts of 'progress' and 'change' with a special attention to spatial and temporal continuities across and beyond the Empire, thereby avoiding the pitfall of assuming that the modern is always what it claims to be: a rupture, a departure or a denunciation of the past.

In one form or another, the essays in this collection all reflect Ottoman reformers' central project of imagining, and implementing – via the novel – an Ottoman modern. The Ottoman modern was not a hybridization of European and Ottoman institutions, ideas and mores, as previously understood. The notion that modernization is quintessentially Western implies that to be modern is to be Western, in other words, that modernization involves to a greater or lesser extent, conformity with Western versions of modernity. Modernization in the Ottoman Empire was therefore understood as largely imitative – either successfully or not. Scholarship in more recent years has gradually disassociated itself from the assumption that modernization necessarily entails westernization, instead proposing to conceive of Ottoman modernization as a hybridization measured along the spectrum from imitation and adaptation on one end and rejection on the other. This formula, however, like its forebear, distorts the nature of Ottoman modernization. Our theory of translation more accurately captures the subtle registers of Ottoman modernization as a process of imagining and implementing modernity. This process was rooted in a re-evaluation of existing institutions on the basis of whether or not they had the capacity to generate and sustain modern institutions, ideas and subjectivities.

Reformers were constructing the modern from a wide menu of available options – some long-standing, 'traditional' conventions, as well as an array of new options, generated both domestically and internationally. The dangerous preoccupation with 'origins' of ideas and institutions were not theirs. Whereas we, as historians of modernity, unquestioningly accepted European claims to have generated modern institutions and ideas at face value, Ottoman reformers understood modernity as a civilizational level, universally accessible, which in no way precluded cultural difference. In other words, what scholarship has typically rendered as 'imitation' or 'rejection' was in fact a much more complex process of constructing the modern from both existing and new possible options. Reformers were committed to generating the 'citizen' as a necessary prerequisite for modernity – but the new subjectivities of the 'Ottoman citizen', while certainly sharing many aspects of the European citizen, were different in important ways. Moreover, Ottoman reformers were convinced that their own vision of the Ottoman modern was no pale imitation of European modernity, but rather a much improved, more moral, more socially just, authentically Ottoman modernity. Essays in this volume are attentive to these nuances, and convey the nuance and subtlety of the Ottoman modern as imagined and conveyed, didactically, to the Ottoman reading public.

The novel of reform, the novel as reform

The nature of reform changed throughout the Tanzimat period, as reformers' ideas about modernity and modernization evolved. In large brushstrokes, Tanzimat reform was characterized by administrative, economic and military centralization and rationalization. By the third quarter of the century, reformers were convinced that government accountability, citizenship and equality were imperative for the strength and wellbeing of the Empire, particularly in the face of aggressive European imperialism. Reformist ministers tended to come from the ranks of the Foreign Ministry and had experience and knowledge of similar rationalizing and centralizing reforms in Europe.

The rapid spread of print capitalism also enabled public discourse on questions of reform, and provided a platform for the emergence of a reform-minded intelligentsia. Reforms were enacted from within the government at a legal and institutional level, but were also discussed and debated from outside the government in new public mediums. Many of the most famous reformist intellectuals chose newspapers and novels not only as new platforms in which to discuss, debate and advocate for reforms, but also as new platforms that were particularly suited to the creation of new publics. Reformers turned to the newspaper and the novel to *reach* new audiences, but equally to *shape* new audiences. They viewed the project of reform not only as a top-down enterprise of institutional changes, but also as a project of creating new citizens. Ahmet Midhat Efendi, in his celebrated 1875 novel *Felatun Bey and Rakım Efendi*, deployed strategies from Victorian literature to create agency in his readership, not only modelling citizenship through the content of the novel, but allowing the readers to participate and practise agency through the act of reading itself.[4] The public, reformers believed, needed to be imbued with new, modern, sensibilities and dispositions; individuals' attitudes, behaviours and values needed to be shaped. For this reason, no other medium better embodies the vision and values of the 'modern Ottoman citizen' than the emerging Ottoman novel.

Defining what the 'Ottoman novel' might be – and, even more so, when such a thing might have emerged – is a much more arduous task than what could be expected, one for which the notions of 'birth' or 'rise', often used in literary studies to account for the beginnings of a given novelistic tradition, prove largely inoperative.[5] The difficulty is twofold: first, should the gradual emergence, during the nineteenth century, of long fictional narratives in prose – what is commonly recognised as 'the novel' – be described as the more or less organic transformation of 'indigenous' forms already present in the Ottoman literary repertoire as well as in its oral tradition or, rather, as the irruption of a predominantly *new* form whose inclusion into Ottoman belles-lettres was largely the result of contact with the West? If we decide to opt for the latter and emphasize a process of cultural and aesthetic rupture over the idea of an unbroken continuity through time, where and when do we situate it? Scholarship on the emergence of the novel in the Ottoman Empire has, until quite recently, been particularly keen on identifying which text might be considered the 'first Turkish novel', guided as it was by a quasi-fetishistic obsession with the idea of 'origins', at the expense of more textured approaches that would account for the complexities of a process of crystallization and slow sedimentation that was nothing short of sinuous. While mainstream scholarship traditionally identified authors like Şemsettin Sami, Ahmet Midhat Efendi or Namık Kemal, who all published their first novel between 1872 and 1874, as the first generation of Ottoman novelists, the rediscovery in the late twentieth century of Hovsep Vartanyan (Vartan Pasha)'s *Story of Akabi* (*Akabi Hikayesi*, 1851) and of a handful of other original novels published in Armenian-scripted Ottoman Turkish in the 1860s, prompted a change in outlook. Some scholars point out that the first examples of novel-writing in Turkish had in fact started to appear two decades prior; the fact that they were written in the Armenian script rather than in the Arabo-Persian alphabet usually used to render Ottoman Turkish, and predominantly – yet not exclusively – for consumption by a small 'minority' group, had prevented their inclusion in traditional periodizations of late Ottoman literature. By the same logic, an even more inclusive conception of what the notion 'Ottoman novel' might cover would require that we extend this quest for the 'origins' of the genre and include not only works composed in

Ottoman Turkish (in a variety of scripts) but any novel published within the Empire in any of its multiple languages, thereby dating the emergence of novel-writing to, at least, a decade before *Akabi* and three decades before the first Arabic-scripted Turkish novels, with the publication in 1842 of the first Greek novel published in Istanbul, Grigorios Paleologos' *The Painter* (Ο Ζωγράφος).

In this volume, we choose to stay away from these debates and prefer to frame the novel of the long Tanzimat period as a medium invested with the full range of meaning of translation. Novels, as a new literary form 'adopted' from Europe, were often at first translations of European, typically French, novels. They also, however, were deployed as a means of translating between cultures, between ideas, moralities and institutions. Ottoman novelists understood their own project of translation as not simply literal translation, but also the rendering of ideas between cultural contexts. They appropriated the novel as a form in order to explore and convey their ideas of the Ottoman modern. The novel was an ideal didactic tool to convince their new public audiences of the benefits of this 'new Ottoman modern' – to embody the new Ottoman modern in the characters of the novel. Novelists invited their audience to empathize with characters, to be drawn into their plots, and in so doing, to both experience and participate in the construction of their own new, explicitly modern subjectivities. Novels were designed to convey and imbue readers with modern values, sensibilities and dispositions – they were the site of the construction of new Ottoman citizens. The novel was thus both the site and motor of translation.

Essays in this book explore the translation of the novel form and its deployment in the late Ottoman cultural context. Authors closely observe the project of modernity as Tanzimat novelists themselves viewed it, and offer an exploration of their terms of engagement, their solutions and their intentions. Collectively, the various contributions suggest new ways of understanding the motivations, intentions and strategies deployed by Tanzimat authors as they innovated and created an Ottoman modern. Investigating both the poetics and the politics of translation (paying particular attention to notions of gender, class, and ethnicity) as they were deployed in the Tanzimat novel, the essays in this volume trace the performative dimension of translational choices, shed light on the tensions resulting from the constant negotiation of authorial agency and collective aesthetics, and study the role performed by the interplay of translation and original novel-writing in the elaboration of a new literary culture that served as a vehicle for political and social reform ideals.

Essays included in this volume emphasize ways in which the Ottoman novel must also be read from outside of a strictly literary perspective in order to understand ways in which both form and content were harnessed to larger Tanzimat objectives. Approaching the Tanzimat novel from a variety of disciplinary vantage points (history, political science, comparative literature, and related fields), this volume illustrates ways in which the novel both translated the profound social, political and economic changes at play during the Tanzimat, and mirrored the various processes of 'translation' around which they were articulated. As editors, we invited the volume's contributors to think about 'translation' as a methodological lens on the Tanzimat period and to frame novels published in the period as both the sites and motors of this cultural practice.

At the nexus of history and literature, form and function

Ottoman Culture and the Project of Modernity encourages dialogue between and across disciplines in the 'reading' of the Tanzimat novel. To this end, we invited historians and literary scholars to share their techniques and approaches. Historians often use novels as illustrations – as textual 'images' that accompany analysis of historical context. Historians therefore tend to be primarily concerned with reading the novel as a product and reflection of context. Literary scholars, on the other hand, are much more concerned with examining literary technique and applying literary analysis. We gathered together a group of historians and literary scholars to consider the novel at the nexus of these two approaches, both contextual and literary. All the authors were asked to reflect on ways in which they read the Ottoman novel, but also how literary technique often intersected with and reinforced didactic objectives.

Ottoman Culture and the Project of Modernity was written expressly with the general reader in mind. To this end, the authors have avoided jargon or references that the general reader may not be familiar with. With the notable exception of Ahmet Midhat Efendi's famous novel, *Felatun Bey and Rakım Efendi*, no other Ottoman novel is available in English translation. The lack of

Ottoman novels available in English required authors to share thoughts and approaches to the Ottoman novel, specifically and as a genre, without assuming, or requiring, any prior familiarity.

In her contribution, **Zeynep Seviner** explores an unusual moment for language and literature between the beginnings of the cultural reformation and the burgeoning of nationalist movement. Marked by what is retrospectively known as the 'decadents debate', the turn-of-the-century Ottoman literary field witnessed the creation of an experimental language, drawing both from the syntax of classical poetry and metaphors of the contemporary French novel. Though short-lived and extensively criticized, this new language opened the space for the mixing of dissimilar elements from past and present to make possible a form of non-identitarian writing shortly before the irreversible rise of nationalism. Seviner tracks the polarized opinions on the functions attributed to literary language and the implications of this polarity on understandings of intralingual translation, of the novel genre, and finally, on the relationship between imagination and morality.

Five of the chapters of the present volume are dedicated, in part or in their entirety, to various aspects of the work of late-Ottoman novelist Ahmet Midhat Efendi, the first Ottoman *littérateur* to cultivate the novel genre in a systematic fashion. Although devoting so much of a volume to a single author might seem excessive, the importance of Ahmet Midhat in terms of his enormous novelistic output, which truly sets him apart from the general corpus of the Ottoman novel, alone justifies this choice. Additionally, beyond the sheer number of the novels he published, a detailed study of Ahmet Midhat's œuvre is also of particular relevance to a volume like the present one in that, as an occasional translator of novels and, even more importantly, as a journalist, publisher and pedagogue preoccupied with the idea of reform, he stands out as a distinctive embodiment of the Ottoman modern, one marked by a selective and ever critical engagement with the West.

In his contribution, **Melih Levi** shows that, since many Tanzimat-era authors of original novels were also translators of foreign novels in Ottoman Turkish, the project of authorial self-fashioning went hand in hand with the practice of literary translation. Therefore, this intimate relationship had important implications for the reformist objectives that writers such as Ahmet Midhat and Recaizade Mahmut Ekrem endorsed as a necessity for the betterment of

Ottoman society. By placing an emphasis upon the representation, in Tanzimat novels, of acts and processes of literary translation whose fluctuating degree of accuracy threatened the main plot structure of their novels, Levi shows that, by foregrounding translation as a process that unsettles notions of textual stability, Tanzimat novelists repeatedly acknowledged that there is no such thing as a 'finished' text and that, in doing so, they invited their readers to experience the process of translation and to take an active part in the production of meaning.

In her essay, **Monica Ringer** explores the binary distinction between *alafranga* (European) and *alaturka* (Turkish), that is, the ostensible guiding grammar of Ahmet Midhat Efendi's novel, *Felatun Bey and Rakım Efendi*, and its eponymous anti-hero and hero, Felatun and Rakım, respectively. The common tendency in the historiography of modernization in the Ottoman Empire is to assign it to a binary option: either imitative and inauthentic Europeanization or reactionary maintenance of an antimodern authentic 'Turkish.' Ringer suggests that we move away from reinforcing these binaries, or even from attempts at hybridization, and instead move to underscore the greater complexity of Ottoman modernity as a process of translation. She suggests that translation allows us to understand Ottoman modernity as a process of negotiation between multiple traditions, institutions and mores – some of them European, some of them Ottoman – and that the resultant construction of an Ottoman 'modern' is primarily a rejection of a similarly constructed Ottoman 'tradition.' She demonstrates how various combinations of characters associated with the two principle characters, Rakım and Felatun, suggest the nuance and complexity of navigating between tradition and modernity in the Ottoman Empire.

One of the central goals of Ottoman reform in the Tanzimat period was the transformation of the Ottoman subjects into citizens as part of the reconstruction of Ottoman imperial identity as a pluralistic national identity. Reading Ahmet Midhat Efendi's 1875 Novel *Felatun Bey and Rakım Efendi* together with the 1871 political testament of the Tanzimat statesman Ali Pasha, **Owen Green** highlights both top-down and bottom-up strategies for cultivating citizens, as well as the methods that these two intellectuals saw as the most conducive to political and social reform. In those two texts, citizens, envisioned to be the basis of both the sovereignty and the cultural character of the nation, were tasked with creating reforms that would be both effective and desirable for the nation through what can be described as a series of 'translations', to adapt earlier Ottoman precedents and material drawn from the imperfect example of European modernity in order to create a distinct Ottoman modernity. Morality, a concept which itself was in flux from communal religious moralities into that of a shared public, national morality, was to serve as the lens through which these 'translations' were refracted in order to ensure that they produced beneficial and effective changes.

Examining Ahmet Midhat's *Amusing Tales* (*Letaif-i Rivayat*), a very popular and successful series of stories and novellas which appeared between the years 1870 and 1894, **Holly Shissler** analyses how, by choosing France as the setting for a number of these stories, Ahmet Midhat showed a deep commitment to developing an enterprising spirit in the lower and middle classes, the classes that he saw as the productive and moral backbone of society. Midhat's French stories, like his Ottoman ones, thus promoted these values, but also allowed the author to explore some themes and settings in a way that was more acceptable to his Ottoman audience if set in France rather than at home in the Empire. The descriptions of new cultural practices, notably the ones that encouraged cross-gender sociability, constituted a valuable source of information about European culture while at the same time pointing out some of the perils of Western materialist modernity.

Analysing the adoption of modern science into the Ottoman modernization process through the lenses of the Tanzimat novel, **Ercüment Asil** argues that the making of the Ottoman modern cannot be explained by the simple juxtaposition of science and technology with the traditional Ottoman moral frame. Rather than a simple 'dualism' of the modern and the traditional, the Ottoman modern involved complex processes of socio-cultural negotiations in the search for an authentic modern. The novel was a major medium through which the boundaries and nature of this authenticity were negotiated. In this context, the Ottoman 'scientific literature' emerged as an amalgamation of science fiction as a literary genre and as a means of disseminating modern science and its authority to the Ottoman reading public. Ahmet Midhat Efendi's *A Scientific Novel, or American Doctors* provides an example of the subtle discussions around questions of the authority and authenticity of modern science and of the Ottoman tradition of knowledge. Like many other Ottoman and Muslim intellectuals of the era, Ahmet Midhat's primary strategy in encouraging the adoption of modern science was to differentiate between science and morality as two independent entities so as to construct a modern Ottoman morality conducive to the modern sciences.

In his essay, **Benjamin Fortna** explores Mehmed 'Mizancı' Murad's 1891 novel *Turfanda mı yoksa Turfa mı?*, a work which highlights the wide imperial and, indeed, trans-imperial possibilities of the late Ottoman period, when horizons had been expanded by the telegraph, the railway and the steamship, a mode of transportation that marks its presence from the novel's first pages. Amid these rapid changes, the novel introduces its central character, an earnest young medical doctor named Mansur, who comes to the Ottoman capital from North Africa via France. As an Ottoman Turk with a French education, Mansur brings a fresh perspective to exploring questions of individual and collective Ottoman identity and the main problem facing the over 600-year-old Empire: How can the state be saved? Perhaps more than any other late Ottoman novel, *Turfanda mı yoksa Turfa mı?* strives to link the personal with the political, in particular the broader fate of the late Ottoman Empire. Mansur's adventures in the state bureaucracy, in medicine, and in love are all subsumed under the larger question of how best to perpetuate and even revivify the Ottoman Empire and, by extension, the Islamic community for which it served as the symbolic centre.

In her essay, **Neveser Köker** offers a critical reading of Ottoman Armenian bureaucrat Vartan Pasha's novel *Akabi Hikayesi* (*The Story of Akabi*) arguing that the work illustrates the dictates of conversion as a logic of political belonging. Experienced and understood through the lens of the converter (not the potential convert), conversion allows imperial subjects to reimagine the communal self as politically and morally superior to its others. It also fosters in these subjects an inherent scepticism of the (potential) convert's ability to see the necessity of such radical change, and to follow the newly acquired beliefs, spaces, practices and community in the right way. *Akabi Hikayesi*'s plot of tragic romance rooted in the religious differences of its main protagonists captures the affective, socio-cultural, and political challenges of this mix of politico-moral hierarchy and mistrust of the individual's capacity for personal and political transformation.

Ayşe Polat's contribution examines two short novels by late Ottoman intellectual Celal Nuri where the author engaged with the 'woman question'. Analysing two texts centred around the figure of an unhappily married Turkish woman and an Italian prostitute respectively, Polat shows how Celal Nuri deployed the novel as a 'motor of change' to mirror the problems of post-First World War Ottoman society and to illustrate cultural norms governing women, family and sexuality. She argues that in his writings on the 'woman question', Celal Nuri advocated reforming the institutions of family and morality to rebuild social order.

Finally, three contributions examine late Ottoman prose from the point of view of current debates around the notion of 'world literature', arguing for the relevance of the late Ottoman novel to these theoretical discussions. In his essay, **Ali Bolcakan** situates the novel of the Tanzimat period broadly defined against the backdrop of contemporary scholarship on translation, Ottoman cosmopolitanism, imperialism and (post)colonialism and proposes that the very corpus of the late Ottoman novel should be rethought to include novels composed in languages other than Ottoman Turkish and that the literary historiography of the Tanzimat period must be uncoupled from that of the Turkish Republic's.

In his essay, **Etienne Charrière** challenges the notion that the selection of foreign novels slated for translation into Ottoman Turkish during the Tanzimat era happened 'at random,' as well as that the notable absence of canonical Western texts in the repertoire of foreign works of fiction translated during the period should be seen as the mark of an aesthetic 'disconnect' between the Ottoman reading public and its Western European counterpart. Shifting away from an exclusive focus on translations of foreign prose fiction into Ottoman Turkish, Charrière examines the dominant trends in the translation of Western novels in another of the Empire's literary languages, Greek, the language into which an important number of foreign works – although not all them – were first translated in the Ottoman Empire and shows how these trends, far from pointing to a 'disconnect,' in fact largely mirrored developments in the realm of novel publishing in Western Europe itself. In addition to showing how attuned the Ottoman market for fiction was to its Western European counterpart, he also highlights the internal coherence of the Tanzimat-era translation landscape, underlining the ways in which the practice of translation cut across linguistic and communal boundaries within the Empire.

Özen Nergis Dolcerocca points out, in her essay, how the nineteenth century, as the age of global canonization, played a significant role in the historiography of world literature, which associated the non-European literatures of the epoch with the universal imitation of Western literary forms and norms. Defining the nineteenth-century Ottoman literary field as a complex multilingual literary system, Dolcerocca shows that the Tanzimat authors and translators formed networks of dissemination and circulation that is incompatible with centre-periphery cartographies of world literature. By foregrounding examples of regionally marked translational concepts, practices and institutions, her essay embeds Tanzimat literary translation practices in questions that drive the field of comparative literature today. It proposes the Tanzimat novel as a new model for thinking about literary comparativism outside of national and universalist paradigms.

Notes

1 Fuat Andic and Suphan Andic, *The Last of the Ottoman Grandees: The Life and the Political Testament of Âli Paşa* (Istanbul, Isis Press, 1996), 33.
2 Andic and Andic, *Political Testament of Âli Paşa*, 34.
3 Ahmet Midhat Efendi, *Tarik*, 1898.
4 Ahmet Midhat Efendi, *Felatun Bey and Rakım Efendi* (trans.) Melih Levi and Monica M. Ringer, (Syracuse, 2016). See also Cemal Demircioğlu, 'Translating Europe: The Case of Ahmet Midhat as an Ottoman agent of translation,' in *Agents of Translation* (2009); Zeynep Tufekcioğlu, 'The Islamic Epistemology in a Western Genre: Ahmet Mithat Efendi's *Esrar-i Cinayat*, the First Detective Novel of Turkish Literature', *CLUES* 29 (Fall 2011): 7–15; and Nuket Esem, 'The narrator and the narratee in Ahmet Mithat', *Edebiyat: Journal of Middle Literatures* 13, no. 2 (2003): 139–46.
5 The scholarship on the development of the novel during the period of modernization of the Ottoman Empire is as abundant in Turkish as it is scarce in other languages. Writing this introduction – and this volume at large – with an audience of non-specialists in mind, we have elected to list only a few notable sources available in English, in their order of publication (excluding English-language sources exclusively dedicated to Ahmet Midhat, listed above): Ahmet Ö. Evin, *Origins and Development of The Turkish Novel*, (Minneapolis: Bibliotheca Islamica, 1983); Robert Finn, *The Early Turkish Novel: 1872–1900*, (Istanbul: The Isis Press, 1984); Nurdan Gürbilek, 'Dandies and Originals: Authenticity, Belatedness, and the Turkish Novel', (*South Atlantic Quarterly* 102 (2003): 599–628); Jale Parla, 'The Object of Comparison', (*Comparative Literature Studies* 41, no.1 (2004): 116–25); Azade Seyhan, *Tales of Crossed Destinies: The Modern Turkish Novel in a Comparative Context* (New York: The Modern Language Association of America, 2008).

1

Thinking in French, writing in Persian: Aesthetics, intelligibility and the literary Turkish of the 1890s

Zeynep Seviner

On 22 March 1897, the prolific writer, literary critic and journalist-entrepreneur Ahmet Midhat Efendi (1844–1912) published a controversial article in *Sabah*, featuring a story of dubious credibility where a well-read friend reports to him in frustration that he has great difficulty understanding the latest literary publications. He asks Ahmet Midhat, 'is it my inability to grasp the meaning of what I read, or is it their inability to say what they mean?' to which Midhat responds reassuring him of his cognitive faculties and iterating that there really is something fundamentally wrong with the current trends in literature. He joins his 'friend' in accusing young writers of employing highly peculiar language impossible to comprehend for a great many well-educated people, and likens them to French decadents, a group of contemporary writers and artists known for their adherence to an aesthetic of artificiality.

Ahmet Midhat's article seems to have opened a can of worms, as a series of articles appeared in response, collectively forming what is now widely known as the 'dekadanlar tartışması' (decadents controversy), which spun for about four years and featured various discussions on language, the representation of reality and the general function of literature. This debate was so central to the history of late Ottoman literature that, in his memoir, Hüseyin Cahit (1875–1957) remarked, 'to summarize the whole commotion on decadents would be to write our recent literary history.'[1]

Midhat's take on the latest trends in literature does indeed represent a moment of collective anxiety about the written register of the Turkish language, now disseminated more widely than ever before.² If an increasing number of people were to read these texts, not only in groups and in social settings but also in the solitary comfort of their rooms, how could their impact on readers be controlled? Worse still, how could one prevent potentially harmful misunderstandings when clarity of meaning was not something authors were interested in ensuring?

Further into the article, Midhat presents the reader with a 'sample sentence' written in what he argues to be unnecessarily ornate and opaque language in the fashion of the *Servet-i Fünun* writers he seeks to criticize. Written in extremely ornate prose, the sentence advises those who are afraid of the sound that the rollers of a sailboat make to simply abstain from getting on a sailboat in the first place: 'Those who are frightened of the rattle of rollers with a blue-coloured fear should refrain from hauling the load of their humanly materiality onto a rocking vehicle with open wings.'³ Highly metaphorical language and complex syntax deliberately paired with the trivial nature of the given advice renders the statement hilariously absurd. The translation into English fails to do justice to some of the semantic peculiarities and extreme neologisms deliberately embedded into the text by Ahmet Midhat, who argues that the very same idea can be rendered in a much simpler and more intelligible language like this: 'Those who are afraid of the rattle of the rollers should abstain from getting on a boat.' ('Makara hırıltısından pek korkanlar yelkenli gemiye binmekten içtinap eylemelidirler.') He then advises his 'friend' to read in a Persian-heavy Turkish but think in French in order to comprehend the article he has been frustrated with. The friend responds, 'Reading in Turkish and thinking in French? What a disgrace! [...] While we are striving to simplify the language, these [young writers] keep ruining it. What kind of language is this? What kind of expressions are these? They make us long for Veysi and Nergisi!'⁴ He concludes his rant by mockingly adding that, because of these young writers, Emile Zola's vulgar descriptions of disgraceful conditions of humanity will begin to count as literature, which he compares to the work of an eighteenth-century Ottoman poet by the name of Sururi (d. 1814), and claims that the new 'nonsense' would surpass even that in its absurd irrelevance.

The way Ahmet Midhat used the term decadent – to imply both a synchronic move towards the immorality of French literature and a diachronic one towards the transgressions of Ottoman classical literature – points to a general concern about these young writers' disarrayed borrowing from multiple sources rather than a fear of excessive literary westernization. More significantly, however, Ahmet Midhat saw the real danger, not so much in the appropriation of the morally offensive nature of both literary traditions, as in the free-style recontextualization of the borrowed signs of Divan literature that once made a particular kind of sense. The new similes, formed using words from Arabic and syntax from Persian (i.e. the reservoir of Divan poetry), had been in a sense the zombified versions of their classical counterparts; they looked like them to an extent but were nevertheless something else entirely. Midhat's choice of term also reflects this disturbing semi-intelligibility: a term difficult to define, decadence was, in a nutshell, 'appealing but dangerous, liberating but perhaps too much so, pleasurable but self-indulgent, exciting yet perverse and destructive.'[5] Elements of decadence, albeit acceptable to a certain extent, would pose serious danger were they to become the operative principle of textual production, thus would need to be pathologized and discouraged. This tendency of pathologizing in excess was not only in line with late-nineteenth-century positivism as exemplified in the fields of psychiatry, anthropology, sexology and criminology, but also exemplified elsewhere in Ahmet Midhat's writing, the most telling of which was his novella co-written with Fatma Aliye, *Hayal ve Hakikat*, where the female character is diagnosed with hysteria by the author himself.

As troublesome as it was for a figure like Ahmet Midhat, who saw no point in engaging with the classical tradition in any shape or form, this experimental play with words played a vital role in the creation of a new aesthetic, which, in its subversive engagement (which was more than Ahmet Midhat's deriding indifference), traversed a longer distance towards modern literature, not despite but because of this very interest. The lack of an appropriate training in classical literature gave these young *littérateurs* both blind courage to awaken its dormant phraseological possibilities and an earnest recognition of its continued – albeit vilified – presence in their midst. This is perhaps best exemplified in Recaizade Mahmut Ekrem's *Araba Sevdası* (A Carriage Affair), published in 1896 but written in the preceding decade, the story of a young bureaucrat who is parodied for his inability to correctly encode and decode speech acts to communicate with his environment. His self-claimed expertise in French and eagerness to experiment with Divan poetry drives him so far from spoken language that it causes him to mistake a prostitute for a high society lady. Yet, in the farcical persona of the protagonist, Bihruz Bey, Ekrem notably turned the mirror towards himself and his immediate environment, in one of the first and most notable acts of introspection of modern Ottoman literature. It is from this place of self-examination, both as an individual and a member of society with a certain kind of (however unlikable) historical baggage, that these writers opened a space for the possibility of dissimilar elements from past and present coming together, mixing and mingling in various ways.

This is not to say that these elements were to be conserved exactly as they were, but that one would find new modes of existence in their convergence. According to Charles Bernheimer, the term 'decadent' also contains this contradiction. 'Decadence appears on the one hand to erode meaning, on the other to insist on its value and relevance,' he argues, '[a]esthetically and politically, the first tendency is modern, disruptive, experimental, whereas the second is conservative and nostalgic.'[6] This contradiction has allowed Nergis Ertürk to read this as Ekrem's indirect gesture towards the 'promise of non-identitarian, egalitarian writing,' which was inspired by the mid-nineteenth century practice of writing Turkish using non-Turkish writing systems such as the Armenian and Greek alphabets, a promise that was ultimately left unfulfilled, as nationalist forces steered literary production towards a monoscripted and monolingual direction in the following decades.[7] This aborted bit of literary history, however, allowed for the emergence of the modern Turkish novel, characterized by non-judgemental depictions of diverse psychological states rather than cautionary lessons told via two-dimensional characters.

The short-lived proliferation of this new type of interaction with language was closely connected to important changes in the field of education. The standardization efforts in education aiming to train a new bureaucratic class had started during the reigns of Abdülmecid (r. 1839–1861) and Abdülaziz (r. 1861–1876), with the foundation of the Ministry of Public Education in 1857 and the coming into effect of The Regulation of Public Education (*Maarif-i Umumiye Nizamnamesi*) in 1869, and culminated during the reign of Abdülhamid II when education was truly turned into a tool of government control over the moral education of its citizens. While Abdülhamid largely envisioned this standardization as a project of authoritarian-Islamic modernization, this vision was ironically challenged and rendered largely ineffective through a multitude of choices built into the system and the emphasis on the individual engagement with the material. This built-in multitude allowed Halit Ziya (1865–1945), one of the young writers criticized in Midhat's article, to become the first Muslim student to attend the Armenian Mekhitarist School in Izmir, despite considerable criticism from fellow Muslims towards his family.

Another of the distinguishing features of these educational reforms was a new emphasis on the modern textbook, which allowed students to own the course materials and take them along wherever they went. It was the Hamidian concern for control within the Ottoman borders that accelerated the promotion of textbooks following their introduction into the Ottoman space of education during the Tanzimat period, and this helped replace what was an educational tradition based on oral transmission of knowledge with one based on the ownership of printed material. Textbooks also became instrumental in steering discussions on literature, as exemplified in the role of Recaizade Mahmut Ekrem's *Talim-i Edebiyat*, intended as a textbook of secondary education. More importantly, however, these books were a gateway to book ownership for many students, allowing them to purchase, keep, care for and display books as commodities, and engage with them in their own time. Reading had become an individual activity practised in solitude.

The first generation to experience book ownership as children was also the same generation that found themselves as targets of Ahmet Midhat's criticism two decades later. They had gathered around the *Servet-i Fünun* magazine founded in 1891 by Ahmet İhsan (1868–1942), and, under the mentorship of Recaizade Mahmut Ekrem, turned it into one of the most influential publications in the turn-of-the-century Ottoman Turkish literary scene. From a young age, these writers owned books and were exposed to a variety of reading material and educational influence, starting at home. Halit Ziya recalls that some time before he was a student of the Mekhitarist School, he spent many nights listening to his father read from Hafez, and enrolled in *rüşdiye*, a school of secondary education for Muslim pupils, where they read 'three chapters of the Golestan and a Persian grammar, a bit of Turkish grammar, a two-hundred page Ottoman history [...], and finally, the most important subject in school, Arabic ... a path we followed reading a few lines a day [...]' He adds, '[i]n the end the youth who emerged with this load of information would neither be able to speak one four-word sentence of Persian to an Iranian tea seller nor understand a ten-line article in an Egyptian newspaper.'[8] The frustration with the quality of education as well as a general lack of interest in these languages would drive the young Halit Ziya to a foreign-run school where he believed he could learn 'more important things about life.'[9] In fact, he stops reading Turkish novels completely after having reached a certain level of competence in French.[10]

If the young writers of *Servet-i Fünun* did not reach the same level of proficiency as the previous generations in Arabic and Persian grammar, they maintained an interest in the lexical diversity that these languages provided. In an essay entitled 'Against [Arabic] Derivatives' (Müştaklara Karşı), Halit Ziya argues against the utilization of grammar rules dictated by Arabic – such as pluralizing 'alim' as 'ulema', per the rule of broken plurals in Arabic, instead of 'alimler', using the Turkish '-ler' suffix – but endorses word-borrowing. He maintains that 'there is no harm in having loan words in a language, the real harm stems from obeying the foreign rules that those words may bring from their languages of origin.'[11] In a similar vein, Ahmet Reşit (1870–1956), writing under the pseudonym H. Nazım states, in partial response to Ahmet Midhat's initial accusation, that 'while we have nothing but respect for the folks that truly studied Arabic – for they have spent their time effectively in pursuit of a valuable skill – we cannot accept that one must learn Arabic in order to write in proper Turkish.' He adds, 'The assistance Arabic language provides for ours can only encompass – and only to the degree we see fit – nouns and compounds; it can never go so far as to affect syntax and style.'[12]

These young writers' general stance towards the lexical wealth that Arabic (and, by extension, Persian) provided for the Turkish language is best exemplified in the amateurish amazement of Ahmet Cemil, the fictional poet in Halit Ziya's *Mai ve Siyah* (1896) who feels stuck in the composition of his poetic masterpiece. 'The work was progressing very slowly [...] At one point, he found the idiom too limited. New ideas needed new words. [...] He immersed himself in dictionaries and marvelled at all that he found there. Why have these been buried within these pages, he wondered.'[13] Embracing and using these forgotten words created a distance from the language that is already in circulation and obstructs intelligibility, in a way not too dissimilar to the case of Ottoman classical poetry where, as Nergis Ertürk points out, '[the] interpretive indeterminacy [...] was a crucial condition of possibility for the development of Ottoman Turkish as an imperial composite and cosmopolitan language.'[14] In fact, in the universe of Divan poetry, a certain sign can simultaneously send one in two different, yet equally valid, directions of meaning and the richness of the text comes precisely from this multitude, difficult to render into both other languages and more vernacular registers of the same language.

This productive ambiguity, turned onto its head in Ahmet Midhat's advocacy for intelligibility, was part and parcel of the classical poetry's expressional spectrum and what made it possible for it to contain two seemingly contradictory tendencies; an almost profane sensuality and an excessive devotion to religion. In *Poetry's Voice, Society's Song: Ottoman Lyric Poetry*, Walter Andrews advises against the reduction of this deliberate ambiguity to mere internal contradiction. 'We must realize that the two patterns are not necessarily mutually exclusive,' he argues, 'nor do they in any way require that a person choose to behave consistently according to one or the other, with the apparent proviso that the contextual requirements be consistently observed.'[15] For example, while excessive emotionalism warranted in the poetic universe may be a threat to certain social functions, it was also the path to a transcendent ontological reality that could be communicated only partially, and only through the expression of the personal experience that runs against the communality of mainstream Islam. The individual emotionalism permitted in this universe in fact provided exceptional freedom for self-expression in a society where religiosocial norms allowed little to none.

Yet, this freedom of expression was only possible for those who were well versed in the tightly-controlled figurative realm of classical poetry. While the poetic vocabulary was not necessarily part of the spoken language – though it had impacted it – it had strong ties to the literary tradition and inhabited a semantic domain whose borders were drawn by this very tradition, with a limited number of tropes reoccurring in different form in almost every poem. With a history that can be traced back to pre-Islamic Arabo-Persian traditions and first introduced in Anatolia in Persian, the vocabulary of Ottoman classical poetry was fixed early on and saw only small changes later on. This stands in stark contrast with the possibilities that *Servet-i Fünun* writers availed themselves of when browsing lexicons to discover forgotten words and reuse them with little to no concern about how they had been utilized previously, although the classical tradition had in fact already been challenged by the previous generation of Ottoman literati, Ahmet Midhat himself being one prominent figure to do so.

Two of the best known novels penned during the few decades preceding the start of the decadents debate, the above-mentioned *Araba Sevdası* and Namık Kemal's *İntibah* (Awakening, 1876), feature descriptions of the garden – the space of gathering and poetic recitation, as well as a recurring metaphor in classical poetry – in an effort to undo the semantic tradition of the previous centuries. At the mention of roses, a well-known image of that poetic universe, Kemal famously wrote, 'perhaps because of my excessive engagement with Eastern imagination, I always recall the nightingale when I think of the rose. I know indeed that it is not in love with the rose, yet one could tell that the poor bird nurtures a tremendous amount of love in its tiny heart. His affections are however for his own freedom for he is unable to live on let alone sing when trapped in a cage.'[16] Building upon Kemal's rebellious replacement of the rose with freedom, Ekrem further disturbed the classical poetic universe by replacing the lyrical descriptions of the garden with the bureaucratic precision of a land registry officer. In Kemal's and Ekrem's descriptions of it, the garden had already ceased to be a space where participants could grasp at higher truths in a collective mystical experience and where each object was the reflection of an otherworldly counterpart. It had now become a modern locale delineated in metres, approximated in walking time, where lyricism could only happen in the realm of new national ideals.

In contrast with the previous generation, the writers of *Servet-i Fünun* almost never confronted the older poetic universe head-on, possibly because of their lack of knowledge of and, by extension, interest in it. In their search of new words, these writers did not directly meddle with the vocabulary of the classical poetry but rather availed themselves of its greater lexical reservoir. Even though the inaccessibility of their language was already at least as discomfiting as that of the classical poetry, the individual arbitrariness of their semantic connections rendered it even more so, particularly because these connections were fuelled by an affection for French literature – an affection that, however, collapsed two opposing ideas, Zola's documentarian approach to reality and Verlaine's symbolic aestheticism. They sought to both explore human nature and produce beauty in language, tendencies that ran counter, or at least remained indifferent, to Ahmet Midhat's agenda of ensuring the diffusion of morally-driven messages within society at large. This lack of concern often caused their writing to be misunderstood, ridiculed and even pathologized, most prominently because of their utilization of colour to express emotion. In *Şehir Mektupları* (Urban Letters), city documentarian and journalist Ahmet Rasim (1864–1932) sarcastically wrote, 'Have you heard? A new disease has been discovered in Europe. It attacked Paul Verlaine first, then spread to his friends: a tendency to see everything in black. [...] It is caused by microbes that attack bulbus medullae, gather on the tissue of nerves where images form – like ants around sugar – and cause the person to see everything in black. This certainly leaves a mark on his writing as well.'[17]

As some of his other works show, Ahmet Rasim's tongue-in-cheek diagnosis of French symbolism was largely meant as a criticism for *Servet-i Fünun* writers who were also affected by this 'epidemic', which essentially pointed to a deep dissatisfaction, not only with the society around them but also with the language available to them to express the various shades of this unease. Neither the cosmopolitan Ottoman used in different configurations in bureaucracy and literature nor the vernacular Turkish mirroring spoken registers proved apt to reflect the emotions that they nurtured. In a response to Ahmet Midhat's initial accusation, Süleyman Nesip (1866–1917) wrote, in defence of Cenap Şahabettin's (1870–1934) poetry, 'I cannot deny that at times they employ oddities excessively. One can certainly argue Cenap Şahabettin Bey particularly goes too far in this endeavour [...] Yet, apart from a few peculiar expressions, his innovative work is rich with pleasant ideas.' Later in the same article, Nesip asked, 'How can these meanings, emotions, this poetry be expressed in the language of the public? How can one explain to them, in their limited tongue, things they would not comprehend?'[18] In another response to Midhat's accusations, Cenap himself showed concern regarding the formation of new expressions for the honest reflection of new emotions through which 'the writer/poet tries to find his own soul in the mirror of words'. Without a new vocabulary, Cenap added, his words would be stillborn, mere tatters of the budding passions of his soul. In contrast, a poet who can rebel against the rules of syntax and morphology 'can breathe something other than the limited air it provides, [...] collects all of his lexical knowledge in his mind, bends and moulds the words, crushes fixed expressions with the hammer of his pen, batters the well-known styles like an angry hammersmith, moulds the debris of expressions into a new shape. His pen thus bears precious new words, unprecedented expressions, new sentences, an impatient new language ... *something truly literary*.'[19]

Style thus emerged as an important element in the undoing of established conventions and created a new register for the language that enabled *Servet-i Fünun* writers to refract their individual responses to the changing world around them. This subjective rule-bending proved disconcerting, not just to Ahmet Midhat, but to all parties concerned with maintaining cognitive commonality across Turkish speakers. In a contribution to this discussion, Tepedelenlizade Hüseyin Kamil echoed this concern and advised younger generations against such deviations in the search for fame: 'If we all execute whatever we please in the name of progress, the condition of our new literature that we are working so hard to ameliorate will collapse into complete disarray.'[20] A fall into the disorder of arbitrary signs is also one into unintelligibility, a result of the cognitive disjunction between multiple semantic universes inherent in the same language, threatening to take over each other's space. In *Against World Literature: On the Politics of Untranslatability*, Emily Apter assigns this phenomenon the term 'untranslatable,' an attribute of '[w]ords that assign new meanings to old terms, neologisms, names for ideas that are continually re-translated or mistranslated, translations that are obviously incommensurate,' and an epithet that evokes foreignness, and by Lacanian extension, paranoia, 'an experience of speaking in a foreign language that one does not understand.'[21]

In an article written some years later, Halit Ziya maintained that the stylistic conventions established by the *Servet-i Fünun* generation, though they were initially perceived as foreign elements dangerously penetrating the language, nevertheless generated unprecedented stylistic possibilities that informed modern Turkish literature in the decades to come. 'If one were to take an article by Cenap Şahabettin and to translate all words and compounds that seem awkward in today's language but not touch the ideas presented,' he observed, 'one would see that though the language has changed quite a bit, style has not, neither has the literary value of the text.'[22] His forward-looking legitimization of stylistic experimentation was reminiscent of its mirror image, that is to say *Servet-i Fünun*'s search for precedents in linguistic transgression, perhaps best exemplified in Ahmet Hikmet's article entitled 'Eslafta Dekadanlık ve Şeyh

Galib' (Decadents among Our Forerunners: Şeyh Galib) where he cast the eighteenth-century poet as the first decadent and renamed the followers of the decadents movement 'Galibiyyun'.[23] In a similar vein, Cenap Şahabettin argued that the language of contemporary French *littérateurs* was referred to as 'decadent' not because they represented a diseased emotional universe but because of their interest in honouring the poetic style of the previous generations. 'Just as a child cannot speak without first imitating his parents,' he observed, 'a poet cannot form his personal style without first imitating others.'[24] One may in fact argue that Galib's efforts in undoing the relationship between signs and their abstract signifiers was one precedent for the writers of *Servet-i Fünun*, and in that sense, their sources of influence were not merely drawn from abroad. In contrast to what Ahmet Midhat would have one believe, foreign did not always mean 'non-Ottoman.'

The half-concealing, half-revealing and rule-bending literariness that emerged as a result of this experimentation with what came before stood in contrast with the instruction-manual bluntness that Ahmet Midhat advocated for in his work. The kind of literary language, which, in David Damrosch's words, 'either gains *or* loses in translation,' was precisely what Midhat perceived as dangerous, as it would imply uncontrollable misinterpretations and transformed meanings even – and particularly – across different registers of the language.[25] As he stated, 'the reason why I don't like the language of the decadents is because it is really difficult to translate it into *our Ottoman*. This is not even all. These texts are also impossible to translate into English or German.'[26] Giving Zola's oeuvre as an example, he added, 'these cannot even be translated into French, the very language to which they supposedly belong.'[27] Elsewhere, he denied that his work had anything to do with literature, encouraging people who 'look for art' to go and read Recaizade Ekrem's and Halit Ziya's texts. In his metafictional novel *Müşahedat* (Observations, 1891) where he inserted himself into the storyline as one of the main characters, he called himself a *muharrir* (writer) and not an *edib* (*littérateur*), thus denying both the traditionalist definition of literature as 'the sum of all texts an educated person should know,' and the modernist one of the belles-lettres or imaginative literature.[28] The defiance that allowed him to freely mould the world outside to his moral instruction while presenting an illusion of truth gained him the epithet of *hace-i evvel* (the first teacher), yet his tight hold on his readers' perceptions never allowed him much room for delving into the internal worlds of his characters and he remained, throughout his writing career, a reporter and a judge more than a psychologist, presenting characters easily categorizable along clearly-drawn moral lines and whose fate matched their personality traits.

Ahmet Hamdi Tanpınar famously drew attention to this problem, which he identified as a lack of 'psychological investigation'. 'The Muslim East has been little preoccupied with the human soul,' he argues, 'even though there are some who sought to deepen their self-knowledge methodically, but such inquiry never became part of general education.' He contrasted Islamic faith with Christianity where the confessional tradition enabled the development of introspection, 'an investigative eye turned inward toward the self'.[29] It is in this contrast that the distinction lies between the seemingly investigative yet already all-knowing morality of Ahmet Midhat in *Müşahedat* (1891) and the self-mocking self-awareness of Recaizade Ekrem in *Araba Sevdası* (1896), two of the most important novels of the late Ottoman period, the former spreading to everyone its self-assured truthfulness, the latter inviting the willing parties to step out and notice their own internal inconsistencies. Ekrem's invitation provided a foundation for the beginning of what is known today as the *Edebiyat-ı Cedide* movement, formed of the very young writers who became the target of Ahmet Midhat's criticism a few years later. In *Hikaye* (1891), a treatise on the novel genre penned shortly before his move to Istanbul and the beginning of his work with *Servet-i Fünun*, Halit Ziya wrote that 'stories [novels] are scales for the human life that allow us to process the most peculiar of human emotions, the most telling instances of the human condition. They provide an arena of investigation for matters concerning the psyche.'[30] Initially a phenomenon of poetry, the formation of new signs to express new emotions - which resulted in the unintelligibility Ahmet Midhat referred to in his initial article – was central to the deepening of the introspective tendencies of the novel as a genre. In fact, prose soon proved to be the more fertile ground for the proliferation of these signs as it did not have to struggle as much with the predetermined signifiers of the classical poetry and their multilayered systems of signification.

In the fight between two registers of the same language, Ahmet Midhat's journalistic street-speak and Ekrem's (and his pupils') idiosyncratic take on the Arabo-Persian vocabulary, the latter would lose its grip during and after the

Second Constitutional Period, as the literary language became increasingly superimposed with that of the national vernacular and the possibility of multilingual, non-identitarian writing increasingly impossible. After the turn of the century, the process of vernacularization would build itself on Midhat's decidedly public language that gained value through its very intelligibility to as many members of a linguistic group as possible, rather than cross-referencing to other linguistic spheres to produce an individualized language. The Turkish vernacular was, in Sheldon Pollock's words, a stay-at-home language, which defined itself through 'ever-increasing incommunication' with anything outside itself, rather than 'unbounded and potentially infinite in extension.'[31] The definite casting of Ottoman literature in the first decades of the twentieth century as the irrelevant literature of a forgone age signalled both a turn to the West as the main source of influence in the formation of the national literature, and the displacement of the short-lived prominence of the cosmopolitan presence of *Edebiyat-ı Cedide*, the first literary movement that 'turned toward the West', but in a way that would remain uninterested in sculpting a national identity. While Tevfik Fikret (1867–1915), the prominent *Servet-i Fünun* poet, wrote 'my home is the earth, my people humankind', echoing Victor Hugo's proclamation in *Les Burgraves* (1843), such a sentiment was replaced with Ziya Gökalp's national romanticism that denied individualist cosmopolitanism in favour of a sort of westernization whose main aim was to defy the West while freeing the language and the culture from the unwanted cultural influence of Arabic and Persian, thereby helping place the Turkish nation in the constellation of Western nations.[32] Gökalp would indeed echo Ahmet Midhat's opinion on what he perceived to be a form of excessive imagination and experimentation in literature: 'Our aesthetic sense should be cultivated by translating Western classics into our own language. The classical literature of Europe is a healthy literature. The kind of literature created by decadents and fantasists is morbid. The Ottoman life [i.e. the second generation of westernizers] copied this sick literature because Ottoman society was senile. The Turkish nation, which has emerged intact out of its ruins, is young, in its infancy even.'[33] In this view, other languages and cultures are only to be appreciated from a distance as an exotic other rather than anything worthy of emotional involvement.

This view of *Servet-i Fünun*'s cross-lingual experimentation would crystallize after the foundation of the Turkish Republic. Even as an author known for his cosmopolitan tendencies, Ahmet Hamdi Tanpınar criticized the work of Recaizade Ekrem, arguing that 'it is hard to admire Ekrem Bey's writing today. His poetry, stories and criticism are but a distant memory in our intellectual and artistic history; they belong to a period of crisis and were representative of the sensibility of their time.'[34] The surviving members of the *Servet-i Fünun* themselves joined in the criticism of their late-nineteenth-century work during the first decade of the Republican period. In an article entitled 'Hakları Var' (They Are Right), Halit Ziya endorsed the early Republican criticism of the *Servet-i Fünun* literature as overly adorned and replete with heavy vocabulary: 'it was an illness of the time to write as if your text would get better as you moved away from proper Turkish.'[35] An embittered call for recognition accompanied this post-imperial self-criticism, as Halit Ziya accused the nature of the vocabulary then available to himself and other *Servet-i Fünun* writers and what he called 'an Eastern knack for language play.' 'Still,' he argued, 'the *Edebiyat-ı Cedide* phenomenon blazed a new trail in the language of prose, like that of a shepherd whose footprints become the riverbed for rivers to flow down from the hills.'[36]

Many poets and novelists in later generations have identified the members of the *Edebiyat-ı Cedide* movement as their predecessors. In the generation following that of the *Servet-i Fünun* authors, poets connected to the *Fecr-i Ati* (Dawn of the Future) movement expressed admiration for Halit Ziya's character Ahmet Cemil, the fictional poet in *Mai ve Siyah*. In an article published in *Servet-i Fünun* (reestablished under the name *Uyanış* after the foundation of the Republic) in 1930, Reşat Fevzi observed that these young poets behaved like Ahmet Cemil, walked up and down Istanbul's Babıali Avenue with a few books in French tucked under their arms, and frequented various libraries sporting their long hairstyles. 'It was as if,' he commented, 'there appeared a new physical form for poethood.'[37] Some decades later, novelist Oğuz Atay drew attention to Halit Ziya's particular interest in 'broken lives', 'stories of individuals who dared to deviate away from the status quo, experienced disappointment as a result, yet never became victims of fate', and thus found parallels between his own masterpiece *Tutunamayanlar* (The Disconnected, 1972) and Halit Ziya's *Kırık Hayatlar* (Broken Lives, 1923), both referring to those who ventured outside the boundaries of the socially acceptable.[38]

In its short life sandwiched between the Tanzimat and the Second Constitutional periods, the *Edebiyat-ı Cedide* authors' experimentation with language showed that vernacularization was not an unsurprising consequence of the natural course of literary history; rather, it involved the active annihilation of certain practices of attachment – particularly cross-lingual and non-identitarian ones – as exemplified in Ahmet Midhat's position in his initial article. Nergis Ertürk drives this point home best when she argues that writing reform was cast as an integral part of the national project not because nationalists saw language as a practical tool to reach their aims, but as a potentially subversive instrument that could undo what they aimed to accomplish, 'as a threatening, uprooting *force*, generative of unseen consequences without end.'[39] (Ertürk: 27). In other words, what is often formulated in social history accounts of the period as a drive towards a representation of the national speech in writing was instead a conscious effort to drive out foreign elements and homogenize an otherwise multilingual population. Contrary to this observation, İlker Aytürk has emphasized, '[i]t is only natural that all mass movements have utilized and continue to utilize vernacular languages. That is the only way the leaders and ideologists of such movements make sure that they reach the maximum number of potential followers.'[40] As such, such an effort did not aim to enlarge the audience so much as it did to shrink it.

Echoing Sheldon Pollock's work, Beecroft points out that a vernacular language is 'not simply a question of ease of use or the ability to communicate more effectively,' though it is often presented in this way – as seen in Ahmet Midhat's emphasis on intelligibility – rather 'this choice is an aesthetic one, with the potential for political overtones, where authors writing in the vernacular construct a narrower audience for their work, and, through that construction of an audience, construct some sort of cultural community.'[41]

I would like to suggest in conclusion that this deliberate distancing from the semantic devices of the cosmopolitan past constitutes a major reason why we often find the aesthetic–intellectual realm confined within that of the political – without a cosmopolitan language that would keep it distinct. In a similar vein, Beecroft observes, 'there is reason enough [...] to note [...] that, in distancing themselves from their classical and cosmopolitan pasts, both China and Europe also eliminated a particular possibility of intellectual autonomy, separated from the political realm by the use of the cosmopolitan language.'[42]

The near-annihilation of the aesthetic space by the political would lead to a widespread scholarly perception of the former Ottoman territories, in Victoria Holbrook's oft-quoted words, 'as an exclusively sociological area where humanities never happen.'[43] This view further enforces the invisibility of the aesthetic realm, obfuscating literature's capacity to subvert linguistic boundaries and to challenge the monolingualism of social institutions. A major aim of literary studies should be to actively recognize and reclaim these pockets of aesthetic resistance against easy identitarian associations, an invitation resounding Apter's criticism of the field for falling short as anti-capitalist critique, 'because it insufficiently questions what it means to "have" a literature or to lay claim to aesthetic property.'[44] This sort of reclamation would not only reveal the conditions behind the literarily innovative moments in their entirety but also goes against the still prominent critical position that reduces literature in the non-Western contexts to a secondary presence that necessarily has to submit itself to the political.[45]

Notes

1 Hüseyin Cahit, *Kavgalarım* (Istanbul, 1910), p.119. All translations from Turkish are mine unless otherwise indicated.
2 Benjamin Fortna notes that '[w]hereas only an estimated 439 titles had been published in Ottoman Turkish prior to 1839, in the less than two decades following 1876 over 3000 titles appeared in that language.' See Benjamin Fortna, *Learning to Read in the Late Ottoman Empire and the Early Turkish Republic* (London, 2011), p.171.
3 'Harhara-i meakırdan bir havf-ı ezrak ile müstehif olanlar per ü bali küşade bir merkeb-i randebada maddiyet-i beşeriyeleri barını ihmalden isticnab etmelidirler.' Ahmet Midhat, 'Dekadanlar', *Sabah*, nr. 2680 (22 March 1897).
4 Veysi (d.1628) and Nergisi (d.1635) are two seventeenth-century poets, *personae non gratae* among the literary circles of the nineteenth century because of their adherence to excessive adornment, particularly in rhymed prose.
5 Charles Bernheimer, *Decadent Subjects: The Idea of Decadence in Art, Literature, Philosophy, and Culture of the Fin de Siècle in Europe* (Baltimore, 2002), p.3.
6 Ibid., p.55.
7 Nergis Ertürk, *Grammatology and Literary Modernity in Turkey* (Oxford: Oxford University Press, 2011), p.67.

8 Halit Ziya Uşaklıgil, *Kırk Yıl* (Istanbul, 2008), p.90. Part of the translation of this passage is taken from Benjamin Fortna, 'Education and Autobiography at the End of the Ottoman Empire', *Die Welt des Islams* 41/1 (2001), pp.1–31.
9 Halit Ziya Uşaklıgil, *Kırk Yıl*, p.170.
10 Ibid., p.187.
11 Halit Ziya Uşaklıgil, 'Müştaklara Karşı', *Sanata Dair* (Istanbul, 2014), p.75.
12 H. Nazım, 'Musahabe-i Edebiye 38', *Servet-i Fünun*, nr. 370 (14 April 1898), pp.86–7.
13 Halit Ziya Uşaklıgil, *Mai ve Siyah* (Istanbul, 2008), p.176.
14 Ertürk, *Grammatology and Literary Modernity in Turkey*, p.187.
15 Walter Andrews, *Poetry's Voice, Society's Song: Ottoman Lyric Poetry* (Seattle, 1985), p.142.
16 Namık Kemal, *İntibah* (İstanbul, 2006), p.5.
17 Ahmet Rasim, *Şehir Mektupları* (Istanbul, 2012), p.130.
18 Süleyman Nesip, 'Dekadanlar', *Tercüman-ı Hakikat*, nr. 5740–5742 (23–25 April 1897).
19 Cenap Şahabettin, 'Yeni Tabirat', *Servet-i Fünun*, nr. 330 (8 July 1897), emphasis added.
20 Tepedelenlizade Hüseyin Kamil, 'Mehmet Celal Beyefendiye Cevap', *Resimli Gazete*, nr. 26 (6 May 1897).
21 Emily Apter, *Against World Literature: On the Politics of Untranslatability* (New York, 2013), p.35.
22 Halit Ziya Uşaklıgil, 'Edebiyatta Hayat', p.123.
23 Ahmet Hikmet, 'Eslafta Dekadanlık ve Şeyh Galib', *Servet-i Fünun*, nr. 393 (22 September 1898). Some decades later, Ahmet Hamdi Tanpınar would also draw attention to the particular kind of care Şeyh Galib showed for language quoting this couplet: 'Tarz-ı selefe tekaddüm ettim/Bir başka lisan tekellüm ettim' (I surpassed the style of my precursors/I spoke in a different language). See Ahmet Hamdi Tanpınar, *Edebiyat Üzerine Makaleler* (Istanbul, 1998), p.179.
24 Cenap Şahabettin, 'Dekadizm Nedir?' *Servet-i Fünun*, nr. 344 (14 October 1897).
25 David Damrosch, *What is World Literature?* (Princeton, 2003), p.289.
26 Ahmet Midhat, 'Klâsikler ve Hüseyin Sabri', *Tercüman-ı Hakikat*, nr. 5912 (2 October 1897), emphasis added.
27 Ahmet Midhat, 'İcmal-i Edebisi Muharririne', *Tercüman-ı Hakikat*, nr. 6326 (5 December 1898).
28 In *An Ecology of World Literature: From Antiquity to the Present Day*, Alexander Beecroft observes that most definitions of literature across the world, including those of *wenxue* in China, *bungaku* in Japan, *edeb/adab* or *kayya* in the greater Middle East feature a tension between these two aspects. See Beecroft, *An Ecology of World Literature*, p.10.

29 Ahmet H. Tanpınar, *Edebiyat Üzerine Makaleler*, p.60.
30 Halit Ziya Uşaklıgil, *Hikâye* (Istanbul, 2012), p.20.
31 Sheldon Pollock, 'Cosmopolitan and Vernacular in History,' *Public Culture*, 12 .3 (2000): p.594; p.606.
32 Tevfik Fikret, 'Haluk'un Amentüsü,' quoted in Orhan Koçak, '"Westernisation Against the West": Cultural Politics in the Early Turkish Republic,' in Kerslake, Öktem, and Robins (eds), *Turkey's Engagement with Modernity: Conflict and Change in the Twentieth Century* (New York, 2010) p.305, where he also draws attention to this double-bind.
33 Ziya Gökalp, *Turkish Nationalism and Western Civilization Selected Essays of Ziya Gökalp* (Crows Nest, 1959), p.268.
34 Ahmet H. Tanpınar, *Edebiyat Üzerine Makaleler*, p.225.
35 Halit Ziya Uşaklıgil, 'Hakları Var', in *Sanata Dair* (Istanbul, 2014), p.17.
36 Halit Ziya Uşaklıgil, *Mai ve Siyah*, p.704.
37 Reşat Fevzi, 'Fecr-i Âtî Nasıl Bir Teşekküldü' *Uyanış/Servet-i Fünun* (1930).
38 A video of the Oğuz Atay interview can be found here: https://www.youtube.com/watch?v=I2X6UWLnFJs
39 Ertürk, *Grammatology and Literary Modernity in Turkey*, p.37.
40 Aytürk, İlker, 'Turkish Linguists Against the West: The Origins of Linguistic Nationalism in Atatürk's Turkey', *Middle Eastern Studies* 40:6 (2004), pp.1–25.
41 Beecroft, *An Ecology of World Literature*, p.148.
42 Ibid., p.226.
43 Victoria Holbrook, *The Unreadable Shores of Love: Turkish Modernity and Mystic Romance* (Austin, TX, 1994), p.1.
44 Emily Apter, *Against World Literature*, p.16.
45 One of the best-known examples of this trend is Fredric Jameson's 'Third-World Literature in the Era of Multinational Capitalism', *Social Text* 15 (1986).

2

How not to translate: Cultural authenticity and translatability in Recaizade Mahmut Ekrem's *Araba Sevdası* and Ahmet Midhat Efendi's *Felatun Bey ile Rakım Efendi*

Melih Levi

Novels published during the Tanzimat period featured characters who actively negotiated their cultural identity by adopting mannerisms considered either *alaturka* or *alafranga*. While the former connoted a traditional, Turkish and, at times, Islamic set of values, the latter referred to the direct imitation of European, especially French, manners. Traditionally, scholars of late Ottoman prose have framed these two competing series of identity markers as evidence of the pedagogical agenda of Tanzimat-era novelists and of their effort to offer cautionary tales against the dangers of haphazard imitation to their readers.

In this study, I turn to the question of language and provide an analysis of the very acts of translation themselves that take place within these literary works. Most Tanzimat novelists were translators as well as authors of original works. Thus the project of authorial 'self-fashioning' always went hand-in-hand with literary translation. This intimate relationship had important implications for the reformist objectives that writers such as Ahmet Midhat and Recaizade Mahmut Ekrem endorsed as a necessity for the betterment of Ottoman society. While it would be tempting to associate this attempt at self-fashioning as being limited to an authorial enterprise, I argue that, for the authors in quesiton, it also constituted a *translational* one. Specifically, by placing an emphasis upon acts and processes of literary translation whose fluctuating degree of accuracy threatened the main plot structure of their novels, these authors turned the unavoidable pitfalls of literary translation into narrative elements that continuously undermined or obfuscated their authorial intentions. Most importantly, by foregrounding translation as a process that unsettles notions of textual stability, Tanzimat novelists repeatedly acknowledged that there is no such thing as a 'finished' text. In doing so, they invited their readers to experience the process of translation and to take an active part in the production of meaning. This hermeneutic liberty stood in clear contrast with the more overtly pedagogical agenda of these novels. Such contrast is quite useful because translation, then, often serves as a subversive undercurrent, which at times contradicts the apparent moral objectives of the narrative. The process of self-fashioning that readers were invited to contemplate involved a continuous reexamination of the acts and decisions that engendered the illusion of authenticity and faithfulness that translation was supposed to achieve. Conversely, a similar volatility contaminated what characters in Tanzimat novels often conceptualized as either their 'local', 'Ottoman' or *alaturka* identity and its French or more generally Western counterpart.

By asserting the instability of both the objects and products of translation, Ahmet Midhat and Recaizade Mahmut Ekrem explored a dialectical, rather than teleological, relationship between agency and culture. In their works, particular actions and expressions were not presented as ends in themselves, nor were they designated as markers or signifiers of any 'authentic' cultural identity. They were, rather, clusters of tension (economic, social, ideological), which served to justify the valuation of certain phenomena as 'authentic'. Such a dialectical movement is crucial to understand how and why Tanzimat novelists opted to include long-winded processes of translation in the very plot of their works. This study will analyse Recaizade's *Araba Sevdası* (The Carriage Affair, 1898), whose protagonist Bihruz Bey dramatically fails in his attempts to translate literary excerpts and poetry in a letter addressed to his lover. In his case, the source texts are untranslatable due to an obvious lack of necessary knowledge, and yet they gradually become translatable as other characters get involved and reading becomes a more public enterprise. The second part of this study will turn to Rakım Efendi, the protagonist of Ahmet Midhat's *Felatun Bey ile Rakım Efendi* (Felatun Bey and Rakım Efendi, 1875), Bihruz Bey's quasi-polar opposite. For polyglot Rakım, Sufi poetry is at first elegantly and effortlessly translatable. Yet, as the story unfolds, his successful translations turn out to be the largest impediment against narrative closure and threaten to undermine his persona as a teacher and intellectual. Both characters run into conflicts when it comes to cultural representation engaging with the 'Other'. In Bihruz's case, it is about the dangers of translating *from* a culture without a slightest understanding of its traditions and in Rakım's case, the dangers of translating *into* a culture without paying any attention to the forms and methods of reception.

Recaizade Mahmut Ekrem's *Araba Sevdası* is a story of infatuation. Bihruz Bey, the protagonist, falls in love with Periveş Hanım after catching a glimpse of her during a public outing. Bihruz's feelings are based on erroneous assumptions regarding Periveş, who is neither noble nor wealthy as her young suitor originally assumes. Even though they do not exchange a single word, Periveş quickly becomes the object of Bihruz's desire. Bihruz plans to impress her by writing a letter. 'According to him, a love letter addressed to someone like Periveş Hanım, who comes from a *nobl* [noble] family and must have received a perfect education, should also include expressions, *sentimants* [sentiments] that are *nobl* and thus it was imperative to consult writings on this subject in French.'[1] This letter and its contents become the central plot element for the rest of the novel. Bihruz cannot make up his mind about what to include in the letter. Can he turn to Turkish literature for quotation, or is it more noble and appropriate to invoke the French canon? To what extent does he need to translate? To what extent does he need to understand the pieces of literature that he intends to quote from? With such indecisions, Recaizade gradually moves the reader's attention away from public spaces (i.e. outings, social encounters) towards the realm of language. More specifically, Recaizade devotes a substantial portion of the novel to a catalogue of literary excerpts and to Bihruz's attempts at translating them. In doing so, he foregrounds language as a more reliable record of the dialectical negotiations taking place between intention and meaning.

The nature of Bihruz's reckless infatuation with Periveş Hanım is captured by his repeated reference to her as 'blonde'. Through its repetition, the adjective becomes the signifier not for Periveş herself but for the structure of Bihruz's desire and attraction. The description of the young woman's physical features with this italicized, 'foreign' word calls attention to a recurrent linguistic gesture which aims to maintain a degree of enchantment with a constructed object of desire. Ultimately, such continued code-switching to refer to an individual becomes superfluous. Structurally, however, it helps make Bihruz's claim for authenticity emerge as the central theme of the novel. The linguistic realm is where the imaginary constitution of the blonde girl's identity is deconstructed. In other words, the comedic errors in Bihruz's readings and translations demonstrate the structure of his desire and how it culminates in the creation of an idealized feminine identity. From there on, the novel becomes a chronicle of Bihruz's attempts to communicate his desire by writing a love letter. Yet, this communication proves much more difficult than expected and involves a long-winded journey through some canonical works of Turkish and French literature.

Bihruz conceptualizes the choice between literary traditions with such ignorance and arbitrariness that it becomes impossible to maintain a conversation between them. All possibilities are manipulated and subsumed under the imaginary object of his desire. The choice, if there is one to begin with, is not, ultimately, between two traditions or cultures. It is rather the illusion of choice that drives Bihruz's thought process. In the following sections, I demonstrate how this very choice is idealized at the cost of its objects.

Early on in the novel, the narrator informs his readers about a choice Bihruz makes between an *alafranga* and *alaturka* education. As part of his upbringing, Bihruz receives tutoring in French, Arabic and Persian. However, his Arabic and Persian tutors quickly decide to drop him because they feel 'belittled and denigrated . . . Only Monsieur Pierre, the French tutor was allowed to continue given his age and ability to handle his student with tact. In fact, his compensation was increased from four to six liras.'[2] In fact, as the narrator soon makes clear, despite the explicit financial arrangements to accommodate a change in pedagogical circumstances, Bihruz's French education remains nearly non-existent. Monsieur Pierre, who knows 'how to handle his student with tact' becomes a confidant-of-sorts for Bihruz and whenever he brings him readings from French literature, they simply serve to boost his ego and complement his romantic sensibility. The narrator is careful here to pair a social concern such as education with Bihruz's financial situation. The two are intimately connected, for, in this novel, cultural investment is like financial investment in that both are exhaustible and can be consumed. Recaizade is strongly attuned to how culture, when used purely as a marker of one's class or social standing, turns into a marketable asset, an economic value rather than a pedagogical one that can be internalized.

This categorical way of understanding and analysing society is an integral part of Bihruz's perspective. When thinking about carriage rides through the district of Kadıköy, he sees it as a clash of opposites as he assumes Kadıköy to be populated only by middle class. According to Bihruz, Istanbul is

> divided into three classes ... the first one included people like him, the *noblesse,* or in other words the *civilisé* class consisting of the nobles and the elite, the second was the *bourgeois,* the middle class which were rather coarse and did not have a great handle on civilized discourse, and the third consisting of craftsmen ... so had Bihruz divided the quarters and neighbourhoods of Istanbul and for some reason, mistakenly placed Kadıköy in the second category when it should have been in the first.[3]

Such descriptions are important because they point to the narrator's urge to either verify or challenge Bihruz's analysis of the societal structure of Istanbul. Once again, Bihruz's misconceptions or incomplete knowledge leads him to make baseless inferences about Periveş and her social position. Despite the rigidity of the structures that colour his perception, they do not play a role in regulating his behaviour. Even though he places himself into the *noblesse* category, he is certainly not capable of the kind of civilized discourse which he deems characteristic of this class. To begin with, Bihruz fails to formulate his own sentiments and opinions. He plagiarizes from literary sources in order to appear cultured and capable of producing an 'authentic' discourse. The instability of class distinctions or the striking discrepancies in Bihruz's overview of societal structures underline once again the arbitrary valuation of self-fashioning. One's class identity is valuated based on extrinsic rather than intrinsic categories, which means that the recognition of class occurs primarily through explicit markers rather than the specific processes of self-fashioning undertaken by individuals.

So far we have pursued two mutable markers in the novel: language, and class. Bihruz does not possess proper knowledge about either, a fact that the narrator is keen to highlight. However, the absence or presence of knowledge is not any more important than the very question of knowability. In Bihruz's case, choices are illusory and have to be made between false objects emptied of their content and whose meaning is only temporarily activated. When the objects of choice are in such flux, the rhetoric around choice becomes the only reliable and stable tool. Hence, *Araba Sevdası* becomes a chronicle of this absence of a stable referent. In the last part of my analysis, I shall highlight this absence through an analysis of Bihruz's failed attempts at translation, which subsequently results in the loss of any ground for objective judgement.

Upon deciding to write a letter to Periveş, Bihruz sees fit to include 'a few pretty *poésies* or a *couplet*.'[4] At first, he considers Turkish poetry rather coarse and not quite fitting for this occasion. Later, he contemplates translating from French poetry or love manuals like the popular *Le secrétaire des amants* (1886). However, Bihruz worries that 'for *en vers* (verse) translations, Turkish would be inadequate and as for *en prose* (prose) translations, they wouldn't be beautiful anyway.'[5] Still, he gives it a try, picks a few couplets and attempts to translate them into Turkish. The results are not entirely satisfying, since there are several lines of the original that remain untranslated or are translated in such a convoluted way that they become unrecognizable. He returns once again to Turkish poetry but this time with more frustration: 'Ah! What to do! The Turks never had a decent poet!' Here the narrator steps in once again to dispute this claim: 'Bihruz Bey had heard from *alafranga* folks like him this talk about there not being a decent Turkish poet and the impossibility of reciting poetry in Turkish.'[6]

As readers, we of course know that Bihruz does not have the linguistic capability to understand or enjoy the nuances of Turkish poetry given that he never acquired an education in Arabic and Persian in his youth. The same is true for French, for the narrator makes it clear that Bihruz's French tutor, Monsieur Pierre continued the lessons purely for financial gain and was little more than a prop in Bihruz's household. In fact, when Bihruz falls in love and brings it up in conversation with his teacher and asks him for more examples of romantic texts, Monsieur Pierre starts to realize the danger of a reckless literary education and worries that Bihruz will start imitating, in speech and in action, the infatuated characters of the romances he reads. But upon sensing Bihruz's frustration with his cautionary statements, he decides not to risk losing his job and continues to feed Bihruz examples of blind desire from French literature. Lacking a proper and critical understanding of the Romantic movement in French poetry, Bihruz considers their amorous rhetoric to be exemplary.

Bihruz finally picks up the poet Vasıf and his book of poems, *Divan-ı Eş'ar*. His initial take on Vasıf's poetry is dismissive and critical, for he finds his images and metaphors to be disturbingly rough and quotidian. Bihruz's decision to turn to Vasıf is not the result of a sophisticated selection process. Vasıf, a poet of the eighteenth century, was heavily influenced by the distinctive pedestrian style of Nedim, one of the most important classical poets of the Ottoman Empire. The apparent simplicity of Vasıf's poetry makes him one of the only poets Bihruz can tackle without extensive dictionary use. Yet, even with Vasıf's poetry, Bihruz's attempts to translate go tragically wrong. He is entirely lost when it comes to words of Arabic or Persian origin; he continuously approximates them to find similar-looking or -sounding words in the dictionary. For almost a dozen pages, Recaizade quotes excerpts from Vasıf, provides his own translations at times, and recounts Bihruz's long-winded attempts and failures. In this way, Recaizade puts the spotlight on the very process of translation of translation, showcasing the various caprices of language and possible errors. The emphasis on the process is a way to get the readers to decide what constitutes a good or appropriate translation. However, the texts are simply untranslatable with Bihruz's level of education and linguistic aptitude. The process depicted in this episode, then, is rather an inquiry into the possibility of turning an objectively inconceivable task into a possible one. To succeed, Bihruz will need to disassemble the original and mutate its parts thoroughly to authorize his own translation.

Bihruz takes a quatrain from the book, which begins with the praiseful line: 'Bir siyeh-çerde civândır' ('She is a swarthy youth.')[7] Mistakenly reading the first two words as one, 'bersiyeh,' he consults dictionaries to no avail and concludes that it cannot possibly be a bad word. He misreads the next work as well. He reads 'çerde' as 'cerde' and learns from the dictionary that it must refer to a yellow horse. Excited about the reference to 'yellow,' he concludes that the poem must be written for a *blonde*, ignores the rest of the definition and decides to include the quatrain in the letter. Afterwards, when he does not get a response to his letter and stops seeing Periveş altogether, Bihruz starts to worry about the poem and whether its content might have offended her. He goes around asking for help to translate it more properly but in his *alafranga* circles, no one is able to help him decipher the meaning. Their attempts are so farcically preposterous that the original poem becomes a distant echo. They take the non-existent word 'bersiyeh' and stretch it to 'persiye' and 'persillé' which refers to cheeses like Roquefort with green stains on them. Once these theories are exhausted and the poem starts to turn into an infinitely-translatable object, one of his friends exclaims: 'Come on now, let us see this poem so that we can find the word. We don't even know where and how it's used!'[8]

This discussion offers a compelling challenge to contemporary theories of translation which are keen to make a direct association between translation and interpretation. There is no denying that all translations are also interpretations but the question is about whether one ought to treat translation as a positive or a negative form of freedom. *Araba Sevdası* calls attention to the dangers of a positive mode which considers the text an object that can be stretched freely in any and all directions. The assumption of infinite translatability denies the possibility of there ever being an original. Recaizade himself is not an essentialist when it comes to culture. Even when the original poem is retrieved and the character takes a look at the original poem, the main issue persists. Namely, the 'literal' meaning of the text becomes available to Bihruz only in assisted translation and any aesthetic enjoyment or appreciation is not possible due to his larger ignorance of the poetic tradition. Even though Recaizade does not privilege the original poem, he seems to be advocating for authenticity and context which might generate varying degrees of translatability in a work. Recaizade suggests a dialectical movement between translatable content that one can work through and decipher, and an untranslatable content that is very much defined by conditions of access. The translatable and the untranslatable are not necessarily features of the original but features that are disclosed throughout the process of translation. What is (un)translatable in a text announces itself through the work of translation. Hence, while not advocating for an essentialist conception of translation or cultural influence, Recaizade makes a convincing case for there being limits of translatability which are revealed through specific acts and situations, and which always emerge in dialectical tensions.

In Ahmet Midhat Efendi's *Felatun Bey and Rakım Efendi*, translation is also one of the key elements in the narrative. Rakım Efendi, who is valorized as an exemplary and self-made man, makes money as a teacher and a translator. One of his most important sources of income is the English Ziklas family. Rakım teaches Turkish to their daughters, Jan and Margaret. He uses Hafez's poems, translates them into Turkish with ornate commentaries and, over time, the English girls begin to admire them and even prefer them to British Romantic poetry. After engaging with such amorous content, however, one of the girls, Jan, falls madly in love with Rakım. The relationship is obviously impossible since Rakım is already engaged to his Circassian slave, Janan. Ahmet Midhat blames Rakım for inciting such emotions in Jan and bringing her so close to death's door. The question that emerges from this context is almost the opposite of the one in *Araba Sevdası*. Rakım, after all, proves himself to be a competent teacher, reader and commentator of poetry. Unlike Bihruz, he is capable of translating poetry with great mastery. Now the question is not so much translating *from* but translating *for*. Rakım neglects to think about translation as a way of communicating information that can be misused, misinterpreted or misunderstood depending on the receiver and context. He neglects to add a critical element to his translation in order to form distance-generating mechanisms which would prevent reckless mystifications of the original texts. The aura of authenticity is created as a result of the emotional expectations of the reader and not in conjunction with historical and literary context. It is surely inconceivable for a reading not to shape itself according to the expectations of the reader, however, like Recaizade, Ahmet Midhat also argues for a dialectical tension between such expectations and comparatively objective information about the text and its cultural position.

The ninth chapter of *Felatun Bey and Rakım Efendi* starts with an evaluation of the novel's overall development: 'Things continued along as usual. That is, Rakım continued to fulfil his duties as a translator, writer and teacher. If there was an apparent modification in the state of affairs, it was the slight change in the way the English girls treated him.'[9] Here, we are at a turning point and the 'slight change' is a mere synonym for the most important conflict in the novel. Despite the narrator's assertion, things are not 'continuing along as usual.' The narrator contradicts himself and tries to suppress a narrative problem that has been hinted at throughout the book. The change in the manner of the English girls is, in fact, an alarm bell for the impending calamity that will result from Rakım's teaching of love poetry. The contradictory statement at the beginning of this chapter demonstrates the amount of psychic investment the narrator has had to make so far to control a situation that has been engendered and overlooked by Rakım Efendi himself.

By 'psychic investment' I refer to two processes. First and foremost, the narrative wants to move in one direction but it is continuously pulled into an impasse. The narrator, as seen in the sentence above, makes an effort to downplay the gravity of the situation. There can be multiple explanations for such unremitting suppression. Most importantly, it threatens Rakım Efendi's position as the exemplary character, idealized in most, if not all, situations. The narrator is obviously not impartial in his treatment of the novel's protagonists, and this particular situation involving the English girls risks disturbing the moral compass of the narrative. The narrative registers this development as a shock and tries to soften it with phrases like 'slight change.' Second, this psychic investment reveals itself through a *libidinal* structuring of the narrative. Rakım Efendi experiences varying degrees of sexual attraction to most female protagonists in the novel. His attraction to Janan is constantly repressed (mostly on moral grounds) and is quite obviously worked out through his relationship with other characters. For example, the English family invites Rakım to join them on one of their boat rides. The narrator describes the English girls' attractive sailor outfits:

> Rakım found himself resting against the elder sister, and the younger sister resting against him. This gave Rakım more delight than anything else. Yes, do you suppose he gave their parents any cause for concern? Well! So . . . Rakım had such urges too, eh! Why shouldn't he? Did we introduce Rakım to you as someone who doesn't understand appetites, masculinity, and femininity? Besides, the pleasure he felt was totally emotional and conscientious, and since he never thought of turning these desires into reality, he engendered no mistrust.[10]

Notice the extent to which the narrator goes out of his way to reassure readers that Rakım's pleasure poses no moral conflicts since it is ultimately not turned into action. There is a negative foreshadowing here. The narrator seems to be casting a misleading confidence vote for Rakım, as if to delegitimize any narrative expectation that would risk Rakım's moral integrity. This cautionary style sets the stage more decisively for the impending calamity at the end. Thus, it is crucial to recognize the division of moral control between Rakım's actions and the narrator's commentaries. In other words, the production of readerly judgement is caught up and to some extent engendered by the narrator's effort to keep the libidinal economy in check. It is ultimately the collapse of this system, this control mechanism that will necessitate a new mode of agency.

So far critics have treated the novel from a rather one-dimensional perspective: the narrator mocks Felatun and idealizes Rakım. *The tone* of the narrator does seem to suggest that Rakım is a model character. However, the narrative structure suggests a different reading which brings Rakım down from the position of an ideal character. One of his major flaws ends up posing the single, largest threat to the linear movement of the story. Rakım, who is repeatedly acclaimed for his success as tutor and translator, ends up stumbling in both respects. The narrator explicitly suggests that there is a fundamental problem with the way he teaches Hafez to his pupils, and Rakım, too, occasionally worries about his pedagogy. In the rest of this chapter, I'll demonstrate how the novel registers the tension that gradually builds up as a result of Rakım's failure, and through that, elucidate the role translation plays in the novel.

At the beginning, Ahmet Midhat creates specific instances for the sole purpose of valorizing Rakım as a skilled teacher and tutor. For instance, Felatun repeatedly attempts to undermine Rakım's linguistic abilities but each instance works only to confirm Rakım's knowledge. In the third chapter, Felatun confronts Rakım in front of the English family, casting doubt on his ability to teach. Felatun claims that Rakım made errors while teaching the alphabet to the English girls. Rakım, however, has taught it correctly: Felatun, we learn, was not aware of the additional three letters used in Ottoman Turkish (p, ç and z). A similar incident takes place later, this time involving a translation issue: at a dinner, Felatun tries to show that Rakım has mistranslated a song. He claims that 'brunette' means 'blonde' in French. But once again, Rakım *is* correct. When it comes to alphabetical, lexical translation, Rakım seems to never fail. He's got a good grasp of various languages. He has, in other words, the raw material one needs to do things with and across languages. These early scenes in the novel do not only confirm Rakım's linguistic abilities but also situate language in the intersection of public and private realms. Benjamin Fortna argues that 'reading bears an iconic quality for the individuation of society in the modern period. Both the widening access to literary and the increased emphasis on individual as opposed to collective reading has had profound implications in the political, religious, economic and social fields.'[11] The linguistic disagreements between Rakım and Felatun are resolved in the public realm and they both carry echoes of institutional pedagogy. The narrator lists the letters and writes the alphabet, like a classroom teacher writing on the blackboard. Ultimately, it is not in the public but in the private realm that

Rakım fails as a teacher; and Ahmet Midhat emphasizes their inseparability for modernized education.

How does Rakım fail as teacher? From the very beginning, Rakım is aware of presenting Hafez without providing any context or background regarding the poems' philosophical content. Rakım recognizes the danger in teaching poetry with the sole purpose of serving one's passions. But he also takes a pleasure from seeing the way his pupils respond to the poems.

> **Jan** English poetry never makes one thirsty for love. I used to like French poetry more but now that I've learned Turkish, I've given up on French poetry as well.
>
> **Margaret** Me too. What is a poem for if it doesn't ignite a fire in you?
>
> **Rakım** What are you saying? I've never heard you talk this way before.[12]

Like Felatun's, the girls' engagement with another culture is founded on fancy. They too end up consuming the resources of another culture until it starts to consume them. Rakım fails in his attempts to provide a more nuanced understanding of Hafez's poetry. The girls are blindly selective in their taste: they find some verses unworthy of recording in their notebooks, and simply ask Rakım to skip them. The discarded verses often have overt Sufi content. The girls are only interested in an explicit and raw expression of desire, for 'they didn't have a grain of mysticism in their nature, their minds were unable to access the delights of the spiritual world.'[13] As teacher, Rakım Efendi is aware of venturing into dangerous territory and makes this known to his pupils: 'Since you are so enthusiastic about poetry ... I could show you some Persian poems and even translate some of the better Ottoman ones; however, I fear you might take advantage of this much independence.'[14] It clearly gives Rakım pleasure to see that he can charm and impress, even if this means appropriating and reducing his own culture. The pleasure he takes from this activity is evident in the following lines:

> As he read, he employed a fine Shiraz accent, turning the Persian language around in his mouth as if he were savoring candy. Although the girls weren't able to comprehend the meaning yet, they admired the sweetness of the pronunciation when Rakım translated the poem and conveyed its meaning. The girls, whose amorous feelings had already been awakened, were intoxicated.[15]

Critical appreciation and content are sacrificed almost entirely to induce passions and leave impressions. That Rakım encourages such reckless enjoyment is clear from the way he translates the poems. Even if it is standard procedure to offer commentary on a poem by embellishing its various images, Rakım takes it to an extreme, knowing that it is precisely his ornate commentaries which move the English girls. By reserving such substantial space for both the poems and Rakım's long, elaborate translations, Ahmet Midhat suggests textual comparison as the basis for the use of readerly *judgement*. While an informed Ottoman reader may appreciate the nuances and bravado of Rakım's readings from a distant, critical perspective, the English girls evidently fail to qualify their immediate, emotional responses. Aesthetic distance for Ahmet Midhat is central to the activity of translation. Ultimately, Rakım's way is not the right way to translate. Later, when Jan falls to her deathbed from lovesickness, Rakım recognizes his error: 'Ah, see, isn't it Hafez's poetry that brought her to this state? I couldn't predict that it would have had such an impact. How she listened to and absorbed the most passionate couplets with a fire in her heart! Now I realize she was poisoning herself with them.'[16]

Rakım's deceptive tone is reminiscent of Felatun's regretful remarks at the end of the novel. He had seen it coming but chose to look the other way. Felatun's farewell words upon encountering Rakım and learning about Jan's sickness are infused with irony and some degree of truth: 'There, you see? This is as good as philosophers like you can do. You say, "we should protect our honor, we should protect our decency", and give such young girls tuberculosis and then abandon them.'[17] His criticism is rather well-placed and calls attention to the double standard in Rakım's behaviour. This entire plotline has often been ignored by literary critics, even though it precipitates the conflict that takes up almost the entire second half of the book and provides the biggest threat to the healthy resolution of the primary relationship in the novel: between Rakım and Janan. For Ahmet Midhat, while transmitting and adapting meaning, translation has to maintain a degree of critical distance.

Felatun Bey and Rakım Efendi marks an important moment in Turkish literary history because it is one of the first times that an author uses a libidinal narrative structure to explicate cultural and societal relations. The attraction of different cultures plays a structuring role in the claims one can make about the authenticity of one's own culture. Self-definition is not only a question of what and what not to take from another. It is also, and more so, a matter of understanding the structure of attraction one comes to feel for *the other*. For the idea of self can only be woven out of a structure and the activity of translation ought to assert a dialectical relationship which ultimately emphasizes *translatability*. Without a dialectic, culture turns into a mere commodity and any claim for authenticity amounts to a frivolous negation of culture altogether. Ahmet Midhat's concept of authenticity is only possible through establishing certain distance-generating mechanisms. Put differently, the very possibility of theorizing the right amount of translation or a balanced cultural adaptation depends on being able to develop critical frames for authenticity to begin with.

The overt didacticism of Ahmet Midhat's narrators and their attempts to fashion a readership do not produce a meaningful agency. That is, the narrator's interjections are a performance and never a secure moral compass. Where agency emerges most forcefully is when the narratorial voice *fails* to deliver a convincing moral judgement. In *Felatun Bey and Rakım Efendi*, this happens due the narrator's failure to create an undercurrent critical of Rakım's teaching. The reader has to invent this form of agency in the absence of a narratorial modelling and endorsement. If Ahmet Midhat is able to fashion 'an authentic readership', it is because the reader has to *assess* Rakım's translation and determine what is authentic about Hafez and Ottoman culture by maintaining a critical distance. Ahmet Midhat's ideal citizen is one who can feel entitled to make claims of authenticity only if and when they can establish distance-generating mechanisms. It is therefore difficult to agree with Ahmet Evin's analysis of this novel, which holds that 'certain ideas gleaned from Europe are translated and adapted into a particular Turkish context to such an extent that they are altered beyond recognition.'[18] Quite the contrary, Ahmet Midhat describes the *process* of translation, the *translatability* of ideas and customs in order to reject the illusion of complete alteration or transformation.

To conclude, I return to the question of whether the act of translation offers the opportunity to exercise a positive or negative form of freedom. Much contemporary scholarship in translation studies tends to idealize the positive aspect by dismantling the obsession with an original and insisting on the infinite proliferation of meaning, a position which strategically ignores objective struggles or impediments which may inevitably impede such boundless liberty. For Ahmet Midhat and Recaizade, however, it is the negative aspect that lays the foundations for a healthy society. The acts of translation, which occupy a central position in the two novels discussed in this chapter, are failures in their own rights. Nevertheless, the absence of an authorized translation gives authors the opportunity to foreground the objective structures which enable or disable one's exercise of freedom. The coexistence of relentless narratorial interference with the negation or suspension of translational agency helps to foreground these structures. The tension and interdependence between the two enterprises – authorial and translational – do not discredit authenticity as a concept altogether, but render it credible only when they manage to establish grounds for a strong dialectical objectivity.

Notes

1 Recaizade Mahmut Ekrem, *Araba Sevdası* (Istanbul, 2017), pp.60–1.
2 Ibid., p.22.
3 Ibid., p.27.
4 Ibid., p.67.
5 Ibid.
6 Ibid., p.69.
7 Ibid., p.77.
8 Ibid., p.121.
9 Ahmet Midhat, *Felâtun Bey and Râkım Efendi* (Syracuse, NY, 2016), p.110.
10 Ibid., p.32.
11 Benjamin C. Fortna, *Learning to Read in the Late Ottoman Empire and the Early Turkish Republic* (New York, 2011), p.3.
12 Ahmet Midhat, *Felâtun Bey and Râkım Efendi*, p.57.
13 Ibid., p.100.
14 Ibid., p.57.
15 Ibid., p.58.
16 Ibid., p.126.
17 Ibid., p.127.
18 Ahmet Ö. Evin, *Origins and Development of the Turkish Novel* (Minneapolis, 1983), p.95.

3

Beyond binaries: Ahmet Midhat Efendi's prescriptive modern

Monica M. Ringer

Ahmet Midhat's most famous novel, *Felatun Bey and Rakım Efendi* (1875), has long been read as a critique of superficial westernization in the Tanzimat period exemplified by the contrast between the two eponymous characters, Felatun and Rakım. In this reading, Felatun, a dandy and spendthrift, represents the inauthentic *alafranga* man, the westernized fop; Rakım, the hard-working modest teacher and family man, the authentic *alaturka* Ottoman. Binaries of West versus East and traditional versus modern are often welded together into a super-binary: the modern West versus the traditional Ottoman. In this manner, modernization's possible discourses are limited to discussions of the authentic as inimical to 'Western' or 'modern', which in turn forces modernity to be understood as inauthentic and Western. The prevalence of these assumptions have distorted our understanding of the Tanzimat project.

I propose that we read this novel differently. *Felatun Bey and Rakım Efendi* does posit a binary represented by Felatun and Rakım, respectively, but not a binary between West and East, nor between Traditional and Modern, nor even between *alafranga* and *alaturka*, but instead between different possible new Ottoman moderns. We need to re-read *Felatun Bey and Rakım Efendi*, and to re-read the Tanzimat project largely conceived, not as one of westernization – a project framed and limited by the narrow possibilities of imitation or rejection – but instead as a project of introspective re-evaluation and reform – a re-evaluation of Ottoman institutions and traditions, in the context of a useful comparison with Europe. The historiographic construction of a linear movement of ideas from Europe to the Ottoman Empire must be replaced with a more nuanced understanding of the Tanzimat as primarily a period of self-reflection, self-assessment and change. The project shifts from: what can we adopt from Europe beneficially? – which suggests that adoption is the objective – to: what do we want to change?, what do we wish to retain?, and, what might we learn from Europe as an empirical example of one possible articulation of modernity? These questions shift the discourse away from adoption to one of translation. The Tanzimat was not a project of the *adoption* of Western modernity and/or the *rejection* of Ottoman tradition, but a project of *translation* from Ottoman 'tradition' to Ottoman 'modern.'

Turning back to the two central characters in the novel, Rakım represents a productive synthesis between tradition and modernity and Felatun represents a destructive one – each of them a possible modern – but Ahmet Midhat clearly presents one version as superior to the other. It is thus not that Felatun is Western and Rakım not, but that Felatun adopts negative, destructive qualities of the West, whereas Rakım adopts positive, constructive, ones. Similarly, Felatun is less selective in which Ottoman customs he follows, maintaining practices inimical to the modern, whereas Rakım discards Ottoman conventions that are unproductive. Felatun abandons Ottoman tradition, only to find himself stranded in the shoals of superficial Westernization. Rakım, conversely, deftly navigates between tradition and modernity, safely arriving on the shores of a productive Ottoman modern.

Nowhere is Ahmet Midhat's project of translation more evident than in his treatment of female characters, and there are lots of them – in fact, female characters disproportionately populate the novel. Of the characters who speak in the novel, as opposed to being referenced or implied, such as Rakım's father, there are ten female characters: Janan, Josephine, Pauline, Mihriban, Mrs Ziklas, Fedayi, Rakım's mother, the Ziklas daughters Jan and Margaret, and a secondary character in the Ziklas' Greek cook. By contrast, there are just six male characters: Rakım, Felatun, Felatun's father, Mr Ziklas, the doctor, and a peripheral character of an Armenian who hires Rakım to do secretarial work and loans him French books at the outset of the novel.

Much of the translation between Ottoman tradition and Ottoman modern occurs through the relationships that Rakım and Felatun have with two central pairs of female characters. The first pair consists of Janan, Rakım's Caucasian slave girl, and Mihriban, Felatun's younger sister. The second pair consists of

Josephine, Rakım's French mistress, and Pauline, Felatun's French mistress. Notice the pairings here between two Ottoman women – one associated with Rakım and one with Felatun – one who is presented as a good model and the other bad; and two French women – again, one associated with Rakım and one with Felatun – one who is presented as a good model and the other bad. Rearranging the pairs, we have the two women associated with Rakım serving as positive models and the two women associated with Felatun serving as negative models. Of these women, two Ottoman and two French, we have as positive models one Ottoman and one French, not two Ottoman or two French. The positive female models clearly do not map onto binaries of West versus East. How then should we read them? One might consider rearranging the two pairs in the following way: first, take the two Ottoman women, Janan and Mihriban. Janan manifests advantageous Ottoman and admirable European qualities. Mihriban by contrast, manifests disadvantageous Ottoman and injurious European qualities.

Janan displays qualities of Ottoman-ness that are praiseworthy, yet also adopts some positive European characteristics: she is educated in traditional Ottoman and new French ways: she learns French, but enjoys learning Turkish more, she avidly learns the piano; she is thrifty and modest and makes her own clothes. Moreover, she models companionate marriage – predicated not just on education, but also on independence and a capacity for friendship with her partner Rakım. Theirs is not primarily a physical relationship, nor one based on subservience or dependency. Janan, mirroring Rakım, can be read as making productive choices from this menu of options – Ottoman and European.

Mihriban, in contrast with Janan, but like her brother Felatun, is uneducated in either Ottoman or French terms, spendthrift and irresponsible. She eventually marries a man who is described as a father to her – so she, unlike Janan, is not able to hold up her end in a companionate marriage of equals. Mihriban's failings are largely attributed to her father, an Ottoman gentleman, but a misguided and ignorant one, hopelessly smitten with irrelevant European fashions and status symbols. He provides a 'neither-nor' upbringing to his children, Mihriban and Felatun – 'neither-nor' in that it is neither a solid European education, nor a solid Ottoman one, but rather one that leaves his children ignorant and morally adrift, with the consequence that they are ultimately unable to make good choices. Mihriban's failings are also thus her father's and are cast as Ottoman failings – failings to make good choices about what to safeguard or not of Ottoman tradition.

Mihriban is the daughter of parents who represent the worst of choices. Her father loses himself in superficial Westernization, irrelevant at best and dangerous at worst, and her mother is absent as a consequence of harmful Ottoman traditions. Ahmet Midhat explicitly names these traditions – lack of education for girls and child marriage – when he has Mihriban's mother die in childbirth at the tender age of fifteen. It is not that Mihriban's mother is herself to blame, but that her death forecloses her daughter's possibilities. Mihriban is the child of Ottoman traditions that ought to be abandoned, and European practices that ought not to be embraced.

It is worth noting not only the sorts of techniques Ahmet Midhat employs to convey to his readers the choices available to them, the possible models of emulation, but more critically, the techniques he uses to enable them to make decisions themselves, to provide them with agency of thought and wisdom. Ahmet Midhat carefully educates his readers, before allowing them to choose for themselves. In order to make clear to his readers his position regarding Mihriban – the product of the worst case scenario of negative Ottoman and European practices – Ahmet Midhat deploys a technique that he repeats throughout the book at important moments – the direct, rhetorical question. In fact, he even begins the novel this way – the very first sentence is a question: 'Have you heard of Felatun Bey? You know who I'm talking about ...'[1] – thereby inaugurating a mentoring relationship with his readers from the very first line that he sustains throughout the novel. As part of the narrative of Mihriban's parentage, Ahmet Midhat describes the loss of her mother immediately after her own birth. Yet in the middle of his narrative, he interjects a question directed at the reader: 'These things happen ... what else can we say?'[2]

The posing of this question signals a change in voice. Ahmet Midhat the narrator dons a different hat – that of teacher – and in so doing invites the reader to grapple with the premature death of Mihriban's mother by the very flippancy of his question: 'These things happen ... what else can we say?' This is a direct provocation, obliging the reader to decide if, indeed, there *is* anything else to say, and thus enabling the readers' own response to facilitate the development of their own capacity to choose, and to choose wisely. Returning to the pairing of women, and their relationship with the eponymous characters, we can read the two French women as examples of positive European qualities improved by beneficial Ottoman ones, versus negative European qualities unredeemed by Ottoman ones, respectively. Josephine, Rakım's French mistress, and Pauline, Felatun's French mistress, serve to amplify Rakım and Felatun's choices. Josephine is educated and modest, an accomplished pianist who provides lessons to private pupils. She performs, but only for friends, never in public – unlike Pauline, Felatun's actress mistress, or in the less euphemistic language of Ahmet Midhat, a 'theatre slut.' Josephine likes to drink, but again, among friends and in moderation – something Ahmet Midhat condones by the fact that Rakım, too, adopts this formula. She is independent, of spirit and of means, supporting herself and making her own choices. Josephine is also first and foremost a friend to Rakım and Janan; her consideration for them is always placed before her desire for Rakım. In sacrificing her own happiness for theirs she proves herself to be what Ahmet Midhat describes as a 'sincere' friend and is rewarded, in turn, with their genuine friendship and with being the first to hold their newborn child as the book closes.

Pauline, on the other hand is a horrible friend: two-faced, devious, manipulative, self-interested and ultimately the architect of Felatun's financial demise. She is coquettish, ill-mannered, overly familiar and sexually, though not romantically, available – the exact opposite of Janan, who becomes Rakım's beloved well before they begin a physical relationship, or Josephine, whose relationship with Rakım, though physical, is always primarily one of friendship. Although dangerous to society, and certainly to Felatun, Pauline is not independent – she is 'run' by men who only seek to use her, financially and sexually. Lest his audience succumb to her exotic French charms, Ahmet Midhat clearly condemns her, by indicating Rakım's reaction of distaste for her immodesty in comparison with his beloved Janan. Ahmet Midhat writes: 'Rakım was taken aback when he heard Felatun talk this way (of the delights of Pauline). Rakım wondered what wisdom there was in putting up with these French ladies when Ottoman ladies, despite their solemnity and price, offered so many delights.'[3] This point is driven home ten pages later, when Rakım thinks back on this argument with Felatun, and muses to himself, 'Spare me, you fool! How could you know what is delightful in this world and how to enjoy it? You live like a slave with that flirtatious actress of yours!'[4]

Morality, ethics and friendship lie at the heart of the contrast between these four female characters: Janan and Mihriban, Josephine and Pauline. Ahmet Midhat identifies morality as more of an Ottoman quality than a European one. Josephine, as a result of her long stay in Istanbul, or perhaps also as a result of Rakim's beneficial influence, displays Ottoman moral habits and attitudes. Ahmet Midhat's position on this is most evident in the daybreak scene where Josephine, having spent the night at Rakım's house in order to depart early on a boat trip and picnic up the Bosphorus, breakfasts with Rakım's household – himself, Janan and his surrogate mother and Arab slave, Fedayi. Josephine is invited along on this excursion since she, according to Ahmet Midhat, 'couldn't bring herself to take pleasure' in the 'woman-chasers' and ostentatious consumption enjoyed by the likes of Felatun and Pauline that is described in great detail in the preceding chapter – a viewpoint she explicitly shares with Janan. Over breakfast, Josephine exclaims: 'I am really enjoying this. Rakım, can I tell you the truth? Everything about the Turks is better than the Europeans.'[5] Although Rakım, ever moderate, opines that there is good and bad in both Ottoman and European customs, Ahmet Midhat as narrator intervenes on the side of Josephine, helping the readers draw the 'correct' conclusion:

> As Josephine liked taking full advantage of the world, she paid particular attention to those things that sweeten our existence. She proved her point regarding Europe's disagreeable aspects but couldn't find such disadvantages in the ways Ottomans lived.[6]

Janan and Josephine are capable of making their own choices, but choices informed by their sense of responsibility for themselves, and towards others. These characters earn their independence and freedom of choice by means of education, but an education that includes morality. It is significant that Janan is allowed to make her own decisions only after she becomes educated and mature enough to consider the effects of her choices on others. Ahmet Midhat is clearly indicating the importance of freedom and choice, but freedom and choice tempered with social responsibility. It is this particular combination of agency, choice and morality that Rakım models, and which is replicated in the two women that are primarily associated with him, Janan and Josephine.

Conversely, Pauline and Mihriban lack agency, precisely because they lack morality and social consciousness. They are independent, but an independence that is socially destructive since it is not tempered by consideration for others. Ahmet Midhat points specifically to Mihriban's irresponsible independence, again posing a question directly to his readers: 'How about that? Are you surprised at Mihriban Hanım's independence?'⁷ Yet, Ahmet Midhat does not leave the question unanswered – he is not prepared to allow his readers to make their own choices yet – so immediately intervenes, answering his own question: 'Don't be.' This question/answer technique here makes clear Ahmet Midhat's intention of denouncing Mihriban's independence, but attributing it to her not having had a mother's influence – in other words, signalling that Mihriban has not been adequately raised; morally she remains immature, a child. As a result of their absence of morality, Pauline and Mihriban are not truly independent, not the makers of their own fate, but instead remain confined to the unenlightened mores of their respective societies. Together with Felatun, they represent the un-modern; they lack the education, companionate marriage and morality integral to Ahmet Midhat's vision of the modern Ottoman citizen.

It is also worth noting that Ahmet Midhat, in his deliberate contrasting of these similar pairs of female characters, Janan and Josephine, Pauline and Mihriban, focuses on their *relationships* with Rakım and Felatun, respectively. Rakım's relationship with Josephine is primarily one of friendship, not only leading up to their amorous ties, but pervading their affection and transcending it. Even after they break off their romantic liaison, their friendship for one another, and for Janan, endures. Ahmet Midhat is insistent on their friendship, and lest the reader ever forget, repeats it on nearly every occasion when the two converse. For example, in a prelude to their first awkward conversation, when Josephine prepares to convey an offer from a mutual acquaintance to purchase Janan from Rakım, she begins thus: 'Monsieur Rakım! Do you have any doubts about my friendship?' To which he replies: 'How could I have any doubts?' Josephine repeats her declaration of friendship before advancing to the issue at hand: 'To begin with, we should acknowledge that we don't just love each other amorously; we love each other like true friends. And we care sincerely about each other.' Rakım echoes her sentiments: 'Okay, okay, I agree. Let's see if I understand this correctly. That's certainly how I feel about our friendship, and I'm pleased if that's how you feel, too.'⁸ This scene is also a prelude to the end of their amorous relationship, but the maintenance of their ties of friendship, which occurs the next day. This time, it is Rakım who broaches the subject of friendship: 'Madame, what were you telling me last night? ... Didn't you say, "Don't consider me your mistress, but instead regard me as a friend?"' Josephine agrees, and Rakım elaborates: 'If that's the case, then rest assured, from now on I'll regard you as a friend, a sister, a mother, or whatever you want.' When Rakım then confesses his love for Janan, Josephine, disappointed, assures Rakım of the steadfastness of her friendship: 'I am very happy to hear this even though it goes against my own interests.'[9]

Although not Rakım's biological sister, the relationship between Rakım and Janan closely resembles that of brother–sister. Ahmet Midhat repeatedly emphasizes this familial relationship. It is less important that it be grounded in biology, than that it be extended and practised. This relationship begins with Rakım's purchase of Janan, when he refrains from holding her hand or engaging in sexual relations with her, even though he agrees with Felatun that he has the right to do so, and occupies himself with Janan's physical, educational and financial welfare. Later in the book, in the scene where Janan refuses to leave Rakım's service for a more financially advantageous offer, Ahmet Midhat emphasizes their brother–sisterly relationship in an extensive three-page dialogue in which Rakım insists, no less than four times, that he loves Janan as a sister.[10] Her refusal to accede to this relationship hints at their future romantic ties, and makes clear to the reader that their relationship up to this point has been like that of siblings.

Janan is adopted into Rakım's household and becomes family, much the way that Fedayi has become part of Rakım's family. Both women, while not biologically related, enjoy strong familial relationships with Rakım, and with each other – Fedayi is both Rakım and Janan's surrogate mother; Rakım and Janan behave as brother and sister – and fulfil these functions based on affection, and conscious commitment to each other's welfare. It is through these surrogate familial relationships that Rakım and Fedayi raise and nurture Janan, curing her of her illness and nurturing her into an adult woman, educated both technically (Turkish, French, piano, sewing) and morally so that she is able to make her own decisions. It is only as a full grown, morally mature woman that Janan is able to choose to enter into a reciprocal amorous and sexual relationship with Rakım. It is important, as Professor Holly Shissler notes in her afterword to the English translation of this novel, that it is only after she is fully educated and 'free' that Janan becomes the 'partner' to Rakım, and thus, in Ahmet Midhat's estimation, worthy of becoming his wife. Rakım's relationships with both Josephine and Janan, thus, are primarily grounded in friendship, even as they extend into the realm of the amorous and sexual.

In contrast, the two women associated with Felatun are his French actress lover, Pauline, and his younger sister Mihriban. Unlike Rakım's relationship with women which are grounded in and defined by, first and foremost, strong ties of friendship, Felatun does not enjoy friendship in his relationships with women. Felatun has little to do with his sister Mihriban – they have weak family ties, not enhanced by friendship, affection or a sense of responsibility towards each other. Felatun and Pauline's relationship is primarily physical – and characterized by emotional brinkmanship and manipulation. Ultimately, Felatun is destroyed, morally and financially, by Pauline, but ultimately redeemed, morally and financially, by Rakım's enduring friendship for him.

Friendship is reciprocal in *Felatun Bey and Rakım Efendi* and modelled as constituting the heart of any productive relationship, amorous or otherwise. As in friendship, Rakım models productive relationships and Felatun destructive ones. Yet if we remind ourselves that Rakım and Felatun are also models of alternate Ottoman modernities, we can also read these relationships as alternate syntheses of Ottoman tradition and Ottoman modern. Ahmet Midhat's insistence that this Tanzimat project involved translation between tradition and modernity is clearly evident in his powerful rejection of the assumption that modern values belong to Europe, a point which he makes repeatedly throughout the novel. This point is driven home towards the end of the novel in the scene where Rakım hosts the Ziklas family at his home for lunch.

Ahmet Midhat's literary strategy in this extended luncheon scene masterfully underscores his message of translation and synthesis. Even as he suggests that some Ottoman traditions should be abandoned, he is careful to pair this suggestion with assertions of Ottoman cultural superiority, making it easier for his readers to let go, assured that they are not doing so from a position of cultural inferiority. For example, at the outset of the luncheon, Rakım puts Mr Ziklas alone in a different room, explaining that unlike in the West, Ottoman tradition demands gender segregation. Yet rather soon thereafter, they all agree that this *alaturka* custom has little utility and readily abandon it, instead opting for what Ahmet Midhat describes as a 'mix of some *alafranga* into this *alaturka* style.'[11] Ahmet Midhat moves quickly into a juxtaposition of Ottoman and Western slavery, emphasizing Ottoman practices' comparative superiority and humanity, even as he emphasizes that slaves should be free to make their own choices.

This scene is remarkable in that it reverses the usual roles of modern and traditional, fundamentally and conclusively destabilizing assumptions of the West's superior modernity. Here, we clearly see Ahmet Midhat at his most deft, challenging Western claims of superiority in no uncertain terms. At the luncheon, the Ziklas girls envy Janan, who is presented as in every way superior – in beauty, refinement, education and morals. More significantly, the girls declare themselves willing to become slaves if they could have the diamonds and clothes that Janan had. Even Mr Ziklas joins in their enthusiasm, declaring: 'How wonderful! If I sold my wife and daughters for 2,000 liras each, that would make 6,000 liras. Not bad, eh?'[12] Although he is clearly joking, it is significant that Ahmet Midhat emphasizes the material covetousness and monetarization of family relationships that the Ziklas family indulged in, even as he stresses the familial bonds of slavery as practised in the Ottoman Empire. He also dispels the Ziklas' assumption that slaves are mistreated and confined to the house, underlining the beauty of Janan's diamonds and clothes, and insisting on her physical freedom. As Rakım explains to his guests, Janan 'goes wherever she wants.'[13] Mr Ziklas again demonstrates European enthusiasm for Ottoman slavery, confounding ideas of Ottoman inferiority, by saying to Rakım: 'you describe slavery in such a way that soon I'll want to be sold as a slave myself.'[14]

In this crucial luncheon scene, Rakım exhibits an Ottoman modern, a translation of tradition and modernity. There are Ottoman traditions worth losing and worth keeping, just as there are Western practices worth rejecting and worth adopting. Ahmet Midhat demonstrates that modernity is complex and multifaceted – it is no facile glorification of Ottoman tradition or, conversely, European modernity. When he suggests abandoning some Ottoman traditions, he simultaneously presents another aspect of Ottoman tradition that is worth retaining – that is superior to the West. It is readily apparent that modernity is not conveyed in binaries of Ottoman/West, but rather embedded and animated by new patterns of behaviour that don't explicitly 'belong' to either. Ahmet Midhat identifies some qualities as European or Ottoman in origin, but the very fact that they are, for better and for worse, manifest in *both* Ottoman and French women, Janan and Josephine, suggests that these qualities are not essential, not owned by one or the other society. It is not then so much a question of Ottomans adopting French qualities or French adopting Ottoman ones, as it is a matter of identifying which qualities, in this complex multicultural menu, will form the new 'sensibilities and dispositions' of the modern Ottoman citizen.

In *Felatun Bey and Rakım Efendi*, Ahmet Midhat succeeds in modelling what should and should not be kept, what should and should not be adopted, and what, specifically, is to be gained by the resulting combination of Ottoman modern. Ahmet Midhat acknowledges that change must come from the state in the form of laws, but also that top-down reform must be paired with the generation of modern Ottoman citizens from the bottom up. Citizens must be supported and encouraged by law, but the success or failure of the modern project will ultimately depend on Ottoman individuals' willingness to adopt and embrace modern subjectivities. Modernity cannot be decreed. It is symptomatic of his quest to form modern Ottoman citizens that Ahmet Midhat doesn't simply present these models to a passive audience who watch them pass through the pages, flitting in and out of scenes, but deliberately deploys literary techniques to involve his readers as pupils, to engage them as agents of translation and thus of their own transformation into modern Ottoman citizens. Readers are provided with a rationale, not a prescription. In modelling for his readers, he also involves them in the deliberation and decision-making that they need to develop in order to *become* modern. Ahmet Midhat acknowledges not simply that his readers have a right to understand the advantages of Ottoman modernity, but equally importantly, that his readers as Ottoman citizens must consciously adopt the sensibilities and dispositions of modernity. Readers, as citizens, are thus the subject and object of Ottoman Tanzimat reform. Ahmet Midhat plays a dual role: of impartial narrator and wise teacher. The moments of transition between these roles, when he puts down one hat and dons the other, are particularly worth looking out for, as they signal his own opinion, as teacher, and allow us to trace, literally, Ahmet Midhat's translation from Ottoman tradition to Ottoman modernity.

Notes

1 Ahmet Midhat Efendi, *Felatun Bey and Rakım Efendi: An Ottoman Novel*, Translated from the Turkish by Melih Levi and Monica M. Ringer (Syracuse: Syracuse University Press, 2016).

2 Ibid., p.2.
3 Ibid., p.73.
4 Ibid., p.81.
5 Ibid., p.87.
6 Ibid., p.88.
7 Ibid., p.7.
8 Ibid., pp.53–5.
9 Ibid., p.66.
10 Ibid., pp.62–5.
11 Ibid., p.105.
12 Ibid.
13 Ibid.
14 Ibid., p.106.

4

Cultivating Ottoman citizens: Reading Ahmet Midhat Efendi's *Felatun Bey ile Rakım Efendi* with Ali Pasha's political testament

Owen Green

Beset with rebellions and secessionist movements in the Balkan and Aegean Provinces and the encroaching tendrils of European imperialism, Ottoman Tanzimat reformers sought to stabilize and strengthen the Empire by transforming both the political and emotional relationships between the state and the subjects who inhabited the Ottoman lands. The successes of several secessionist movements convinced many that – regardless of how the state chose to respond to this fact – the fate of the empire lay in the hands of the people. This represented an implicit recognition of popular sovereignty, whereby the continued legitimacy, and very existence, of a state came to be understood to rest on whether or not the state reflected the interests of its collective people, rather than the personal interests of its ruler. For this reason, Tanzimat reformers recognized the existential necessity of ensuring that the concerns of the people were addressed. Such objectives took a variety of forms across the long Tanzimat period, with the debate mostly circling around changing ideas of equality and representation. By the last quarter of the nineteenth century, reformers also recognized the need for the people to be ideologically and emotionally committed to the Ottoman Empire such that they would align their interests with the interests of the empire and act accordingly. Thus was born the need for the Ottoman Citizen.

In a process that can be described as a transformation from subject to citizen, a citizen serves as both the 'subject and the agent of change,' in that they both generate the changes and are themselves affected by them.[1] In the realm of the political, this transformation explains the increased interest on the part of reformers in representational and even consultative forms of government. However, while the impetus for the cultivation of Ottoman citizens lies in the realm of the political, the role for the Ottoman citizen encompassed a much broader spectrum of operation that included social and cultural objectives. Just as the political fate of the empire was recognized to be in the hands of the people through their collective choices to band together, choosing either to secede or to remain and strengthen the empire, so too was the moral and cultural fate of the empire recognized to be in the hands of these citizens. Ottoman citizens were to be bastions of culture, identity and morality, guiding their fellows through the complexities of Ottoman modernity. The proper formation of citizens would serve to ensure that the empire retained its cultural authenticity. The project of the cultivation of Ottoman citizens was not merely a political project, but a comprehensive social engineering project which sought to create a desirable and modern Ottoman society through the full transformation of each individual subject into a citizen.

The process of transition from subject to citizen can be analysed through two works produced in the 1870s, both of which are available in English translation.[2] The first work is the 1871 political testament of Ali Pasha – an important statesman who served many years as grand vizier and is considered one of the main architects of the Tanzimat reforms. He wrote his political testament from his deathbed in the form of a letter to the sultan, Abdülaziz (r. 1861–1876). It details not only his long career and justifications for many of the choices he made over the years, but also provides prescriptive advice for the statesmen who came after him. He thereby presents a model for how Ottoman citizens can be cultivated 'from the top down,' actions that the existing state structures can take to develop its subjects into citizens and incorporate them into the state and national project.

The second work is Ahmet Midhat Efendi's 1875 novel *Felatun Bey and Rakım Efendi*. Ahmet Midhat Efendi was a prolific writer and intellectual of a younger generation than that of Ali Pasha. Ahmet Midhat Efendi is known primarily for producing works designed to teach – whether those taught be schoolchildren or the empire at large. He published numerous other novels, newspaper articles and even a series of textbooks which earned him his epithet, *Hace-i Evvel*, which is translated as 'the People's First Teacher.'[3] In the novel examined here, Ahmet Midhat Efendi presents his readers with a richly detailed tableau of his vision for Ottoman citizens. The ways in which the characters develop and interact with one another model the ways in which the author envisioned individual subjects undergoing the transition into citizens, and, as a component part of that transformation, helping others make the same transition. The model for the development of Ottoman citizens thus presented through the novel, complements the top-down model presented in Ali Pasha's political testament and fills out our understanding of how Tanzimat reformers cultivated Ottoman citizenship.

Beyond their content, these two works continue to complement each other in the information they provide through their format and audience. Both authors took advantage of the power of the press to spread their ideas, but their potential audiences, and the ways in which the audiences could have acted upon the ideas presented in the texts, are different and complementary. The two works, again, aptly span the gap between top-down reform efforts of the political elite, and the bottom-up approach of the growing class of urban intellectuals and the broader literate public. Ahmet Midhat Efendi's work was a novel, and Ali Pasha's political testament, though written in the form of a letter addressed to the sultan, was published as well. It was a style of the time to write letters ostensibly addressed to the sultan, but to publish them in the newspapers to reach a broader audience.[4] In their broader careers both men were known for using language and grammar that was consciously simpler than many of the other modes of writing available at the time, again with the goals of reaching a broader audience.[5] These works can both also be considered examples of what Benedict Anderson has referred to as 'print capitalism' – widely available and financially accessible printed materials that would have circulated among the literate classes and played a role in developing a sense of shared identity among the readership, which in this case resulted in the 'imagined community' of the Ottoman nation.[6]

The novel teaches the reader the path to becoming a modern Ottoman citizen by example, even if it does not provide all the requisite knowledge an Ottoman citizen would need. The author's understanding of the relationship between novels and teaching modernity is hinted at in the content of the text, as well as in the overarching structure and themes of the novel. In a couple of meta-moments, that are brief and not elaborated upon, it is mentioned that

Rakım is writing a novel of his own.⁷ We are not given any information about the novel he is writing, for apparently it was too hastily handwritten for the other characters to read in the brief moment they have with it. The readers of Ahmet Midhat Efendi's novel, however, are almost invited to imagine that it is a novel that is not unlike the one in which Rakım is a character. Given that Rakım's primary role once he attains Ottoman elite status is that of a teacher, it is not a stretch to imagine that this is a hint at the role that the novel is intended to play. This further demonstrates the teaching aspect of Ahmet Midhat Efendi's own novel, and promotes the role of the novel more broadly as a tool for modernization, reform and teaching a much broader sector of the people how to be Ottoman citizens.

When speaking with Felatun and his mistress Pauline, it comes up in the conversation that Rakım is a writer. He explains his work by saying, 'I write all sorts of things! I am a laborer who writes some small novels, plays and some pieces for newspapers.'⁸ These were primarily relatively new mediums to the Ottoman Empire during the reform era, and were mediums of print capitalism, which helped create a sense of common, national identity among the people who read them. This also has resonances with what Ali Pasha says in his political testament about the press serving as a substitute for national representation, which would support the assertion that Rakım's work as a writer is crucial to his role as an Ottoman citizen.⁹

Writing in these modern genres allows Ottoman citizens to reach a broad audience. Ahmet Midhat Efendi's *Felatun Bey and Rakım Efendi* was written in much more accessible language than other works of the time, which would have allowed it to reach a broader audience than other written works. Plays, and especially plays in Turkish, perhaps like some of those which would be written by Rakım, would be able to reach a broad audience also. Plays also had the distinct advantage of being performed in a theatre, and thus these theatre spaces could serve as spaces of networking between Ottoman citizens, when they were all gathered to watch the same play. Finally, newspaper articles, the quintessential print capitalism, were cheap, widely available and short enough to be read out loud and easily shared with illiterate individuals as well. Rakım Efendi's engagement with writing, and the particular types of writing he engages in, especially when compared with the work of Ahmet Midhat Efendi himself, suggests that novels, scripted plays, and newspapers were not only a way of displaying one's modernity and capacity for Ottoman citizenship by producing them, but also a way of bringing others into Ottoman citizenship.

Morality and translation

Beyond the political and ideological transformations Ali Pasha and Ahmet Midhat Efendi advocate, the two men express a shared concern about the vices that can come with uncritically following a European model to determine the parameters of reform. This speaks to the fact that the question of morality and cultural authenticity is essential to any discussion of reform in the mid-nineteenth-century Ottoman context and to the development of the modern Ottoman citizen. While morality is often at the centre of discussions of reform in the long Tanzimat period, it is rarely – if ever – clearly articulated just what an individual Ottoman might mean when they invoke the concept. However, a combined reading of both the articulation of moral concerns in these two texts and each author's suggestions on how to resolve this problem, illuminate at least the role that this nebulous concept was seen to have in reform efforts, as well as some aspects of its shape. We find that while to a certain extent, morality itself – much like the citizen – is in a constructive flux, it also serves as the necessary lens through which all desired reforms must be refracted to ensure the ensuing 'translated' reforms will be simultaneously effective and desirable.

Ali Pasha clearly believed that although reform was necessary, it was important that reform be 'translated' to the Ottoman situation and emerge to truly fit the Ottoman Empire's needs, rather than being a mere act of imitation of Europe. He repeatedly states that the Ottomans should only adopt what is useful to them, but furthermore suggests that adopting things that aren't useful could be extremely detrimental to the people and the empire stating that 'when a civilization is imported and does not evolve gradually from within, people usually acquire more of its vices than its virtues.'[10] When speaking of his work, and the need for such thoughtful, translating approaches to reform he asserts,

> We had to know our people's needs and aspirations, be able to anticipate them, consider the intellectual development of the nation and account for its needs. This was a thankless task, for we had to avoid the trap all Europe and some utopians and short-viewed diplomats were pushing us into.

In their view, we had to introduce to Turkey, immediately and without being prepared, European habits and customs and a European system of government.[11]

Ali Pasha is advocating for gradual and carefully considered reform, but, the way in which he words this is crucial because it illustrates the degree to which Ali Pasha believed the context of the reforms should inform and influence the content of the reforms – the need for reforms to be 'translated' into their new context. He does not suggest that there is nothing that could be learned from the European example, rather that reform can draw on these, but needs to be carefully and thoughtfully constructed to fit the Ottoman situation and people, in essence, 'translated.' The notion that reform would be neither desirable nor effective if reform was imitative rather than creative is not unique to Ali Pasha and can be elaborated upon through exploration of Ahmet Midhat Efendi's novel, *Felatun Bey and Rakım Efendi*.

Having read both Ahmet Midhat Efendi's novel, and Ali Pasha's testament, one cannot help but see the dissolute character of Felatun Bey as an archetype of Ali Pasha's warning that 'when a civilization is imported and does not evolve gradually from within, people usually acquire more of its vices than its virtues.'[12] The core of Ahmet Midhat Efendi's novel *Felatun Bey and Rakım Efendi* lies in a contrast between the two titular characters and their respective families and social spheres, with Felatun providing a poor role model, and Rakım Efendi providing a positive role model. Felatun Bey engages with the European example in a superficial way and the author makes it abundantly clear that he has attained not a real understanding of European culture, but a superficial infatuation with European fashions. Rather than critically examining the behaviours he adopts, he embraces a misunderstanding of the freedoms allowed by European society, becoming a pleasure-seeking womanizer and gambler who loses his entire fortune.

Through the contrasting example of Rakım and his household the novel models approaches to the cultivation of Ottoman citizens from both the top-down and bottom-up angles. One of his relationships in his household serves as a metaphor for the model the author promotes for the relationship between the state and the subjects, as they are guided to transition into citizens, and on the literal levels of the text, Rakım Efendi's interactions with the people around him model the ways that an individual becomes an Ottoman citizen and then brings others into the fold by modelling and teaching a set of essential competencies and sensibilities, including a sense of morality which itself is undergoing a transition from a form of religious communal morality, to a public, civic, national morality. Morality is of such central importance to the way in which Ottomans thought about reform that the contrast at the core of Ahmet Midhat Efendi's novel is openly articulated by the narrator as a contrast in morality. When discussing the implied physical relationship between Rakım Efendi and his French mistress and close friend Josephine the narrator explains,

> We already told you we're not describing the manners of an angel. We're describing the true nature of a young man who knows how to protect his honor and live decently and genuinely *alafranga*. But above all we are describing someone of our times ... Now ... when you look at these two young men [Rakım and Felatun] from a moral point of view ... How perfect! We are offering you two kinds of morality by showing you the behavior of two young men of our time. You're free to choose the one you prefer. You're also free to dislike both of them![13]

While it is clear through the interactions between the characters – and the fact that the overarching contrast between Felatun Bey and Rakım Efendi is articulated as a contrast between two types of morality – that a certain form of morality is one of the essential sensibilities of the ideal Ottoman citizen, and essential to the translation efforts that are reform, the definition of morality that the author builds throughout the novel is complex and needs to be explored in depth. For, despite its centrality to the endeavour of reforms, much like the citizens themselves, we find that morality is a concept understood to be in flux, and having a certain temporality to it. Just as the fundamental difference between Rakım Efendi and Felatun Bey is a difference of morality, the fundamental determinate of the overarching moral arc that is seen to connect the two, is that they are as stated above, 'of our time'.

Towards a new public morality

To get a sense of how the author sees the temporality of morality, and the morality he advocates for his own time, we turn again to an analysis of the behaviours of Rakım Efendi. Perhaps the most crucial dimension of the question of morality in the novel centres around the distinction between public and private spheres; a full examination of the instances of references to this concept, evidences that the particular form of morality that Ahmet Midhat Efendi advocates as an appropriate response to the times in which he and his readers live, is a form of shared public, even national morality among all Ottoman citizens.

The intersection between morality and reputation, and the importance of a new sort of public morality is well evidenced by the anecdotes and commentary about public behaviour in relation to morality, as well as private behaviour. There are several key social spaces that Rakım and other aspiring modern Ottomans, including Felatun Bey, frequent but the ways in which these two young men engage with the spaces and the other people in them are markedly different, and showcase the moral differences between Rakım and Felatun, thereby illuminating some aspects of this temporally determined morality which was to guide the shape of reforms. One of the most explicit examples the narrator provides, is that of the way the two men conduct themselves in the theatre. The narrator gives extensive commentary with regards to the difference between the ways that Felatun and Rakım use the space, contrasting Felatun's superficial womanizing with Rakım's maintenance of a sphere of social contacts, the network of his public reputation:

> It is often said that the theater is the best place to discover the true personality of a young man. Those who saw Felatun Bey at a theater never noticed him entering the married ladies' box to greet them. He was always busy laughing in the boxes of unattended women or those who treated every man as their owner. Rakım on the other hand, would buy his ticket, enter the theater, and survey the people in the boxes. Whenever he stopped by the boxes of nobles like G— Bey to greet them, they would offer him a seat saying, 'Our magnificent son Rakım Efendi, here you are! There is always a place for you here.' He would typically accept the first offer of a seat, and during intermission would ask permission to greet other families in their boxes. When he went around to pay his respects, the people he was seated with would say, 'What a composed young man! He doesn't have any bad habits like drinking or gambling! Honestly, he behaves as well as a girl.' In fact, for a few days afterwards, families continued to talk about Rakım this way.[14]

Here Ahmet Midhat Efendi illustrates the varied utility of a theatre space for modern Ottoman citizens. For men like Felatun the theatre is a place that enables them in some of their worst habits, especially womanizing, but for men like Rakım the theatre is an important social space to interact with one's friends, acquaintances, and their families. One theatre referenced elsewhere in the novel, and likely implied in this scene, is Naum's Theatre. Naum's Theatre was a real opera house, well known and frequented by Ottomans from a variety of religious communities during the Tanzimat period and, as scholarship has evidenced, it served as a crucial point of social integration between Muslim and non-Muslim Ottomans.[15] The output of Rakım's social interactions in the theatre would suggest that Ahmet Midhat Efendi recognized this and promoted the notion that the theatre is also a crucial space for networking with all Ottoman notables of Istanbul and establishing one's reputation, moral and otherwise, in the creation of a shared Ottoman identity. Furthermore, through Rakım's example, we see that the theatre too can be a site of the crystallization of the new national morality, which serves as the lens of citizens' translation-reforms.

To fully recognize the significance of this shift towards a shared public morality, we must turn to a quick analysis of how the novel approaches religion. While religion often serves many societies as a source of moral values, it is crucial that we should not conflate morality and religion, and in the context of the novel, the formation of a public morality is a process that can be seen as occurring in tandem with the secularization of the public sphere. The secularization of the public sphere was not an anti-religious act, rather, it simply consisted of the relegation of religious belief and practice to the private sphere. Throughout the novel the author implies Rakım does not participate in outward displays of religion. While the author does not outright declare this avoidance of public displays of religious affiliation, a couple of references in the text clearly indicate that Rakım does not attend Friday Mosque. Towards the beginning of the novel, we learn that Rakım has an Armenian co-worker at the Ministry of Foreign Affairs who he is teaching Turkish in exchange for access to his friend's collection of European books, and it is stated that Rakım engaged in a voracious pursuit of knowledge such that, 'it was said that even on Fridays Rakım spent his entire day in his Armenian friend's library.'[16] In another instance, the author states that Rakım later transitions to tutoring the English girls on Fridays.[17] Thus it becomes clear that our main model of an Ottoman citizen does not engage in public or communal displays of religious affiliation.

Although Rakım does not publicly practise his religion, and does not attend communal religious events, Rakım does frequently express religious sentiments in the privacy of his own mind and it is important to remember that Islamic learning was an important part of Rakım's education. The narrator says of Rakım's religious education, 'He acquired a substantial knowledge of Hadith and Quranic exegesis. He even dipped into Islamic jurisprudence.'[18] However, the way in which Rakım gained Islamic learning is just as noteworthy as the fact that it remained a significant part of his learning. A comparison can be drawn between Rakım's form of Islamic education, and that of a servant in the household in which Felatun grew up, Mehmet from Kastamonu, which can also be considered an 'Islamic' education.[19] Mehmet from Kastamonu only 'managed to read two dozen of the shorter Quranic verses,' a feat which is presented in a section where the narrator describes Mehmet's level of education in a sarcastic and condescending way.[20] Whereas Mehmet was trained simply to memorize short Quranic verses, Rakım's training equipped him for religious *interpretation*. The importance of this to Rakım's multifaceted education demonstrates that the particular brand of secularism that is aspired to is not anti-religious, rather it challenges the ways in which religion is approached as well as its role in public society.

Thus, through a reading of the ways in which both Ahmet Midhat Efendi and Ali Pasha approach the moral anxieties of reform, we see that the solution they envisioned to resolve these tensions was not limited to a translation of the inspiration that was drawn from the European example of modernity through the lens of morality. Through the example of Ahmet Midhat Efendi's novel, it becomes clear that this lens of morality was itself also subject to a form of translation on the part of the citizens, a translation into a form of national morality, temporally adapted to be suitable for the context of the Ottoman modernity the citizens were creating.

Top-down reform, and representation and consultation in government

Through his political testament Ali Pasha provides us with a clear picture not only of how his desired reforms to the political structure and social institutions of the empire could be implemented, but also the reasoning behind his desired reforms. He identifies the main source of instability in the empire as the feeling among the people – especially but not exclusively non-Muslims – that they are facing injustice because of inequalities built into the current political system, and that they deserve rights that have been denied them. This feeling he believes can arise indigenously, but has also been inspired in the empire's Christian communities by European powers fanning the flames of discontent to serve their own geopolitical ambitions. He believed the secessionist movements the empire faced to be the result of a combination of European interference and the attention the Europeans drew to the inequalities of the Ottoman legal system. In response to this, Ottoman reformers like Ali Pasha and Ahmet Midhat Efendi, advocated for a change of status on behalf of the non-Muslims of the empire from that of protected minorities to fully-fledged members of the state, citizens equal to their Muslim counterparts, by assuming the same rights and responsibilities from the state.

Muslims too would also be more content and prosperous and less likely to revolt, as they too experienced the sting of inequality, primarily wealth inequality since, among the Ottomans, it was primarily non-Muslims who were engaged in the economic opportunities the Europeans brought to the empire, whereas elite Muslims were primarily employed in government jobs. To this effect Ali Pasha advocates the integration of the two – primarily – separate economic spheres that Muslims and non-Muslims inhabited respectively.[21] The breakdown of professional barriers between Ottomans in this way would not only allow for a greater representation of non-Muslim interest in the government, and an alleviation of the wealth gaps on average between the two groups, but would also encourage social interaction and formation of shared identities. Furthermore, Ali Pasha believed that once the reforms were in place, Europe would be forced to respect the Ottoman Empire and no longer try to stir up secessionist movements, as it would remove the leverage they had when using the status of Christians in the empire as a diplomatic pawn.

The top-down model for the transformation of the Ottoman political system, from one wherein the state rules over its subjects to one where citizens guide the direction of their nation, as put forth in Ali Pasha's political testament, rests on the implicit recognition of popular sovereignty, as evidenced by his statement that:

> The diverse interests of minorities could sooner or later lead to the dismemberment of the empire. The state, through education, can and should seek the ways and means of harmonizing these diverse interests and guide them towards the preservation of the unity of the empire. People are interested in their own welfare and security: and one's [homeland] is where one finds them both.[22]

In this evocative passage, Ali Pasha articulates what he sees as the impetus behind transforming subjects into citizens, and presents one portion of his model for how this should be achieved. He presents an implicit recognition of popular sovereignty by explaining one way that the fate of the empire lies in the hands of the citizens, but also shows that although religious minorities and their current understandings of their interests were seen as a real threat to the sovereignty and territorial integrity of the empire in the context of secessionist movements, their true interests were not seen as irreparably different from Muslim Ottomans. This is a rejection of religious and linguistic essentialism which was prevalent both in European nationalisms and the nationalisms Europeans attempted to cultivate among the Christians of the empire. Through the construction of the homeland as simply where one finds welfare and security, this passage demonstrates the way that the form of Ottoman national identity that Tanzimat reformers like Ali Pasha and Midhat Efendi promoted transcends difference.

While in this passage Ali Pasha promotes education as a means of harmonizing the interests of the people with the interests of the state – a concept which will be explored further when we turn to Ahmet Midhat Efendi's novel – through other sections of the text, we see that the exchange of information on the national interest is multidirectional. While citizens must be educated to bring their interests in line with the national interest, so too must the state itself be informed by its citizens because collectively the citizens compose the nation, and the national interest is, rather, the collective interest of the citizens of the nation.

To this effect, Ali Pasha asserts that the empire needs to start taking steps towards a more representative form of government. While in the scope of this political testament he does not directly advocate for universal suffrage or a constitutional system, he does advocate for a representative system formed out of a special assembly appointed by the sultan but informed by a free press as a stop-gap measure until the subjects have been suitably developed into citizens. He asserts:

> It would behoove Your Majesty to appoint intelligent and honest commissioners who would be above reproach .... They would be a check on the administration, identify its shortcomings, investigate their causes, and propose remedies. They would concentrate their efforts on the improvement of the difficulties our population faces ... They would inquire into the relations between Your Majesty's different minority subjects to verify whether they represent a potential source of trouble. They would also investigate and indicate the people's needs and aspirations so that they do not remain unattended. They would be a source of information for Your Majesty and respond solely to You.[23]

He asserts that this assembly can and would act in the interests of the people and would easily be able to ensure that people felt their interests were represented by the state, were loyal to it and identified with it. To ensure that this representative assembly is well informed about the interest and desires of the people, Ali Pasha suggests that press freedoms be open, and the press play a critical role, asserting:

> Under the present regime the press is but a weak link between the Government and the Ottoman subjects, especially those in the provinces who do not know what public interest means ... The press could in the meantime act as a substitute for national representation, since it will be read daily and inform the people. If the assembly in charge of debating and overseeing public affairs were to be made up of uninformed provincials or residents of the capital, it could quickly become a lamentably impotent instrument.[24]

This indicates that the main purpose of the assembly was to be an honest and temporary substitute for a more direct and formal mode of representation, and that it was to become such by being informed by the people through the press. Through this section of Ali Pasha's political testament we glean an understanding of the main mechanisms by which he believed that the interests of the nation could be ascertained and addressed by the Ottoman state, thus providing a temporary substitute for direct enfranchisement and full political representation of the people, with further developments in that direction to be made at some unspecified point in the future.

Ahmet Midhat Efendi's *Felatun Bey and Rakım Efendi*, however, also provides a top-down model for the cultivation of Ottoman citizenship in the empire. Ahmet Midhat Efendi also uses the transformation of a character named Janan across the course of the novel as a metaphor for how he imagines the trajectory of the transformation of the collective Ottoman people from subjects into citizens. When the reader is first introduced to Janan, she is a sickly slave girl, who is purchased by the character presented as the primary example of an Ottoman citizen in the novel, Rakım Efendi. Given the prevalence of the caricature of the empire as 'the sick man of Europe' at the time, Janan's sickness is likely a clue towards the double role she plays as a symbol of the people of the empire. Furthermore, it is possible that the fact that she is a slave at the start of the novel is intended to represent the condition of the people under the parameters of the relationship between the state and the people before the reforms for which Ahmet Midhat Efendi advocates. We can trace the reforms the author is promoting through the trajectory of Janan's relationship with Rakım.

Through the process of her recovery and education, Janan falls in love with Rakım. This easily mirrors the impetus behind education and integration into the system of Ottoman citizenship, as both Ahmet Midhat Efendi and Ali Pasha promote, recalling Ali Pasha's definition of homeland. Furthermore, after she is educated and fully formed as an Ottoman citizen, Rakım hears of an offer from another man to purchase Janan at a price ten times higher than that he paid for her. Rather than making the decision about whether to sell her or not himself, Rakım turns the choice over to Janan, offering to give her all the gifts he has bestowed on her and the money the buyer offers for her as her own personal wealth. This is a crucial turning point in the text both for the development of the relationship between Rakım and Janan, but also in the metaphorical extension of that relationship to represent that between Ottoman citizens and the state. The way that Rakım hands over control of this decision reflects the move to increasingly consultative government, that both Ali Pasha and Ahmet Midhat Efendi advocate. When given the choice to leave, Janan decides to stay based on the love for him she has developed through her healing, and education. The story doesn't end there, though, for their relationship becomes increasingly equal, until he marries her and they have a child together.

Networks of Ottoman identity: The 'bottom-up' approach

One element of Ahmet Midhat Efendi's vision for the spread of the ideals of Ottoman citizenship represents a 'translation' of earlier systems of integration into 'Ottoman' identity. When examining the intersections of religious and Ottoman identities in the novel, it becomes clear that the novel depicts a time when the identity of the elites was a pluralistic Ottoman identity which had strong precedents in earlier Ottoman systems. For example, early in the empire *devşirme* was a system which brought in mostly young Christian boys from the Balkan Provinces and converted, educated and raised them to serve in various capacities. The most promising could come to serve in high offices in the palaces, or in high military positions in the Janissary corps,[25] and in these types of high positions they were considered Ottoman in ways that lower classes of all groups were not. As early scholarship has demonstrated the purpose of the education that these youths received was intended to imbue them with loyalty to the sultan, but also to 'recreate their social identity' and transform them into Ottomans.[26]

Concepts of how Ottoman citizenship worked on the ground level were remarkably similar, both in how they integrated people into the state project and how they relied on systems of patrimony, to these earlier systems of integrating individuals into the Ottoman elite. This is easiest to explore by comparing the presentation of various minor characters in the novel who occupy varied intersections between the major religious groups and those who are considered 'Ottoman.' Although these characters do not play a significant role in the plot of the novel, they illuminate much about Ottoman society at this time, and how each group is perceived in relation to the 'Ottoman' identity, which was in a period of transition between an identity that only encompassed elites who operated on high levels in the Ottoman bureaucracy to encompassing an increasingly broadening sector of the educated population, with increasing emphasis on bringing all the subjects into the fold. The characters' interactions with non-Muslim Ottomans are especially noteworthy, for understanding how Ottoman identity was understood at the time, because many of these non-Muslim characters are considered to be Ottoman gentlemen and are integral in Rakım Efendi's entry into Ottoman identity and society.

One of Rakım's Armenian acquaintances, a gentleman whose name is simply given as 'Mr. G—,'[27] is important to Rakım's development into an

Ottoman citizen because Mr G—, is one of Rakım's first employers.[28] This is a distinct and significant choice and serves to emphasize that, at this time, Ottoman identity was an identity which was at this time primarily concentrated among certain strata of educated elites, but also encompassed elites from many different religious groups. Furthermore, it seems that the choice to refer to this character only by the first letter of his last name and a dash, is a technique that Ahmet Midhat Efendi uses frequently to refer to characters that are intended to be something of a nonspecific type. This would thereby imply that Mr G— was one of many Armenian Ottoman gentlemen, who are accepted as and understood to be Ottoman gentlemen, with all that this identifier entails.

When comparing the system of how individuals become educated and integrated into the Ottoman System as presented in the novel to earlier precedents of education and assimilation into Ottoman identity in earlier periods, the relationships in the novel suggest, that although the exact nature of that education and the groups of people to which the opportunity was open to were in flux, the basic institution of integration into Ottoman society and identity remained familiar, and served as a strong precedent for the institution which transformed subjects into citizens by means of those who had already become such. Furthermore, Rakım himself works as a teacher, and passes on to others much of the requisite knowledge necessary to become an Ottoman.

This process is most obvious when it comes to Janan, as beyond being a metaphor for the collective of Ottoman citizens she serves as a character in her own right. Furthermore, there are stark parallels between her trajectory and earlier Ottoman systems of integration of outsiders into the pre-national Ottoman elite identity. Circassian women had long been a staple of the imperial harem, and many such women rose to one of the most influential positions a woman could attain in the empire, the mother of the sultan, known as the *Valide Sultan,* who ruled not directly, but wielded immense influence as one of the closest confidants of her son. Favoured imperial consorts also occasionally wielded much power through influence, however, whereas a sultan could have changing favourite consorts, he would only have one mother. Much of the power that an individual could attain, especially in the earlier years of the Ottoman Empire, flowed from the individual's level of personal access to the sultan and the ability to influence his decisions, rather than any direct power an individual other than the sultan might have.[29] In this way, in the earlier years of the Ottoman Empire Circassian slave women became some of the most powerful Ottomans after being brought into the imperial harem.

Similarly, Rakım buys Janan and educates her so that she is able to become not only an Ottoman, but also a model for Ottoman women in the nineteenth century. The skills that she learns in Rakım's household are varied and draw, much as Rakım's own education, on European knowledge and skills as well as Ottoman knowledge and skills, including traditions inherited from a shared and intercultural 'Islamic' heritage. However, notably absent from this curriculum is any religious education. Rakım begins by teaching her to read Turkish, clearly one of her most foundational skills for her new life in Ottoman Istanbul. After attending piano lessons at a neighbour's house without Rakım's permission, he finds her a teacher and a piano so that she can learn piano at home. Later in the novel, Janan also learns French, which she purportedly enjoys learning much less than Turkish, but learns just as quickly. Janan also acquires a variety of other skills as well, but these are some of the most symbolic for her development into a model Ottoman woman. Rakım is amazed by her intelligence and capacity to learn, as are all those who witness or hear of her skills. In this way Janan too, models the 'translated' reforms of ideal Ottoman education through the creative synthesis of desirable elements from all the sources available to her.

Beyond Janan's development into a model Ottoman woman from an educational perspective, the development of her relationship with Rakım has implications as well for the meaning of Ottoman citizenship. The model of the household with the nation is a reflexive model, in that just as the household is a microcosm of the nation, so too then must changing dynamics of the nation be reflected in the household. Just as the nation is a consultative system with all members getting input, so too should be the household. After she makes the choice to stay with him, Rakım treats her with more affection, but does not take advantage of his position as her owner, despite his desire for her, and instead waits until he is sure that she loves him as well, frees her and marries her shortly after their relationship becomes sexual. This makes an argument for increased equality between partners and supports the 'companionate marriage' model that Shissler describes in the afterword to the novel.[30]

Conclusion

A close reading of the 1871 political testament of Ali Pasha and Ahmet Midhat Efendi's 1875 novel *Felatun Bey and Rakım Efendi* provides a clear and detailed picture of one of the central political and social engineering projects of the Tanzimat period – the transition from subject to citizen. Ali Pasha's political testament provides a top-down model for the ways in which state actors under the current political system could begin to bring the state towards a more representative and even consultative form of government, aligning it with recognitions of popular sovereignty. Ahmet Efendi's novel, by contrast – while also providing its own top-down model using Janan as a metaphor for the collective citizens – additionally provides a detailed model for the ways that Ottoman citizens can interact with their peers to cultivate their fellow citizens from the bottom up.

The model of the Ottoman citizen that emerges from these texts is one who, as both the subject and agent of reform, engages with those around them and integrates them politically, socially and ideologically into the Ottoman national project.[31] In addition to changes in regulation and leveraging of social networks, a third set of tools that the Ottoman citizen utilizes to aid their fellow subjects in their transitions to citizens includes the exact types of materials that Anderson refers to when he theorizes about the impact of 'print capitalism' on the development of the imagined communities that come to be referred to as nations.[32] Critically, the modern Ottoman citizen utilizes a new form of national civic morality to translate both earlier precedents, and elements of the flawed European example of modernity to create a distinctly Ottoman modernity – and to ensure that the changes they impart upon society are simultaneously desirable, and effective in furthering their collective national interest.

Notes

1. Monica M. Ringer, *Pious Citizens: Reforming Zoroastrianism in India and Iran* (Syracuse, NY, 2011).
2. Fuat M. Andic and Suphan Andic, *The Last of the Ottoman Grandees: The Life and the Political Testament of Âli Paşa* (Istanbul, 1996); Ahmet Midhat, *Felâtun Bey and Râkım Efendi: An Ottoman Novel* (trans.) Melih Levi and Monica Ringer, (Syracuse, 2016).

3 See Shissler's afterword in Ahmet Midhat, *Felâtun Bey and Râkım Efendi*, p.149.
4 Other examples of this form include a letter written to the sultan in 1867 by a supporter of the Young Ottoman movement, Mustafa Fazıl, which was published in French during his exile in Paris. Though there are no remaining copies of the first publication of Ali Pasha's political testament, and the version we have today was reprinted later in a French language newspaper in the empire in 1910, the existence of an earlier print of the testament is attested.
5 Andic and Andic, *The Last of the Ottoman Grandees*, p.27.
6 Benedict R. Anderson, *Imagined Communities: Reflections on the Origin and Spread of Nationalism* (London, 1991), pp.42–5.
7 Ahmet Midhat, *Felâtun Bey and Râkım Efendi*, p.106.
8 Ibid., p.70.
9 Andic and Andic, *The Last of the Ottoman Grandees*, p.56.
10 Ibid., p.34
11 Ibid., p.36.
12 Ibid., p.34.
13 Ahmet Midhat, *Felâtun Bey and Râkım Efendi*, pp.42–3.
14 Ibid., pp.52–3.
15 For the reference to Naum's Theatre in the novel see Ahmet Midhat, *Felâtun Bey and Râkım Efendi*, p.3. For information about Naum's Theatre see Emre Aracı, 'Naum Theatre: The Lost Opera House of Istanbul. Part I', *Turkish Area Studies Review: Bulletin of the Turkish Area Study Group* 17 (2011), pp.5–6.
16 Ahmet Midhat, *Felâtun Bey and Râkım Efendi*, p.10.
17 Ibid., p.19.
18 Ibid., p.11.
19 Kastamonu is a town in North Eastern Turkey, which has long been considered socially conservative. This is where Mustafa Kemal Atatürk, founder of the Turkish Republic, gave his famous 'gentlemen, this is a hat' speech to promote the adoption of his clothing reforms.
20 Ahmet Midhat, *Felâtun Bey and Râkım Efendi*, p.5.
21 Andic and Andic, *The Last of the Ottoman Grandees*, p.48.
22 Ibid., p.47. I have changed the word 'fatherland' to 'homeland' because, although this perhaps could have made sense translating from the French version of the testament, which is what is available to scholars beyond this English translation, the Ottoman/Turkish word *vatan* does not have such gendered implications.
23 Ibid, p.55.
24 Ibid., p.56.

25 The Janissary Corps was an elite infantry component of the Ottoman military. In 1826 the Janissary Corps was abolished and many of its constituent members killed on the order of Sultan Mahmud II.
26 Fatma Müge Göçek, *Rise of the Bourgeoisie, Demise of Empire: Ottoman Westernization and Social Change* (Oxford,1996), p.24; Colin Imber, *The Ottoman Empire, 1300-1650: The Structure of Power* (New York, 2002), pp.148–53.
27 Ahmet Midhat, *Felâtun Bey and Râkım Efendi*, p.15.
28 Ibid., p.15.
29 Imber, *The Ottoman Empire, 1300-1650*, p.13.
30 Ahmet Midhat, *Felâtun Bey and Râkım Efendi*, pp.150–4.
31 For a discussion of the concept of the citizen as both the subject and agent of reform see Ringer, *Pious Citizens*, p.7.
32 Anderson, *Imagined Communities*, 42–5.

5

Perils of the french maiden: Women, work, virtue and the public space in some french tales by Ahmet Midhat Efendi

A. Holly Shissler

Ahmet Midhat Efendi (1844–1912) was one of the preeminent Ottoman men of letters of the late nineteenth century. In terms of both the scope and volume of his output, there really is no other figure in the period to equal him. His importance is multi-faceted: as a newspaper editor and publisher, as a translator of both fiction and non-fiction, as an essayist, and as the author of numerous novels and short stories. Among the sources of his great impact was his editorship of *Tercüman-ı Hakikat*, a daily paper, the longest running in Ottoman history, which was published from 1878 to 1924. The newspaper was important for many reasons, not least that it published the works of many important Ottoman authors, often giving them their first literary 'breaks.' His capacity to produce was prodigious and he participated in most of the important cultural debates of his time, including the restructuring or reform of family life and the concomitant changes in women's education and presence in the public sphere; educational reform; the modernization and simplification of the Ottoman Turkish language; political economy and the question of free trade; the defence of Islam, especially from the attacks of Christian missionaries; and debates about good and bad modernization and the maintenance of Ottoman character and identity, to name just a few of the most important. He was a great popularizer, a fact that magnified his cultural impact even further.

Among his many literary productions, Ahmet Midhat Efendi wrote a very popular and successful series of stories and novellas under the heading *Amusing Tales* (*Letaif-i Rivayat*), which appeared between the years 1870 and

1894. Of these, almost half were set in France. What was the meaning of these French settings for Ahmet Midhat Efendi? Why write such stories? What did he think he could transmit to his audience in this way? In an attempt to address these questions, this essay will consider five stories from the *Amusing Tales* series: 'Suspicion' ('Suizan', 1870, 44 pp.) 'The Haunted Inn' ('Cinli Han', 1886, 160 pp.), 'Double Revenge' ('Çifte İntikam', 1888, 80 pp.), 'The Girl with a Diploma' ('Diplomalı Kız', 1891, 228 pp.) and 'Mother and Daughter' ('Ana-Kız', 1896, 101 pp.).[1]

First and foremost, it should be recognized that Ahmet Midhat Efendi started out as a man of very modest means and, while he had strong views and an educational agenda in his writing, he always needed his work to sell, and therefore he needed it to be entertaining. In this regard, the stories with French settings clearly had a certain exotic appeal for his audiences. He self-consciously wrote in a style that he hoped would be accessible and engaging to a literate but not necessarily highly educated audience. His work therefore contained descriptions of customs and practices to be seen in France that would catch the attention or spark the curiosity of his readership. He described and commented upon numerous aspects of French life, sometimes moralizing upon them, and he often injected a droll or ironic authorial voice while doing so.

Moreover, he adapted and even gently satirized some of the popular writing practices encountered in English and French literature. Three of our short stories are good examples of this. 'The Haunted Inn' is Gothic in style, with many of the hallmarks of the Gothic such as the mysterious or supernatural phenomenon unmasked. In fact, as I have pointed out elsewhere, the plot of 'The Haunted Inn' incorporates or parallels many characteristics of Ann Radcliffe's famous *Mysteries of Udolpho*, which Ahmet Midhat Efendi translated into Ottoman as *Udolf's Castle* (*Udolf hısarı*).[2] At the same time, he gently teased about Radcliffe's famously detailed descriptions of places and landscapes, which, it turned out, she had never seen.

'Double Revenge' and 'Suspicion' are in the short story tradition of Guy de Maupassant and Alphonse Daudet, with their focus on mores and human foibles, and their propensity for a 'shock' or unexpected twist at the end. Thus, Ahmet Midhat Efendi introduced his audience to various aspects of Euro-American literary practice, as well as offering them information about foreign lands.

In fact, many of his works with both Ottoman and foreign settings were translations or adaptions of works by foreign authors, such as Alexandre Dumas or Eugène Sue. Even more frequently, Ahmet Midhat Efendi produced works that avowedly took their inspiration from the works of others, or even from newspaper accounts he had read, and which he spun out into stories of his own in ways that he viewed as suitable for an Ottoman audience. Ahmet Midhat Efendi was quite frank about this practice and his works often include a short preface in which he explains the origin of the story as translated from, adapted from, or inspired by some specific event. As he says in the introduction to another story from the series, 'Two Frauds',

> The basis of the present little novel entitled 'Two Frauds' consists of a little anecdote that I read seven or eight months ago in a French newspaper ... [M]y readers know that even when in 'translation' (*tercüme*) mode, I always carry out a fair bit of modification on the novels that I take from Europe, and afterwards I [can] recommend them to our shared Ottoman morals. For I have learned well that, of the things that come from Europe, the rotten ones are far more numerous than the sound, and the bad number many more than the good. But anyway, when it comes to borrowing (*iktibas*) I take the idea of modification even further ... From them [the stories] I merely take an idea and then I take up my pen and write an entirely new work based on it ...[3]

While it seems clear that these claims are true when he credits a specific source for his inspiration, be it an author or a newspaper article, it is less clear that there really is an external source or inspiration when he claims merely to have heard an anecdote from a friend or to have overheard someone telling a story in a public place. The latter could just as easily be part of a literary convention. In the case of the stories to be examined here, all of them are described as adaptions of French works or as inspired by accounts Ahmet Midhat Efendi learned of either through personal interaction or through newspaper reports.

Yet for all of his desire and need to engage and entertain a substantial audience, Ahmet Midhat Efendi was supremely didactic in all his writing, including his fiction. Not for nothing did he come to be known in the Ottoman Empire as the First Teacher (*Hace-i Evvel*). He sought to educate his public as well as amuse it, and in general his stories have points or morals. Active in an era of dramatic social, political, and economic change, and himself a child of the Ottoman Empire's period of 'Great Reforms', the *Tanzimat,* Ahmet Midhat Efendi's goal was to inculcate a certain set of moral and intellectual attitudes that he viewed as conducive to progress and self-strengthening. The didactic purpose of his work was therefore social more than educational in the narrow sense of imparting specific knowledge (though Ahmet Midhat Efendi was never averse to the latter). His particular focus was an emerging Ottoman middle class: not an upper-middle class of government functionaries, but a traditional middle class of craftsmen and small-time merchants that was in the process of being transformed and modernized. This of course was the class from which he originally hailed. Ahmet Midhat Efendi's goal was to set these people on the road to what he considered a proper modernization, to help them develop a new world that was 'civilized', productive, and conformed to a moral and ethical vision that could co-exist with the demands of the contemporary world, but that still embodied non-materialist values. He especially condemned instrumentalizing others and seeing human relations in purely economic or transactional terms.

His works show a deep commitment to developing an enterprising spirit in the lower and middle classes, the classes that he saw as the productive and moral backbone of society. For Ahmet Midhat Efendi, this meant the spirit of capitalism in an almost Weberian sense – hard work, devotion to self-improvement and to bettering the situation of one's children, thrift, ambition, and a sense that education was important to these ends. This was joined with a rejection of anti-intellectualism, a rejection of tradition in the sense of accepting things as they were, and a rejection of sinecures and rent-seeking as a 'legitimate' means of securing prosperity. It also meant embracing civic virtue and embracing family life of a sort that valorized the intelligence, education and financial contributions of women to the family and society.[4]

His French stories, like his Ottoman stories, promote these values, but they allow the author to explore some themes and settings in a way that was probably more acceptable to his Ottoman audience if set in France than if set in the Ottoman Empire. These included depictions of 'nice' women mixing freely with men, participating in the public workforce, and entirely self-actuating and self-sufficient; the associated questions surrounding sexual morality; depictions of village life and concern for the moral, educational and economic development of the peasantry; depictions of extreme poverty, with occasional implied criticism of inherited wealth and property rights and overt criticism of the lack of charity visible in societies where human relations have been made purely material transactions.

One of Ahmet Midhat Efendi's favourite themes, in both his French and his Ottoman settings, is that of striver or bootstrapper. The French setting allows him to pursue this theme, but with a focus on female rather than male protagonists making the effort. 'The Haunted Inn' is an excellent example of this. The story, Gothic and dramatic, centres on a young village couple – Joséphine and Grégoire Salpet. The first pages of the story establish that they are both very serious, to the point that the other villagers laugh at them. The remainder of the story focuses on the adventures and challenges that face them while they are separated, with special focus on Joséphine's trials and achievements. Indeed, though the story is built around the undying love and fidelity of the young couple, it is Joséphine who is the real hero of the novella. It is true that Grégoire is the one who initially spurs her efforts by promising her that he will get rich 'for her' while he is away performing his military service, and by learning to read and write so as to send her letters. But the story really focuses on her and her efforts to match his endeavours. She becomes literate, undertakes smaller enterprises like sewing and washing, buys chickens and gradually expands her livestock holdings and adds improvements like henhouses and stables to her small plot of land. And, what is more, when she is subjected to a nefarious assault on her virtue, she successfully defends it herself. She fends off her kidnapper de La Roche for a whole year, first by threatening suicide and later through the clever stratagem of pretending to acquiesce to his advances, but saying that she needs a decent time to mourn her fiancé, Grégoire. Through courage, determination and ingenuity, she survives her captivity and is ultimately rescued by her beloved, returning to him untarnished.

This portrait of self-sufficiency is mirrored in 'The Girl with a Degree.' The child of hard-working and thrifty labourers, Julie Dupré has received a good education, but is unable to find employment with her teaching certificate, earned at great familial sacrifice. When her ageing parents can no longer work and earn as before, the family begins to starve. Though she looks high and low for work, Julie cannot secure a job. One desperate day Julie picks up a large bouquet of flowers fallen from a funeral procession. She divides these and sells them on the steps of the theatre that evening while reciting relevant poetry she knows due to her education. She is a sensation and makes good money, bringing cash and food home to her parents. The next day she repeats this performance, and begins to establish a reputation for herself as the educated, poetic flower girl. When she runs out of verses she already knows, she starts going to the library during the day to research new verses she can use. She lies to her parents, saying she has gotten a job as a bookkeeper in a shop. In the meantime, she continues to make a good business of her flowers, making a business arrangement with the owner of a flower shop. Step by step, from literally nothing, she builds a successful business that allows her to support herself and her parents. She brings home food and pays the rent, and she saves. Julie values education for the cultural riches it makes available; both she and her parents genuinely enjoy the literature her education has opened to her. At the same time, it is only when she joins that education to a practical 'street smarts' that it becomes materially effective for her. When the truth about her work is revealed to her parents, Julie asks, 'Is it wrong for a girl who doesn't [even] have bread to eat to sell flowers?' Her father responds, 'No, it is not wrong, nor is it a misfortune to cry about or feel pained about. I would have counted myself even more fortunate if my daughter were a seamstress than if she had gotten her teaching diploma. What's wrong with trade? Why should it be deemed a misfortune? On the contrary, it is one of the most honorable occupations. As long as there isn't any other kind of ugliness touching on your virtue (*namus*).'[5] In this sense the story reinforces Ahmet Midhat Efendi's concern for people of the middling sort, and his conviction that it is they, properly enlightened, who constitute the moral and economic backbone of any society. It highlights the importance he gives both to the work ethic and to the enterprising spirit and, as in other works of his, it points out the perils of relying upon a government salary or sinecure for one's security and advancement. The story therefore distinguishes between the value of an education and the value of a diploma. A diploma is a piece of paper, a good education in good hands always has both intrinsic and practical value.

'Mother and Daughter' is the inverted image of 'The Girl with a Diploma.' A man who is a successful pastry and confectionery chef in a wealthy household marries a strong, virtuous village woman and brings her to Paris, where he is employed. They have a daughter and give her a fancy education and the best of everything, since they can afford to do so. But when the noble employer dies, the family is left high and dry. The parents are enterprising souls, and so the husband and wife begin to bake on their own account, and to sell their wares with a pushcart. Their daughter continues her education, living apart from them as before. Eventually the father dies, but luckily, the daughter, nicknamed Gigique, meets a young financial speculator who is willing to marry her. The husband loses his job and dies shortly thereafter. Gigique is now penniless with a young child to care for. Her mother, Germinie, suggests that together they can take over the pushcart sweet business, but Gigique cannot imagine such exhausting and lowly work for a woman like herself. She decides instead to make her way in the demi-monde, and abandons her daughter to her mother's care. Initially Gigique is quite successful in her chosen world, becoming a well-known figure and even a fashion setter. However, not only are her pastimes unproductive, they are expensive and wasteful. She must always stand at the apex of fashion, so she pays vast sums for outfits she wears but briefly, selling them afterwards at a fraction of the cost. Though she lives 'high on the hog', she does not save; though she is constantly pursued by men, she has no real or lasting relationships with the people around her. Her existence is therefore tenuous. Hers is a failed modernity of superficial worldliness, passing fads and self-regard. Of course, her immorality cannot go unpunished: she contracts a case of syphilis which, left too long untreated, leads to penury and ultimately her early demise. Her mother's old-fashioned village morality and work ethic, combined with the charity of an aristocratic family, just manage to save the young daughter, Louise, from starvation and provide her with a few feminine 'accomplishments'. In the end she contracts an honourable marriage to a man of good character whom she does not know at all, on the recommendation of her benefactor. So, in the absence of an effective modernity, the old paternalist modes take over.

What is striking about these stories is the very active role taken by the women. Joséphine is a totally self-made woman. It is true that she becomes a helpmeet to Grégoire, a similarly ambitious and virtuous young man, but her education, her savings, her business sense, and ultimately the cunning she uses to survive her captivity are all her own. Julie Dupré benefits from the loving household her parents provide and from the formal education they bestow on her, and, like Joséphine, it is love – more even than need – that motivates her to pursue business, and she too does it all on her own. With no capital but her education and her wits she makes a successful business. In 'Mother and Daughter,' the grandmother, Germinie, who has no training in the modern world or in a trade or even in city life, and no book-learning, nevertheless manages, as a widow alone in the world, to keep body and soul together for herself and her granddaughter over a period of years. Even Gigique, the anti-hero of the tale, is remarkably self-actuating. Left as a penniless widow, she takes advantage of her male friendships to enter the world of the demi-monde, and there she does not merely subsist, but helps to establish various newfangled trends, like bicycling for women.

All five of the tales discussed here have something to say about chastity, sexual morality and jealousy. This is to some extent a predictable outgrowth of the focus on women in the world. If women were to be out and about, getting educated, starting businesses and generally organizing their own lives, what would these conditions mean for female chastity and for male honour and possessiveness? In these French stories Ahmet Midhat Efendi shows the sexual virtue of women questioned and threatened, but however much they might be out and about in the world, family love and devotion would protect them. To the extent that they were raised and shaped in the context of family love and as long as these women orientated their activities towards familial devotion – to parents, husbands or fiancés – they maintained a virtuous course.

The very first fiction produced in the *Letaif-i Rivayat* series, 'Suspicion' is a humorous, almost slap-stick story with a 'trick' ending. The narrator is trying to leave Paris to spend the weekend at his country home in the middle of a heavy downpour. All the cabs seem to be occupied, but he sees one going by, makes a frantic leap for it, and bumps heads with a close friend, Simon, who has entered the carriage simultaneously and in the same manner from the other side. They greet each other and the narrator learns that Simon had married his true love, Pauline, about a year ago, even though she came from a much better family than his. The two men decide to share the cab as the friend's house is on the way. As they converse it is revealed that Simon had despaired of marrying so far above his station. Then, consumed with rage as he saw another man, nominally a better candidate, but whom he knew to be a cad, hanging around Pauline, he decided to quit her country estate, where he had been visiting, before he did something he would regret.[6] But in the end, he got the girl, for she made clear to her father that she would commit suicide if he blocked their marriage, and as she put it in her letter to Simon, 'Do you think my father will see accepting you into our family as a humiliation? I don't, because he is not foolish enough to prefer the disgrace that will become known far and wide tomorrow when I kill myself.'[7] Thus immersed in conversation the two men arrive at Simon's home and the narrator is persuaded to spend the night. At home they find Pauline and her cousin, Charles, a good-looking young man, who is there on an extended visit. The four of them pass a marvellous evening of food and conversation that continues late into the night. As the evening progresses the narrator becomes more and more suspicious and outraged at the easy, affectionate interaction between Pauline and Charles. He is ever more convinced that they are improperly involved and he is appalled that his friend, very happily married, is blind to it. The idea develops in the narrator's mind that he must take his gun and kill Pauline and Charles to avenge his friend's honour. Everyone goes to bed, then, in the middle of the night, the narrator hears the wife creeping out of the house to a small cabin on the grounds. His mind swings wildly to a new conclusion – she must be having an affair with a villager! When the cousin follows her out shortly thereafter, the narrator reverts to his first thought. He is full of rage and in an agony of indecision as to what action to take. Just as he has decided to take 'justice' into his own hands, he sees his friend tiptoeing out too! Confronting him, he discovers that everyone is headed for the latrines, having become indisposed from eating too many plums at dinner. This story is very light-hearted with little real character development, but it does invite the reader to reflect on the narrator's propensity to think the worst of the young wife and her cousin, and it also seems to invite the reader to ask why he assumes that a relaxed, friendly interaction in the presence of her husband between a young wife and a close male friend or relative should be the cause of so much alarm. The whole piece is an attack on various conventions like the father who initially puts family standing above his daughter's happiness and refuses to consider a suitor who is known to be upright and energetic, but who comes from a 'nothing' family. But the crux of the story is the friend whose mind cannot free itself from evil suspicions despite the obvious happiness of his friend's marriage and the position of family trust occupied by Charles, and who then contemplates the most radical of 'remedies'. Simon, by contrast, is quietly rational and civilized: driven mad by the presence of another possible suitor for his beloved's hand before their marriage, he decides he should leave before he does something terrible. His attitude towards his wife after their marriage is one of unquestioning love and confidence in her love, and he is unperturbed by the presence of either Charles or his visiting friend from Paris. The story is almost a gentle 'plug' for a somewhat greater social interaction between the sexes. Pauline with her great youth and beauty is not ultimately portrayed as the root of conflict or as an irresistible temptation, nor is the attractive young relation seen as a wolf in the fold – the real 'devil' in the story is the friend with his conventional suspicions, which, perhaps, are a reflection on his own character. Good character, absolute faith in his loving wife, and an enlightened attitude that measures his honour in terms of reality rather than rumours and suspicions, make Simon the man to admire in this story.

'Double Revenge' is a story about what happens when trust is shattered and restraint is not employed. A villager named Lotis gets engaged to a girl from his home town then goes off to do his military service in Algeria. His fiancée, despite being pursued by many in his absence, is faithful to him. He is discharged after being wounded in battle and returns home. They quickly marry as he takes up the job of game warden in the hunting park of a local nobleman. His pension as a wounded veteran plus his salary constitute a comfortable workingman's living. Soon a girl is born, but within a few months the wife gets sick and dies. Lotis is left alone to raise his daughter. She is his only child and joy, and he decides he will attend to her upbringing himself. Thus, the girl is a bit of a wild child, traipsing after her father through the woods, dressed like a boy and swearing like a sailor. She becomes tall, strong, beautiful, fearless and forthright, lacking any semblance of a woman's wiles or a girl's coquettishness. Over time her father is moved by the intervention of the villagers to have her don some more suitable female attire and attend church, and she continues to go to church because often afterwards there is dancing in the village. We discover that Marguerite loves to dance at these after-church events. All the boys in the village follow her about, but she has no interest beyond dancing them nearly to death, for really they are not her equals. Eventually, she goes to a regional fair a few days' travel away in the company of village friends. She meets a young man who is really her match, Antoine Marsil, nicknamed Rock, and they dance the night away, wearing out even the musicians. He buys her wine in one of the tents and asks her if she can like him. She says 'yes' very clearly but then learns that he is a poacher by trade. She feels obliged, for her father's sake, to distance herself from him. He pursues her and she sees a bit more of him at village dances and functions back in her home village, but she never lets it go further because of the impediment of his occupation, which he refuses to forswear for her sake. A short time later she is confronted, once in the woods by her poacher-admirer, once at home by her father, to the effect that she has been seen running around alone with a man. Her father has heard tell of it from gossiping villagers. She denies everything. Who is the interloper? Millefleur, an itinerant painter from Paris. It turns out it is true, she has been having an affair with Millefleur. She is serious about him, but he, an unreconstructed rake, is toying with her. Both her father and Rock, the poacher, follow her into the woods the next day and when they see her and the painter together, they shoot – simultaneously – Rock kills Marguerite, the father kills the painter, Millefleur.

Though technically a criminal and a poacher, Rock is straightforward, hides nothing about his way of making a living, has a manly history of military service as a dragoon, and is honest in his real passion for Marguerite and in his intention to marry her. Millefleur, on the other hand, is a Parisian womanizer with a history of preying on unsuspecting women. How could a woman like Marguerite fall into his trap? Marguerite and Rock are portrayed almost as noble savages, with a natural morality that stands outside the bounds of unfair laws or of a conventional morality. Rock hunts for his living; the fact that this is illegal in France is attributable to laws that are harsh and unfair. Ahmet Midhat Efendi comments that often in Europe forest lands are kept private and closed so the wealthy can hunt for sport, and ordinary folk who hunt for food are seen as thieves.[8] Marguerite, raised outside of society, a fine healthy young animal, has never lied to her father and is naturally both faithful and passionate. However, denied the mate who would have been her true and natural match out of loyalty to her father and due to the laws on poaching, she turns to another choice and is ripe fruit for the picking. She is utterly natural and free of guile, while Millefleur is an experienced rake who specializes in preying on innocent girls from the lower classes. She gives herself to him sexually because to her mind the exchange of words of love is the same as marriage and will inevitably lead to marriage. It is this combination of her loyalty to her father, her inability to pursue her first and natural inclination, her innocence of the duplicity of city-slickers, and her freedom from conventional understandings of morality, that lead her to lie to her father, to become a 'fallen woman,' and finally to fall victim to Rock's jealousy. A certain failure of devotion on the part of Lotis, her father, also contributes to her undoing. Her father never really recognizes either her adulthood or her womanhood until the end. He wants to keep her as his companion, and fails to provide an outlet for this child of nature. He keeps her close, but he does not really sacrifice for her; he gives no real thought to her future, neither educating her nor thinking of finding her a husband. In fact, he imagines no future for her beyond his home. She, in contrast, is devoted to her father and renounces the good man she loves and who loves her, thereby laying herself open to the wiles of a rogue. But Ahmet Midhat Efendi does not impeach her virtue: she gives herself to the rogue with a clear sense that she is giving herself in love to this man forever. Rather he impeaches the city-slicker who deceived her, the society that oppressed the countryside by outlawing local men who hunted for food, and, to a lesser degree, the father who loved her without really caring for her.

The industrious and resourceful Julie Dupré is also victimized by gossip and suspicion vis-à-vis her sexual morality. She is accused of being a prostitute, and maybe even a member of a criminal syndicate by the concierge of her building in 'The Girl with a Diploma.' The concierge and his wife distrust her education and they envy her success in the working world as reported by her mother, and so they spy upon her and immediately draw the wrong conclusions. She is out all hours, she hangs around on steps of the theatre, she regularly goes to the library and to an office on Rue de Richelieu. What can such carryings-on be if not prostitution and criminal conspiracy? This suspicion of theirs is abetted by Julie's foolish shame at the fact that she is making a living in the flower business and not in a higher status job, 'worthy' of her education, like bookkeeper or shop clerk. But in this case family bonds are the motivation for Julie's entrepreneurial efforts, and they do not fail her now. Though her parents experience doubt when the concierge details his accusations to them, they nevertheless defend Julie. When her father confronts her, he begins by saying he recognizes he has no right to demand an accounting of her since he is not the breadwinner, and she quickly responds that he is her father and as far as she is concerned he will always have authority with her. That bond of love and trust is shared and, for Ahmet Midhat Efendi, the proof that the proper moral character is present in both Julie and her parents. When she asks her parents for a week in which to make clear to them what she has been doing, her father replies, 'take 15 days.' Family bonds have kept all of the Duprés on the straight path, even though her parents weren't married and their occasional church attendance was more in the order of taking in free entertainment than of moral uplift or religious instruction. Her uneducated parents are naturally hard-working and they are devoted to each other and their daughter. They are thrifty, they sacrificed for her, and she in turn has the inner resources to save them all from destitution, without the slightest threat to her sexual virtue. The fact that she walks the street at night selling flowers to strangers poses no challenge to her chastity. Her devotion as a daughter is her guide and keeps her safe.

'The Haunted Inn' is all about how Joséphine, motivated by her love for a genuine, hard-working, and loving man, makes her way in the world and then finds herself in a situation where men who should be in positions of trust – a 'great man' from the big city who is a friend of the local priest, and the priest himself – abuse her trust and try to rape her. In 'Double Revenge' Ahmet Midhat Efendi put before his readers the idea that Marguerite's virtue is not bounded by marriage, if marriage is understood as a mere rite or empty contract. In similar vein, the fact that Joséphine, a young unmarried woman, is out in the world is no cause for any shame. The problem is the corruption of the clergy, the immorality and the self-referential vanity of the city-slicker de La Roche, and the ignorance and small-mindedness of the other villagers. When de La Roche kidnaps her, many in the village think that there is nothing wrong with that, really. The general sense is that if he has carried her off, but marries her in the end, there is no problem, especially since he is rich. Some even imagine that Marguerite may have connived at her own 'abduction'. They have no real sense of a woman as a person; if she is materially provided for, what more can she want, what other will can she have? The whole thrust of the story is to strike out at these notions. Joséphine is absolutely virtuous. She cares for money in the sense that she is willing to work hard and live thriftily in order to be prosperous, and she is interested in this entirely in the context of her love for her fiancé and her desire to build a life with and for him. She has no interest in easy money or money for its own sake, and the thought of a high life with another man repels her. Grégoire never loses faith in her nor stops looking for her, despite the wagging chins of the villagers, and likewise she never doubts that he will find her. Here de La Roche and Father Prasil are the great villains who are willing to destroy a young woman on a whim. Her virginity is imperilled in the story, but not her virtue. Though she is a young woman out in the world, Ahmet Midhat Efendi does not describe her as having 'tempted' her tormentors, nor as having been tempted by them. Her moral compass cannot be moved. The story is also an occasion to call into question practices that were still to some degree accepted in the Ottoman Empire, such as bride abduction.

It is 'Mother and Daughter' where we see most clearly a case of fallen female virtue. Angélique, known as Gigique to friends and family, is miseducated. She was given first to a wet nurse and then to a privileged Parisian education that had few practical aspects. Shielded from the hard work of her parents, she came to identify more with the upper classes and had many grand dreams and inflated expectations. Her brief marriage proved something of a sham, not to say a shambles: in a short time, the couple become bored with one another and, though they have a daughter, each lives his own life, with separate social engagements and affairs. A few years later, widowed with a young child, Gigique chooses life in the demi-monde over enduring the 'de-classing' that working with her mother would require. Abandoning her young daughter, Gigique leads a life of high fashion, immoral self-indulgence and sexual licence until a long-untreated case of syphilis lays her low. What went wrong here? Gigique came from an honourable working family, but she never spent any time with them – she went from wet nurse to school. Though her parents loved her, she never felt their warmth and they never instilled in her, by teaching or example, the values of hard work, thrift and family bonds. Thus, she chooses a world of self-regarding image making. She has no real commitments save to her own 'lifestyle.' This is so much the case that when she does encounter her mother by chance on the street years later, in a state of distress so deep that strangers have stopped to help, Gigique, dressed in the latest style and fashionably out riding on velocipedes with a well-heeled admirer, literally runs from her. And so, lacking the moral compass that family love and family ties provide, she floats on a sea of immorality and materiality, and eventually dies of it. Her sin is not being a modern woman out in the world, her sin is approaching the world rudderless. Hers is a failed modernity, and her sexual virtue is an early casualty and the vehicle through which she ultimately receives the wages of sin.

Those who do work are the cornerstone of the successful society of the future for Ahmet Midhat Efendi. As we have noted earlier, he was a great exponent of self-help and of the productive society, and he believed that there was a natural symbiotic and self-reinforcing relationship constituted by devoted family life based on companionate marriage; hard work, industry, and education; and civic virtue. The future of society thus lay not with grandees and coffeehouse intellectuals, but with the likes of labourers, tradesmen, and peasants. He therefore cared deeply for their current conditions and future uplift. But his Ottoman readership was not too interested in stories of the very humble and lowly in the Ottoman Empire (though they could be interested in the stories of successful and established tradesmen). The French settings of these stories therefore offer the opportunity for Ahmet Midhat Efendi to shine a light on the conditions of the poor without losing the interest of his audience. He does not romanticize what he finds there: grinding poverty, worn out workers cast aside, ignorance, envy, small-mindedness, grasping behaviour and an utter lack of human compassion are all too common. And though nominally the stories reveal conditions in France, Ahmet Midhat Efendi uses them to shine a light on the condition of Ottoman poor and rural communities as well.

'The Haunted Inn' is set in a rural village and its protagonists are common peasants, something which, if set in the Ottoman Empire, would not likely garner a wide audience among the Ottoman reading public. The countryside was largely viewed as backward, a place from which to escape. In fact, as Ramazan Kaplan has noted, Ahmet Midhat Efendi wrote some of the first examples of 'Village Literature' in the Turkish language, namely, 'A True Story' ('Bir Gerçek Hikaye') and 'Happiness' ('Bahtiyarlık').[9] But though they had village settings, neither story was deeply concerned with the social conditions of ordinary peasants. By contrast, the 'The Haunted Inn' is concerned with such matters. Its protagonists are a young village couple and the descriptions of village life and of how our young heroine, Joséphine, slowly builds up her little nest egg are quite detailed. Ahmet Midhat Efendi even jokes in an authorial aside that no doubt his readers are not interested in these nitty-gritty agricultural details, but he has already given quite a few of them. He also highlights the mockery of the other villagers for Joséphine's serious and determined behaviour. First, they regard her and her fiancé, Grégoire, as boring and naively 'square' in their commitment to each other, in their embrace of hard work, and in their rejection of frivolous pastimes and premarital experimentation. Later, they lack any understanding of Joséphine's motives as she works to better herself, and they criticize her and poke fun at her as stuck-up and having airs. Finally, jealous of her successes, they gossip about her and imply that the increase in livestock and other possessions must be from ill-gotten gains that have accrued to her as a result of her supposedly running around with men. When de La Roche kidnaps her, no one, other than her mother (and Grégoire upon his return), is the least bit concerned. They are ready to believe the worst of Joséphine – that she has run off with a wealthy paramour – or at best that she was carried off by a wealthy man and this was either with her complicity or she soon made peace with it. They callously repeat these baseless suppositions to Grégoire.

'Mother and Daughter' and 'The Girl with a Diploma' both contain wrenching descriptions of poverty and hunger: days and days of eating thin meatless broth, malnutrition, illness, having to burn one's few bits of furniture (and even furnishings that do not belong to one) in order to not freeze. Hard work and a good, enterprising spirit do not always produce a happy rags-to-riches ending. In 'Mother and Daughter,' Grandmother Germinie works herself nearly to death to support little Louise, but as she ages she can no longer endure the hardships of the laundry or the rigours of pushcart sales. The child sickens before her eyes for lack of food and fresh air. Her final desperate effort selling her homemade sweets from a pushcart is wiped out by a thunderstorm, leaving the exhausted desperate women so undone that she collapses into bitter helpless tears on the street. Julie Dupré's father suffers an injury at work as he gets older and is never as strong or able as before. His wages are cut and cut again, and the family is reduced to penury and starvation. But on the whole, no one cares. The concierge of Julie's building and his wife immediately decide they must not lend any money to the Duprés, and must rather be sure the rent is fully collected. Illiterate and grasping, they quickly begin to be suspicious when Julie starts to make good. Despite having known her and her family for years, they spy on her, think about how to get money out of her, and spread malicious gossip about her. In 'Double Revenge' as well, it is the idle tittle-tattle of the villagers, disguised as 'concern,' that leads Lotis to take up his rifle and follow his daughter to her assignation in the woods.

Ahmet Midhat Efendi asks his readers to look at these people and feel compassion and outrage. He allows them the slightest bit of superiority and distancing by comparing Christian customs unfavourably with Muslim practices, but then quickly brings them back to the harsh realities. The poor suffer, he tells his readers, and in their suffering they are often both ignorant and mean, but at least they live from honest labour and as such, they can, in the right conditions, be re-made and set on the path to success. The vapid pleasure-seeking classes with their rents and sinecures or the immoral artistic types, on the other hand, can never really constitute sound fundamental building blocks for a modern moral society.

We may therefore think about these stories with French settings as touching on many basic themes that are common to Ahmet Midhat Efendi's works with Ottoman settings – all of them concentrating on the basic question of a moral modernity: good versus bad modernization, self-help, companionate marriage, the productive versus the parasitic classes, and the importance of love and family in maintaining a moral outlook. But the French settings allow for a more radical examination of the 'woman question' and also allow for a deeper examination of the values and the travails of the poor in town and country. Julie Dupré might be regarded as a female version of Rakım Efendi, right down to the mother who does laundry. She, child of a family of modest means, receives the benefits of education at great cost to them and, in the end, through ingenuity and hard work, the child makes good use of that education and loyally repays the debt of gratitude owed to the family. But in this case, the child who makes good is a woman. One might even see Joséphine as something of a rural version of this story. Gigique, for her part, has many of the characteristics of Felatun Bey. Her father, though he was hard-working, was something of a dandy and, like Felatun's father, overly enamoured of various urban fashions, including a fashionable education for his offspring. Also, like Felatun's father, Gigique's father spent little actual time with her. The result in her case, as in Felatun Bey's, was an inability to form real sexual-emotional attachments. They use and are used by the men and women around them. Each sees him or herself, and is seen by others, as highly urbane and up-to-date, but each squanders his or her educational and material resources and ends in penury (and in Gigique's case, death). The descriptions of strange practices, like the newfangled fashion of men and women going out on velocipede rides through the parks of Paris and environs, provide interesting colour for an Ottoman readership, and at the same time point out some of the perils of a whole materialist modernity as practised in Europe, which was commonly labelled 'civilization'.

Notes

1 'Suizan', *Letâif-i Rivâyât*, vol. 1, 1287/1870, 44 pp.; 'Cinli Han', *Letâif-i Rivâyât*, vol. 12, 1302/1886, 160 pp.; 'Çifte İntikam', *Letâif-i Rivâyât*, vol. 16, Istanbul 1304/1888, 80 pp.; 'Diplomalı Kız', *Letâif-i Rivâyât*, vol. 19, 1307/1891, 228 pp.; 'Ana-Kız', *Letâif-i Rivâyât*, vol. 25, 1312/1896, 101 pp;. A new collected edition of all the stories in the series, transliterated into the modern Turkish alphabet, appeared in 2001: Ahmet Midhat, *Letaif-i Rivayat* eds., Fazıl Gökçek and Sabahattin Çağın. Sultanahmet, (İstanbul: Çağrı, 2001). All quotations from the stories refer to that edition.
2 Ahmet Midhat Efendi's 'Cinli Han' and especially its Gothic aspects are treated in A. Holly Shissler, 'Haunting Ottoman Middle-class Sensibility: Ahmet Midhat Efendi's Gothic', in Marylin Booth and Claire Savina (eds), *Translation and Circulation in the Late Ottoman World* (Edinburgh, 2019).
3 Ahmet Midhat Efendi, *Letaif-i Rivayat*, p.703.
4 I have discussed the exposition of these values in two of Ahmet Midhat Efendi's novels with Ottoman settings, *Felâtun Bey ile Râkım Efendi* and *Henüz Önyedi Yaşında*. See A. Holly Shissler, 'The Harem as the Seat of Middle-class Industry and Morality: The Fiction of Ahmet Midhat Efendi' in Marylin Booth, *Harem Histories: Envisioning Places and Living Spaces* (Durham, NC, 20), pp.333–60.
5 Ahmet Midhat, *Letaif-i Rivayat*, p.658.
6 Ibid., p.3.
7 Ibid., p.4.
8 Ibid., p.505 and pp.507–8.
9 Ramazan Kaplan, *Cumhuriyet Dönemi Türk Romanında Köy* (Ankara, 1988), pp.3–11.

6

The Tanzimat novel in the service of science: On Ahmet Midhat Efendi's *American Doctors*

Ercüment Asil

In the late eighteenth and early nineteenth centuries, when Ottomans started to systematically adopt European science and technology, they largely conceived of it as an addendum to their established body of traditional knowledge (*ilim*). *İlim* was a concept, which, thanks to religious and scholarly works composed over the course of thirteen centuries, enjoyed immense prestige among both scholars and lay people alike. Although they were foreign in origin, the Ottomans did not hesitate to include these new European sciences within the powerful and prestigious concept of *ilim*. Soon, however, some realized that the newly imported European sciences contained elements that could potentially challenge their worldviews. This constituted a crucial moment for the course that Ottoman modernization would take. On the one hand, Ottoman modernizers wanted to adopt modern scientific rationality, its methods and institutions. They often underlined the ways in which it differed from traditional *ilim* by using the term *fen* (art, practical science). Hence, *fen* emerged as the term which emphasized productivity rather than theoretical or religious and moral knowledge. On the other hand, however, the term *fen* did not enjoy the same long-standing authority as the term *ilim*. Promoters of *fen* thus often appealed to the authority of *ilim* by using both terms together. Thus, by presenting *fen* as an extension of *ilim*, modernizers not only benefited from the already established prestige of *ilim* but they also mitigated the challenge *fen* would pose to established notions regarding science and knowledge.[1]

Yet, the tension between the traditional *ilim* and modern *fen* surfaced every now and then, at the level of worldviews, methods, institutions and social groups associated with them, as in the case of modern *mekteb* schools and the traditional *medrese* schools which existed side by side. The tension and co-existence led some historians to conceive of a 'dualism' in Ottoman modernization: a battle between purely modern institutions and purely traditional institutions that were essentially inimical to each other. However, recent studies, more attuned to the details of the discursive negotiations between institutional and individual actors, have been more successful at capturing the ways in which Ottomans constructed their own modernity. In the pages that follow, I look at the *ilim/fen* pair as a conceptual axis that underlines Ottoman efforts to acquire new scientific methods through a productive discourse emerging from within established tradition rather than running against it.

'Scientific Literature' as a genre

Ahmet Midhat's *A Scientific Novel, or American Doctors* (*Fenni Bir Roman yahut Amerika Doktorları*, henceforth *American Doctors*, 1887–8) is an early example of how the discourse around science, tradition and civilization found its direct reflection in the modern genre of the Tanzimat-era novel.[2] In his novel, Ahmet Midhat clearly endorses the difference of modern *fen* science from the traditional *ilim* science, as shown by its title *Fenni Bir Roman*, rather than *İlmi Bir Roman*.[3] Throughout the novel, he consistently uses vocabulary that does not rely on the traditional prestige of *ilim*, such as, for instance, loan words like *doktor* or *profesör*, collectively described as 'men of *fen*' (*erbab-ı fen*, *fen adamları*). Even the word that Ahmet Midhat uses for 'teacher' (*muallim*) contrasts with the traditional term *müderris*, denoting the type of teacher found in modern institutions of knowledge rather than the one found in traditional schools. In fact, because the entire story takes place in America, a non-Muslim setting, Ahmet Midhat manages to avoid sensitive questions that might have arisen from the use of the word *fen* rather than *ilim*. In that regard, his novel participates in the domestication of the concept of *fen* as a form of modern science that does not rely upon the authority of *ilim*. Ahmet Midhat is able to accomplish this task thanks to the American setting chosen for his narrative, which, due to its geographical distance, must have undoubtedly been seen as more innocuous than an Ottoman setting.

I am of course not arguing that Ahmet Midhat's sole purpose in writing this novel was simply to endorse the term *fen* and reject that of *ilim*. As a novelist, his agenda was first and foremost a literary one; secondarily, it related to the larger discussion around the proper mode of adoption of modern sciences in the Ottoman context. Ahmet Midhat sought to provide an example of the newly imported genre of science fiction, which had been increasingly translated from the Western languages over the course of the previous decade.[4] He also employed fiction as a medium for conveying factual scientific knowledge. For all of these reasons, science and scientific innovation are thematically dominant in the novel.

In order to better conceive of the significance of Ahmet Midhat's attempt to produce a work of science fiction, it is important to emphasize the literary and intellectual context in which he operated. By the second half of the nineteenth century, Ottoman bureaucrats and litterateurs were convinced that scientific education should not to be limited to formal schooling. Science had to be publicly embraced, not only through schools but also via newly available print media such as newspapers and periodicals. Fiction was another such medium. However, this was still a time when literary fiction at large, and scientific literature (*fennî edebiyat*) in particular, remained largely perceived as a potentially problematic mode of expression. On the one hand, some were sceptical of Western forms of literature. On the other, some committed but marginal promoters of modern science cultivated science and scientific rationality to such a degree that they erected modern science as the sole criterion and meter of progress and truth. In a period marked by a concerted effort to impose 'innovation' from the top, by fierce debates around the purpose of literary genres, and by an increasing simplification of language and writing, some of these intellectuals went so far as rejecting the classical themes of traditional Ottoman poetry because they saw them as only fostering carnal pleasures, love and wine and therefore disparaged them as elements of 'disgusting politeness'. In their eyes, legitimate literature had to serve science only; even poetry, a medium for the articulation of the deepest of human feelings had to obey this rule. Accordingly, they composed and attempted to promote what they called 'scientific poetry' (*fennî şiir*).

According to Ahmet Midhat, who was a major promoter of new forms of literature, such criticisms of poetry and experimentation with 'scientific literature' missed the point and did not, in fact, answer the call for literature to become more 'scientific.' He warned that it would be a misunderstanding to think that 'scientific poetry' entailed composing verse on mathematics or natural sciences. This, in his view, only generated ridiculous works. As a corrective to this simplistic understanding of the relationship between science and literature, Ahmet Midhat attempted to define the true nature of 'scientific literature' by providing two interrelated, albeit different, definitions. In the first definition, 'scientific literature' was defined as 'the description of literary imagination based on emotions/sensation stemming from the known sciences.'[5] He cited Jules Verne as a successful example of this new, and promising genre. The second definition was more concerned with the general education of the Ottoman citizenry, a common concern for many Tanzimat-era authors. In this general didactic sense, Ahmet Midhat clarifies that

> literature's being scientific does not mean to teach science (lit. engineering, *hendese*) in the format of literary composition. When we [i.e. Ahmet Midhat referring to himself] come across critical scientific and industrial issues, we will explain them in such a simplified manner that the non-expert, and even women, can understand them.[6]

In his novel *American Doctors*, Ahmet Midhat attempts to realize both ambitions and composes a work of science fiction as much as an attempt to disseminate modern European scientific knowledge among the general public. Throughout the book, Ahmet Midhat's voice is always present and remains largely didactic in tone, as in much of his production. Although *American Doctors* is not, strictly speaking, an original work, it does not constitute a literal translation either. Its plot is largely based on Oscar Michon's comedic story (*variété humoristique*) titled 'Love and Galvanoplastie' (*Amour & Galvanoplastie*), a single-page short story published in 1885 in *Le Figaro*'s literary supplement.[7] Ahmet Midhat read the story multiple times and apparently found it so entertaining that he decided to adapt it for an Ottoman audience. The result, an eighty-page novel, first appeared as a serialized novel in the newspaper *Tercüman-ı Hakikat* (Interpreter of Truth), and subsequently in book form.

While retaining the main plot, as well as some character and place names, Ahmet Midhat's novel diverges in important ways from Michon's original story. Michon wrote the story to address the question of the cremation of dead bodies in the context of public health, a topic debated at the time in local municipal councils in France. Ahmet Midhat, however, recasts the story as an example of the emerging yet ambiguous genre of 'scientific literature' while showing a particular interest in offering a comparison of the American and Ottoman ways of life. Humour, alongside science, must also have played an important role in his choice of the material to adapt as the French original short story is far from constituting a particularly good example of science fiction.

Indeed fantastic elements in the novel are limited to the description of a drug-induced 'fake death' experiment and that of an untried galvanoplastic coating process for human bodies. Apart from these two scientific 'novelties', the novel's primary function is to convey the general concrete scientific knowledge of the time to his readers. For example, Ahmet Midhat intervenes into the narration to describe the dissection of a human body, to explain what galvanoplasty means, how objects can be coated with metals, how people can be turned into plaster statues, and how to check whether one is really dead or not. On occasion, he reaches beyond concrete science and touches upon more abstract issues such as the importance of rationality in every aspect of life. As an example of what he sees as the deep penetration of science in American life, Ahmet Midhat points to the simplicity, and accuracy of the American address system or to the rationality that prevails in the United States in public debates around the issue of cremation. Thereby, the author is able to both convey and explain 'critical scientific and industrial issues in a simplified manner' to the general Ottoman reading public.

In addition to the scientific and humoristic elements, Ahmet Midhat injected an element of love into the novel, and offered a mild dose of suspense as a way to retain his readers' attention. The intimacy that slowly develops between Dr Grippling and Mrs Bowley is juxtaposed with Mrs Bowley's loyalty to her husband. The fact that Dr Bowley is believed to be dead and is therefore at risk of being dissected by the Society for Mutual Dissection per his will adds additional moments of suspense.

Science and morality in Ottoman modernity

The Ottoman modern was often negotiated via discussions of morality and values, which the Ottomans debated explicitly in the press at the time. In that regard, in addition to being one of the earliest examples of the genre of science fiction written in Turkish, *American Doctors* also constitutes an example of Ottoman negotiation of Western civilization and the place of science- and morality-related debates.

The fact that Ahmet Midhat's story takes place in America, not in an Ottoman or Muslim setting, has consequences upon the negotiation of *fen* and its place in Ottoman modernity. While this choice may sound natural today, in the 1880s America constituted a peripheral location for the Ottomans compared to Europe. Therefore, the first chapter of the novel is dedicated to introducing America to the reader – though from a limited perspective. The choice of America as the setting for the novel eliminates the need to discuss the place of Islamic tradition as a source of moral authority. Going back to the interrelation between *fen* and *ilim*, *American Doctors* promotes *fen* without seeking to couple it to the long-standing authority of Islamic tradition. Yet, Ahmet Midhat's defence of *fen* without the recourse to the prestige of *ilim*, does not in any way mean that he neglects the importance of Islam in the articulation of Ottoman modernity. In addition to his work as a novelist, Ahmet Midhat was also an active translator and one of the works that he adapted into Turkish was John William Draper's famous *History of the Conflict between Religion and Science* (1874), which he rendered as *Conflict between Science and Religion: Islam and Sciences* (*Niza-ı İlm-u-Din: İslam ve Ulum*, 1895–1900). In this work, Ahmet Midhat presents Islam, unlike Christianity, as a religion in complete harmony with modern sciences. He was careful to build an Ottoman modernity committed to science existing in harmony, not conflict, with Islam, thereby situating Ottoman modernity firmly within a Muslim context.

At the core of Ahmet Midhat's depiction of America are the concepts of deficiency and excess (*ifrat ve tefrit*), a term which corresponds in his translation to the French term *excentricités*. In his eyes, America is the land of extremes. He therefore details examples that shed light upon the American code of honour, American family life and the place of religion in the American public sphere. However, he also criticizes these extremities as a consequence of modern civilizational processes, which, he believes run the risk of leading people to the brink of manic disorder. Indeed, according to Ahmet Midhat, progress for the sake of progress (*terakki-perestlik*, literally 'progress-worship'), or 'progress-mania', creates, within American modernity, a sense of widespread dissatisfaction that borders on illness. For students of Islamic ethics, it is only natural that the discourse on extremity ended up with a discussion on perfection (*kemal*). Islamic ethics, having its roots in Aristotle's *Nicomachean Ethics*, instructs that perfection is located in the middle between the two far ends of the scale. In the middle of the extremities he described, Ahmet Midhat believed that Americans went far beyond Europe in their building of cities, in their farming policies, in their inventions and in their industrial prowess. In *American Doctors*, scientific and technological advances are the measure of American civilizational perfection, yet they also signal, when taken to the extreme, an absence of morality, the spill of materialism into the realm of ethics.

Throughout the novel, Ahmet Midhat draws contrasts and comparisons between the Ottoman, American and European worlds. Starting with the abundance and quality of doctors in America, he states, in a rather denigrating tone, that they are not like 'Ottoman doctors, who by prescribing sulphate for malaria raised their fee from being free to one *mecidiye*.' As he emphasizes, American doctors are experts in other sciences as well, such as physics and chemistry. In America, by contrast with the Ottoman Empire, those who simply apply what they have learned are called practitioners; professionals are only those who dedicate themselves to furthering, not merely practising, sciences.

Ahmet Midhat's reasoning for providing these details stems from the fact that science had yet to enjoy enough prestige to be able to guide the development of applied professions in the Ottoman Empire, at a time when the contours of what 'science' truly meant remained unclear. In addition, the sciences and industry were largely regarded as independent fields and their connection was vague. Complaints were aired in various Ottoman newspapers and journals of the time on the lack of consciousness concerning the connection between industry and crafts, on the one hand, and the natural sciences, on the other. In the same vein, Ahmet Midhat complains that the majority of Ottoman artisans lack knowledge of the very scientific foundations of their arts. Ottoman scientists, too, he opines, are often heedless as to how their science relates to various crafts. 'However,' Ahmet Midhat comments optimistically, 'we are new [in the sciences],' believing that in the near future science would assume the authoritative and guiding position it had in the West, thereby allowing for significant improvement in the local industry.

Ahmet Midhat provides an idealized picture of what it means to be a scientist. The American scientists that populate his novel are depicted as serious professionals committed to experimentation and who stay away from leisure activities. For example, Dr Grippling is a rather silent young man who, as Ahmet Midhat underlines, thinks and produces more than he speaks. He has 'scientific and industrial zeal.' His house functions primarily as a laboratory for his experiments to further develop the science of galvanoplasty. Similarly, the middle-aged Dr Bowley is also a specialist, who invents various pharmaceutical materials and, like Dr Grippling, he uses his home as a laboratory. Bowley is so committed to science that he even puts his own life at risk in order to discover the effects of drugs on humans. Only in one instance does Ahmet Midhat subtly ridicule the young Dr Grippling as a man characterized by such a firm 'scientific faith' that he believes that any problem can be solved by the use of electricity and that human civilization can only reach a state of perfection by the widespread use of galvanoplasty. This point recalls Ahmet Midhat's questioning of a civilization that he sees as having turned its back on morality. Otherwise, both Dr Grippling and Dr Bowley exemplify the characteristics of the good Western scientist, as shown by their industriousness, their dedication to experimentation and the breadth of their scientific work.

Because of its partially humorous character, the plot of Ahmet Midhat's novel slightly differed from most of the works of science fiction that were available to him through translations from Western languages. As expressed by Mihran Arabajian, an Ottoman translator who was one of the chief promoters of science fiction in the Empire, the genre was expected to adopt that serious tone found in scientific works properly speaking. In the introduction to his translation of one of Jules Verne's novels intended for Armenian readers, Arabajian writes that science fiction differs from other types of literature as it is 'free from unsuitable love stories, from insolent, terrifying and disgusting pictures of deception, horrible crimes which disturb man's mind and imagination' and that a 'wise father can let his sons and daughters read it without reserve.' Johann Strauss has explained that 'almost identical remarks can be found in the edition of the same work in Arabic script,' demonstrating that science fiction was seen as a morally safe area of literature across communities in the Empire.[8] Whether Ahmet Midhat injected romance and suspense simply to keep his readers or because he saw these elements as essential parts of any novel (including science fiction) remains unclear. It suffices here to observe that science was seen as a safe zone which avoided the moral risks that the Ottomans saw as inherent to European modernity.

Ahmet Midhat's discussion of the different ways in which dead bodies were respectively handled in the Western and Ottoman context gave him another opportunity to implicitly criticize the West. The ritual ways in which these two different civilizations care for the dead suggest that while Westerners invest material objects with a sense of eternal remembrance, Ottomans did not give the same value to material traces as forms of affection and respect for the deceased. In traditional Ottoman practice, all of the deceased's clothes and personal items are disposed of or given away to the needy. Europeans, on the contrary, collect pictures taken at various stages of the deceased's life or even sometimes take post-mortem portraits. According to Islamic rules, the deceased must be buried immediately, wrapped with a seamless piece of cloth and interred without a coffin, while Europeans bury their dead in sometimes highly ornamented graves and erect statues or monuments in their honour. These concrete examples that Ahmet Midhat provides to his audience make clear that he sees his native Ottoman culture as superior to European ways, which he perceives as being marked by materialism rather than by spirituality. In this materialist culture, the galvanization of dead bodies championed by Dr Grippling represents the apex of these rituals of post-mortem remembrance. In his words, 'through the art of galvanoplasty, we will eternally preserve the body of this person, the spirit of whom has become mixed with the world of ether.' Here, Ahmet Midhat juxtaposes Ottoman morality with European materialism and leads his readers to conclude that the idea of galvanoplasty is morally abhorrent.

It is probable the passages in the novel discussed above were interpreted by Ottoman readers as reflections of the binary between their 'spiritual' self and their materialist Western Other, which was so frequently employed by Tanzimat-era modernizers who, although they advocated for the selective adoption of a number of Western technologies and cultural practices, nevertheless sought to uphold their own native culture's 'dignity' by emphasizing what they saw as the moral inferiority of the West. In *American Doctors*, one example of this moral critique of Western civilization – represented here by the modern American way of life – is the repeating theme of human relations, notably friendship, plagued by insincerity. Dr Grippling, for instance, devises a way to begin a close friendship with Dr Bowley, who happens to be his neighbour, by praising him in scientific newspapers as an unequalled scientist, to which Dr Bowley responds in kind, noting the superiority of Dr Grippling's solution of galvanoplasty as an alternative to burial or cremation. Thus, the two neighbours embark upon a friendship based on mutual praise in the public forum of the press rather than through 'normal' good neighbourly relations. In Ahmet Midhat's words, 'not only in America but even in Europe, the neighbourhood has no effect on friendship. Neighbours who use the same stairs for forty years remain strangers just as long.'[9]

Ahmet Midhat describes the relationships between his American characters as governed by hypocrisy. The aforementioned account of Dr Grippling and Dr Bowley praising each other's scientific accomplishments in journals and newspapers for purely selfish puporses is one example. But, in fact, Dr Grippling's ultimate goal is to draw closer to July, Dr Bowley's wife. Upon becoming friends, Dr Bowley introduces his wife to Dr Grippling and Dr Grippling responds by extending his hand to her 'as if he considered her to be his sister' – yet another mark of hypocrisy in the eyes of Ahmet Midhat's readers. Both doctors spend hours listening to the relation of each other's experiments despite the fact that neither is truly interested in the other's research. They merely appear to tolerate each other because of their respective hidden agenda, Grippling's interest in July Bowley and Bowley's professional ambitions. As for July Bowley, she, too, appears thrilled to gain the opportunity to frequent Dr Grippling's house where she can delight in the wonderfully shiny statues that adorn it. Another example of hypocrisy and egoism, she neglects to mourn her husband even for a single day after his alleged death and only organizes a pompous burial service as a way to receive praise and approval from the community rather than out of respect or love for her deceased husband. When Bowley's coffin is brought to the grave, his friends deliver eulogies, as was the custom at the time in the West. Yet Ahmet Midhat suggests that their real aim is not to praise the deceased as much as to impress others with their eloquence. This again serves the author's general purpose of showing that, for all their 'backwardness' in terms of scientific and technological advancements, Ottomans are morally superior to Westerners.

Ahmet Midhat emphasizes, as did many other modernizers of the Tanzimat period that the goal should be to 'appropriate the modern sciences and industries as means of economic and utilitarian pursuits.' As Niyazi Berkes explains, in the view of the modernizers, the material and non-material aspects of European civilization could – and should – be approached differently. The 'corrupt' elements of European civilization, some of which were, in the view of Ottoman modernizers, gradually becoming themselves the object of the Europeans' scrutiny and self-critique, were to be rejected altogether and the spread of European materialism had to be kept in check. In Ahmet Midhat's words,

> if we try to Europeanize only for the sake of becoming European, we shall lose our own character. If we, on the other hand, add European civilization to our own character, we shall not only preserve, perpetuate, and maintain our character but also fortify and refine it.[10]

Many other modernizers employed the same strategy deployed here by Ahmet Midhat, which consisted in imagining an abstract – and supposedly universal – morality that could be divorced from material culture. This enabled them to argue that the 'superior' Ottoman morality should remain as the essence of processes of modernisation in the Empire. This separation between 'morality' and 'materialism', which would later be critiqued as naïve, opened up a space that allowed nineteenth-century modernizers to co-opt many of the technical and administrative innovations developed in the West as a way to create a new Ottoman social order imbued with the sense of its own moral superiority.

Though weaker, another strategy used to conjure up this alternative modernity consisted in underlining variations across nations within Western civilization itself. These variations created a theoretical space for discussing yet another, alternative, version of modernity, constructed as the 'authentic' Ottoman modernity. In that regard, an emphasis on what opposed American and European cultures constituted an important argument for the possibility of an Ottoman modernity. For example, Ahmet Midhat discussed in detail the differences between American and European etiquette and codes of morality. In his description, women and men in America were more conservative and more modest than their European counterparts. In the passages of *American*

Doctors where Dr Grippling and July discuss how to produce a full statue of her likeness, Ahmet Midhat details the challenges involved, explaining that moulding the mask of hands, arms, and even the head was easy to manage, but what of her legs and chest? As the narrator explains, models accustomed to pose for painters and sculptors often feel shy and are unable to accept certain poses. Still, Dr Grippling spends time convincing July to pose for a bust of herself. The exchange allows Ahmet Midhat to contrast the more conservative American morality with that of Europe and he notes that 'if Madame Bowley were a Parisian lady and Dr Grippling a Parisian artist, they would have produced every possible variation of statues: naked, in bust, and in any pose,' something that would have been unthinkable in America, especially among the 'aristocrats of the world of science.' The term 'aristocrats of science,' used here and associated with notions of moral uprightness participates in Ahmet Midhat's effort at creating a more positive public image for the figure of the scientist. In doing so, Ahmet Midhat presents to his readers a variety of moral examples within Western civilization itself, suggesting that, in the West too, morality exists on a spectrum. It is precisely this insistence upon the existence of competing degrees of morality within various understandings of Western modernity, as well as the very idea that morality and modernity could and should be divorced that would, Ahmet Midhat hoped, ultimately empower Ottomans to create their own morally superior version of modernity.

I now want to return to the larger context of the tension – and connectedness – between the notions of *ilim* and *fen*. The conceptual ambiguity in the relationship between the two terms was not simply a linguistic one; rather, it was a direct consequence of a highly complex and lively process of negotiation regarding the kind of knowledge that should be included in the prestigious field of the traditional body of knowledge represented by *ilim*, which elements of Western civilization were 'useful,' and how Western science should be adopted in order to help the advent of an authentic Ottoman modernity. In *American Doctors*, Ahmet Midhat promoted *fen* within a setting not legitimized by the traditionally authoritative knowledge that was increasingly associated with, and limited to Islam. He emphasized hard work, commitment and dedication to the experimental spirit of science. At the same time, he frequently differentiated between the material and non-material aspects of Western modernity that produced science and highlighted moral deficiencies and variations in Western modernity. Thus he implied what he saw as the superiority of Ottoman morals and the very possibility of an Ottoman modernity, even superior to the Western one. All of these suggest that the way to the Ottoman modern had to go through assuming a type of *fen* guided by the firm morals implied by *ilim*.*

Acknowledgement

I wish to thank Monica Ringer, her invaluable comments form the development of this paper, and Maria Taiai for helping me to contrast Ahmet Midhat's novel to the French short story, on which it was based.

Notes

1 The academic debate around the usage of *fen* has recently been revised. Early studies, most prominently by Niyazi Berkes, had thought that Ottoman modernizers coined the term *fen* in order to distinguish the new Western knowledge from the traditional Islamic one. See Niyazi Berkes, *The Development of Secularism in Turkey* (Montreal, 1964), p.100. On the other hand, Şükrü Hanioğlu, İsmail Kara and Alper Yalçınkaya, who introduced the aspect of social groups into the debate, have shown that the process was much more complex. See M. Şükrü Hanioğlu, 'Blueprints for a Future Society: Late Ottoman Materialists on Science, Religion, and Art', in Elizabeth Özdalga (ed.), *Late Ottoman Society: The Intellectual Legacy* (London, 2005), pp.29–116; İsmail Kara, *Din ile Modernleşme Arasında Çağdaş Türk Düşüncesinin Meseleri* (Istanbul, 2005), pp.126–97; M. Alper Yalçınkaya, *Learned Patriots: Debating Science, State, and Society in the Nineteenth-Century Ottoman Empire* (Chicago, 2015).

2 Ahmet Midhat Efendi, *Fenni Bir Roman yahut Amerika Doktorları* (Ankara, 2003), pp.547–646.

3 Ahmet Midhat, in one of his earlier articles, contrasted *fen* and *ilim* as certain versus disputable/uncertain knowledge. His example of *fen* was arithmetic while that of *ilim* was history. See his 'İlim ile Fen', *Dağarcık*, no. 1, 1288 [1872], pp.26–9.

4 On the development of science fiction as a genre in Turkish literature, see Seda Uyanık, *Osmanlı Bilim Kurgusu: Fenni Edebiyat: Osmanlı-Türk Anlatılarında Bilime Yönelişin Mantığı ve Gelecek Tasarıları* (Istanbul, 2013).
5 Ahmet Midhat Efendi, *Fenni Bir Roman*, p.551.
6 Ibid., p.552.
7 Oscar Michon, 'Amour & Galvanoplastie,' *Le Figaro, Supplément littéraire*, 29 August 1885, pp.138–9.
8 Johann Strauss, 'Who Read What in the Ottoman Empire (19th–20th centuries)?', *Arab Middle Eastern Literatures* 6.1 (2003), p.52.
9 Ahmet Midhat Efendi, *Fenni Bir Roman*, p.584.
10 Quoted in Niyazi Berkes, *The Development of Secularism in Turkey* (Montreal, 1964), p.285.

7

Mizancı Murad's *Turfanda mı yoksa Turfa mı?* as historical novel

Benjamin C. Fortna

Mehmed 'Mizancı' Murad's novel *Turfanda mı yoksa Turfa mı?*, usually translated as 'The Good or the Bad Seed?' or, alternatively, 'First or Forbidden Fruit?', is generally not among the first to be considered in discussions of late Ottoman literature. Yet this fascinating novel, first published in 1891, holds an important place in that field and, more importantly for our purposes, offers a useful foil to revisit some of the key dimensions of the late Ottoman world. In particular, *Turfanda mı yoksa Turfa mı?* highlights the wide imperial and, indeed, trans-imperial possibilities of the late Ottoman period, when horizons had been expanded by the telegraph, the railway and the steamship, a mode of transportation that marks its presence from the novel's first pages. Set against this technologically altered landscape, the work insists on a similarly wide historical and geographical scope. Like its author, the novel's protagonist arrives from outside the borders of the Ottoman Empire and maintains a focus on the pan-imperial and pan-Islamic despite the pull of local and domestic concerns. Perhaps more than any other major late Ottoman work, Murad's novel strives to link the personal with the political, in particular the broader fate of the late Ottoman Empire. Identification with a range of overlapping identities – imperial Ottoman, trans-imperial Muslim, ethnically Turkish, globally modern, local, etc. – emerges as a key preoccupation of the work as its central character navigates the complexities of the late Ottoman period. Although it may justifiably be claimed that the work does not always achieve a consistent literary standard, the novel's broad scope and overtly political engagement mark it as an important monument in late Ottoman fiction. Revisiting this singular work offers useful insights and important correctives to our understanding of the late Ottoman world and challenges the assumption that the transition from an Ottoman to a Turkish national polity was either expected or even likely in the final years of the empire.

In some important respects *Turfanda mı yoksa Turfa mı?* conforms to the expectations of literary production from this period. First, it chooses the novel, still a relatively young but quickly dominant genre, as its vehicle for addressing its putatively modernist, i.e., reform-minded and progressive, audience. Secondly, it is shot through with the same sort of moralistic and didactic rationale that animates most of the other novels written in the final decades of the Ottoman Empire. Thirdly, like them, it uses a deliberate strategy of drawing rather extended and often exaggerated contrasts between good and bad characters, as if to leave no room for misapprehension on the part of its readers. To the same end *Turfanda* asks its characters to bear considerable demonstrative weight. The twists and turns of its plot generate more than a few contrived scenes, drawing on some of the tried and true narrative devices of its contemporary works, such as, conversation overheard by unintended audiences, parallel love interests and almost impossibly evil machinations, all the while following a relentlessly positive, pedagogical approach to societal and moral improvement.

And yet, Mizancı Murad's work offers a refreshingly distinctive approach. For one thing, the novel is a 'one-off', the only work of fiction written by its author who is better known as a journalist, historian, reformer, sometime oppositional figure and, latterly, adviser to the Ottoman palace. Mehmed Murad (1854–1917) was the publisher of and frequent contributor to the journal called *Mizan* (The Balance), one that served as a focal point of opposition to the reign of Sultan Abdülhamid II (r. 1876–1909) and is forever linked to his name. This adversarial role led to an extended period of exile, first in Egypt and then in Europe where Murad played an important role in the constellation of opposition figures broadly referred to as the 'Young Turks'. Murad's reconciliation with the sultan and his subsequent return to Istanbul to take up a position in the Ottoman government and adviser to Sultan Abdülhamid II amounted to a substantial blow to the opposition movement in exile. That Murad was trying his hand at writing fiction explains some of the rough edges of the novel – as well as its fresh approach – but also helps us to appreciate its heartfelt engagement and the urgency of its ambitious quest to reform the empire, politically, socially and economically, while doing so in what was ostensibly a less overtly dogmatic way. Literacy rates in this period were rising dramatically but from such a low basis that they struggled to reach double digits by the 1890s. By writing a novel, Mizancı Murad was addressing an elite that was expanding in size but was still far from a mass readership.

The slightly odd title Murad assigned to his work is perhaps also a reason for its relatively obscure place in the late Ottoman literary canon. 'Turfanda', a Persian word meaning first fruit but also someone or something new, a novice, stands in questioning juxtaposition with 'Turfa', an Arabic term conveying the sense of food that is either unclean or not fresh; of a person it can mean disgraced or despised. The subtitle *Millî Roman*, often translated, incorrectly as I shall argue, as 'National Novel', takes us into even more interesting nomenclatural territory. As we shall see, it leaves considerable room for interpretation, but at the very least suggests a new, and unprecedented political orientation. The dichotomous framing of the main title ostensibly offers two clear choices, but also hints at ambiguity: are the protagonist and his at times awkward ideas and plans to be considered as good seed or bad? The question imposed by the title also suggests the rather conflicted view of the hero towards the object of his intense energy, namely, the Ottoman Empire that he has loved and idealized from afar and the messy and at times distinctly unappealing aspects of its daily workings that he encounters, as we shall soon see, from the moment he approaches its capital.

The main vehicle of the novel and principle bearer of its considerable demonstrative, reform-minded weight is its central hero, Mansur Bey. In fact, a later version of the book, published in 1972 in Latin script and 'purified' (in other words, condensed and simplified in places and frequently converted to modern Turkish vocabulary) was entitled simply 'Mansur Bey.' Mansur possesses many qualities but perhaps the most distinctive are his intense, uncompromising nature, his clear agenda to reform the empire along lines inspired by a combination of his Western education and his innate love for the Ottoman Empire, and his visceral reactions to his surroundings, which serve as a kind of moral barometer for his personality. Amidst the many flighty characters that populate the pages of late Ottoman novels, Mansur, with his intense feelings, his 'electric' impulses, his clarity of focus in dedication to his cause, and his unwillingness to accept the *status quo*, stands out as a vivid if often awkward figure.

From the first chapters, readers of *Turfanda* are given to understand that the novel's central figure is complexly configured with respect to his place in the Ottoman world. Scion of an old Turkish family with established roots in Algeria, the novel's protagonist Mansur Bey is presented as both undisputedly an indigenous Ottoman with a long-standing and illustrious pedigree – 'the Ibn Galibs were in origin Arabized Turks and Ottomans'[1] – and conspicuously an outsider. Mansur had left his native Algeria to be educated in France and at the opening of the novel is depicted as entering Ottoman lands for the first time alongside a group of mostly foreign travellers. On arrival in Istanbul and on many subsequent occasions, the earnest Mansur feels obligated to insist on his Ottoman and, indeed, his Turkish lineage, as for example, when his interlocutors attempt to patronize him or indicate that, having become a 'Frank', he must be ignorant of local customs and social expectations. His responses can reach comic proportions, as when he insists on sitting on a cushion on the floor and not on a chair ('I didn't come here as a Frank. You can regard me as the purest Ottoman'[2]), when considerable awkwardness arises over the manner in which he should greet his cousins, or when his Istanbul-based uncle, offended that his nephew stayed in a hotel, insists that Mansur stay in his mansion and thus clashes with Mansur's 'firm resolution' to follow his own path and wants 'to owe nothing to anyone'.[3] From a young age his burning passion had been to make his way to Istanbul, capital of the Ottoman Empire and seat of the Caliphate. He narrowly tolerated being in France for his years of study on the grounds that he needed only to obtain a useful *métier* in order to accomplish his ultimate goal aiding the twin hallmarks of Ottoman service, *din ü devlet* (religion and state). It is interesting to note that unlike many literary characters' fawning embrace of all things Western European, ranging from ethnic nationalism to fashion, Mansur remains devoted to his indigenous Ottoman-ness even while a student in France. In other words, although he spends his formative years in the West, he conspicuously avoids what Mehmed Murad sees as falling into the trap of cultural alienation; despite the clear attraction of some attributes of the West, cultural and, indeed, political westernization is not the inevitable outcome for this novel's protagonist. Mansur is thus constructed both to have the outsider's perspective necessary to form a dispassionate, critical attitude to the Ottoman world and, paradoxically therefore, to be deemed by some as insufficiently native to understand let alone effect change in his original but now adoptive homeland.

Perhaps in order to solve this existential riddle, Murad has Mansur's character insist frequently on his Turkishness. Mansur often has need to identify his family origins as Turkish and to demonstrate through his behaviour and speech that he is a true Ottoman Turk. He also waxes rhapsodic over the life that he finds in Anatolia amid the upstanding Turkish folk. If, however, the novel's modern-day readers began to gather the impression that Mansur was going to emerge from its pages as a bona fide Turkish national(ist) hero, they would be greatly mistaken. While it is true that there are a number of instances of ethno-racial stereotyping in the novel, including some that make for distinctly unpleasant reading, including that of Mansur's aforementioned Jewish hotel agent, his uncle's Armenian lawyer, and the pejorative references to Circassians among the military figures, these are never specifically contrasted with the attributes of other ethnic groups and certainly not with Turks in particular. Conversely, the hero's affection for his Turkish ethnicity should not be mistaken for the kind of chauvinistic ethnic adherence that would prove so disruptively successful after First World War. To state Mansur's approach more positively, his Ottoman identity is inclusive of all of the empire's constituent groups even if prejudices and stereotypes inhabit his portrayal of them.

Here readers can easily be misled by the label *Millî Roman*, usually translated as 'National Novel', found in the book's subtitle. To render *millî* as national reduces its much broader Ottoman meaning to the narrower usage that later became commonplace. In the late Ottoman period, when the subsequent splintering of Ottoman territory into numerous nation-states was far from assured, the term *millî* connoted a sense of shared patrimony and inclusiveness among the different Ottoman Muslim ethnicities, sometimes referred to as 'Ottomanism'. Collapsing this inclusive sense of Ottomanism into a 'Turkish' national identity was ultimately convenient for the Turkish Republic and its founders, but it elided the variety of the Ottoman Muslim experience, that included, among others, ethnic Turks, Arabs, Kurds, Circassians, Albanians, etc. This is precisely one of the places where, in light of the longer sweep of Ottoman and Turkish history, *Turfanda* can be most helpful. As a corrective to the tendency so strongly emphasized by Turkish Republican historiography, Murad's novel ought to be read as a passionate statement *against* the simplistic reductionism that would have the Ottoman-to-Turkish transition so seamlessly and seemingly naturally understood. The Ottoman Empire of Mansur Bey is not one that so easily transforms into a national monoculture as the translated term 'national novel' incorrectly implies. Yes, Mansur does insist on his Turkishness but he does so in spite of his mother's Circassian origins, his years in an Arab land, his French education, and, most tellingly, his undisputedly pan-Islamist inclinations that keep him aware of and interested in the plight of his fellow Muslims outside the Ottoman lands. Yes, Mansur writes rhapsodically about the goodness of the Turkish villagers whom he lives among (and dedicates considerable effort to modernizing) but he is also concerned with the fate of non-Turkish Muslims both inside and outside the empire's former or current borders. The novel's remarkably broad geographical scope, encompassing North Africa, Western and Eastern Europe, Anatolia, Greater Syria, and the Sudan, stands as a pointed contrast to the reduction from imperial to national and in this case from polyglot, multinational Ottoman to Anatolian Turkish. Mansur's unwavering support for and dedication to the Ottoman Empire and the Islamic world beyond its borders clearly supersedes identification with any single ethno-national group.

The novel's opening passage sets the scene and the tone for the rest of the novel. Usefully for our purposes, it establishes several of the dominant themes that mark Mansur Bey and his singular agenda throughout the remainder of the book. Mansur's particular vantage point as an outsider with a strong familial and ideological attachment to the empire reflects the autobiographical stance of the author. Mansur's *vita* has clear parallels with that of Mizancı Murad who was born of Muslim parents outside the Ottoman Empire – Murad was born and raised in Russian-controlled Daghestan, the fictional Mansur in French-ruled Algeria – and received a mix of Islamic and Western-style education before graduating from the Gymnasium in Sevastopol, after which he moved to the Ottoman Empire, the source of his childhood hopes and dreams. The introductory passage quickly reveals Mansur's uncompromising attitude, most obviously in his physio-psychological profile which becomes especially apparent in his visceral reactions to the unexpectedly incorrect or even immoral aspects of life in Istanbul. The opening scene also introduces, if somewhat indirectly, what will be perhaps the strongest and most persistently concrete of his desiderata for improving the empire, namely, the imperative of spreading modern-style education throughout the Ottoman lands and, indeed, throughout the Islamic world. Like many of his real-life contemporaries, Mansur Bey considers modern-style education as a cure-all for the empire's many ills. We will return to the specific attributes of Mansur's educational campaign below but for now it is important to underscore the degree to which educational reform is crucial to Mansur's overall plans to revivify the empire.

Temporally, the opening scene of *Turfanda* is set on a Spring day in the mid-1860s and thus towards the end of the Tanzimat period (1839–1876) that preceded the reign of Abdülhamid II. This staging was politically prudent because the sultan was notoriously sensitive to criticism of his rule; government censors were vigilant in monitoring publications both inside the empire and abroad. Physically, the book opens with its protagonist set in motion. Mansur is first encountered on board a steamship approaching Istanbul from the Black Sea port of Varna. The ship is named 'The Volcano' (Volkan), a hint at the smouldering, latent energy concentrated in Mansur – and perhaps the sense that the empire is dangerously close to explosion. The protagonist is first described as standing on deck, deep in thought, resolute and ready. So deeply absorbed is he in his ruminations that he appears almost oblivious to his surroundings. At this point he is approached by one of his fellow passengers, a Frenchman who mistakenly assumes Mansur to be a compatriot. Expecting Mansur to be an experienced traveller through the Straits of the Bosphorus, the Frenchman asks him about the particular point the ship has reached in its passage down the waterway. Mansur, motionless, fails to take notice of his interrogator. When a repeat of the question proves equally fruitless, the Frenchman moves away with a Gallic shrug. Mansur remains 'nailed to the spot', 'constant' in his fixity. The point is made: unlike the dilettantish tourists around him, Mansur is a man on a mission.

The object of Mansur's intense concentration is, of course, his destination Istanbul, which exerts an attraction over him that pulls him forward 'like an electric current', and his plans to contribute to the Ottoman cause. While the rest of his shipmates chatter away on deck, our protagonist continues to be oblivious to their discussion and is instead frozen in posture, holding onto the railing with a powerful grip. Only once does Mansur move even a little and this in an involuntary way, a sure sign, as succeeding pages will make clear, of Mansur's deep-seated feelings and conscience. The first such barely perceptible movement occurs when members of the nearby crowd, discussing the various sites coming into view along the shore, allude to symbols of the foreign presence in Istanbul. They point to some of the places associated with either foreign embassies, such as their summer residences in Tarabya, or shoreline villas that had been sites for the signing of unfavourable treaties with the Foreign Powers, such as Hünkar İskelesi or Balta Limanı, signed in 1833 and 1838, respectively. Mansur's twitching in response to these locations indicates the presence of a counter current to the narrative otherwise running through the hero's mind. The much more positive train of thought had been steadily building during the course of the novel's opening pages, revolving around affirmative and often romanticized ideas of the Ottoman state and its former days of glory, Mehmed II's 1453 conquest of Istanbul, for example. It is as if the strains of a powerful symphony that has been building in Mansur's imagination are suddenly halted by the discordant reality of more recent years. Another shock, one that appears to shake Mansur even more, occurs when the ship passes before Rumeli Hisarı, the fortress built by Mehmed the Conqueror on the European shore of the Bosphorus. Seeing this more-than-four-hundred-year-old fortress had even caused a rare smile to cross Mansur's lips and encouraged him to resume his daydream about the heroics of the conquest of Constantinople. But then he hears two of the passengers describing the modern building not as he had hoped as an Ottoman edifice but rather as Robert College, the American missionary establishment whose prominent buildings dominated the skyline above. Mansur reacts with utter disbelief.

Further disillusionment awaits Mansur as he enters the city for which he has been longing since childhood. He is approached by a shabby Jewish agent, shilling for a hotel. Mansur disapproves of the fact that the room price is cited in foreign currency instead of the local 'kuruş' but reluctantly consents to be taken to his hotel, which bears another dismayingly foreign name, Amerika Hoteli. To Customs where Mansur is discomfited less by the overly familiar nature of the Customs clerk than by his statement that the books in Mansur's suitcase ought not to contain harmful material. The clerk makes the brusque assumption that an educated man like Mansur wouldn't be carrying such things and so does not even search his books, another source of irritation for the protagonist who would have preferred to see procedure carried out and regulations upheld even if it meant personal delay. Likewise, the muddy streets, the chaos of an accident during which Mansur looks in vain for an authority figure, the heavy presence of foreign-language signs, and the coldness of his hotel make Mansur's first contact with the city heavily dispiriting. From his hotel window Mansur looks out toward the horizons and, spotting Mount Olympus (Keşiş Dağı) near Bursa, the first Ottoman capital, again conjures up rather stereotypical images of the greatness of the Ottoman past, one defined by military conquest and expansion. He contrasts the present weakness of the empire with its former glories yet sees in them the promise for a somewhat inchoate revival as a modern, capable state. Onto this needed transition he imposes his own personal trajectory; the time has come for him to say goodbye to his childhood and to resolve to dedicate himself to 'religion and state'.[4]

Mansur's plans to serve the empire invoke science and modern-style bureaucratic efficiency. (Later on, the novel will reveal a third, demonstrative dimension, when he sets up both a model farm in Anatolia and a new school in Beirut.) On the one hand he intends to devote a considerable part of his time and remarkable energy to practising medicine in Istanbul with his trusted colleague Mehmed Efendi (while working as a consultant in the Medical School and also serving as a doctor for the Refugee Commission, another sign of Mansur's awareness of and attention to the broader problems of the empire at this stage in its history). Although it is never stated explicitly, the implication is that the empire's problems are medicalized and thus require the services of Doctor Mansur. His medical knowledge goes hand-in-hand with his advocating a scientific remedy to the empire's ills, of which education is the prime example. A medical doctor by education, Mansur opens a practice in an old quarter of Istanbul where he sees patients, many of them on a *pro bono* basis. Meanwhile, while not dedicating his time and effort to healing the empire, Mansur enters into the imperial bureaucracy in order to try to make it run efficiently. In this latter venture, specifically in the Foreign Ministry where Mansur had hoped to harness his linguistic abilities and overseas experience to the service of the state, he predictably encounters numerous obstacles that will be familiar from other critiques of Ottoman officialdom. Mansur quickly finds that his fellow bureaucrats are self-serving, overly accepting of the *status quo*, and conspicuously lacking in Mansur's devotion to improving his beloved empire. The scribes sit around eating sherbets and desserts, waste time on seemingly endless breaks, and are far too many for the work at hand. Mansur is particularly irked to learn, for example, that when applying for a position, the would-be scribes emphasize their own particular circumstances and needs instead of how they might best serve the Ottoman state. Mansur, appalled by this wasteful standard operating procedure, declares that he would go mad if forced to remain in such a setting. Not for the last time, Mansur's remarks read less like driving forward the novel's plot than delivering a programmatic political message. Like several of his ficitional peers, Mansur here demonstrates the modernizing spirit on display in the late Ottoman period most conspicuously through a modern approach to time-consciousness and the growing physical presence of regulated time. One could even say that Mizancı Murad inaugurates a tradition that continues into the Republican era where it is most famously evoked in Ahmet Hamdi Tanpınar's 1962 novel *The Time Regulation Institute*.

Mansur's solution for the empire's ills is both simple and profound. On numerous occasions throughout the novel he advocates for reform via the spread of education. This mantra-like solution appears time and again, as Mansur confronts the unpleasant reality of the empire. Indeed, some passages of the novel appear as thinly disguised policy statements and advocacy, as if Mansur were the direct vehicle for Mizancı Murad's advice to the Ottoman government and general public. In this respect the novelist's agenda was hardly out of step with the times. Rather it seems to be channelling the concern for educational reform and implementation that was manifested throughout the upper levels of the Ottoman bureaucracy. Like many advocates of late Ottoman educational change in government and in private circles, Mansur cites the success stories of the Western nations in harnessing education, invoking countries like Prussia and Russia as models to be emulated. As with his forceful critique of the deep problems besetting the Ottoman bureaucracy, Mansur advocates a formula for reform that takes the best of 'how things are done in Europe' and blends it with an appropriate Ottoman sense of morality and exigency. Nearer to home, he refers pointedly to the Western missionary presence in Ottoman lands, which he sees as an important spur to domestic educational expansion. In all of its recommendations, Murad's novel is largely in tune with the gradualist reform agenda of Sultan Abdülhamid II that strove for a modern Ottoman morality that would channel both 'traditional' Ottoman values and militate in favour of a highly utilitarian bent.

Yet Mansur's educational advocacy has more than a purely policy-related dimension. When he receives a large sum of money by way of inheritance, he attempts to open a school in Qayrawan, the long-standing centre of Islamic studies in Tunisia. When he is refused permission due to what he refers to as Franco-Tunisian 'intrigue', he turns his attention to Beirut. This school represents Mansur's effort to blunt the effects of the missionaries' schools in the empire. But even within the Ottoman realms, setbacks confront the protagonist. After the local officials resist his Beirut plans, he turns to Istanbul but has to wait for three months to receive permission. And this while American missionaries are granted the right to open a school in Diyarbekir within a single month! Like real-life Ottoman educationalists, Mansur finds that the deck is stacked against him by the conditions of the day. For him, whatever ills pervade his beloved empire can only be cured by education. 'The only thing missing is education. How powerful will it be when it has spread!'[5]

In an interesting sub-theme to his insistence on the ameliorative power of education, Mansur completely rejects armed resistance as a recourse to overturning imperial encroachment. When, for example, Mansur's contemporaries advocate supporting armed resistance to the French colonialists in North Africa, Mansur strenuously rejects such militancy in favour of a peaceful focus on education and gradual improvement. It is not that Mansur is 'soft' on the question of standing up to the injustice of the Great Powers – on one occasion he writes strident columns in three Istanbul newspapers in protest at Russian and Austro-Hungarian machinations in the Balkans, which provoke an international incident – but Mansur is careful to choose a form of protest that does not risk further loss of Muslim life. In this sense it could be said that Mansur's repsonse to the long-standing issue of territorial loss displays the sensibilites of the 'modern' Ottoman citizen who realizes that a bellicose response would merely exacerbate the problem. In a long debate with his uncle Salih Efendi, Mansur urges Salih to think of the people whose lives would be ruined in the event of an armed conflict against the French in Algeria. Eventually Mansur is able to convince his uncle of the wisdom of his quietist approach but at the time Mansur's idea of opening a school in Qayrawan, which he labels a *millî mektep*, prompts the nefarious Raşid to claim that Mansur is no longer a Muslim but has become French or even a Freemason.[6] Mansur's use of *millî* indicates that his programme is in fact a Muslim one that is designed to serve the larger Muslim community (*millet*) and not one of its ethno-national sub-groups.

Another noteworthy dimension of the approach to education in the context of the fate of the empire is Mansur's stance on local and, indeed, national particularism. Mansur argues that the rush to create independent countries is flawed: 'I don't know what "Serbia" means', he claims.[7] He says that if you go to ask the people in the villages, their lives have changed for the worse since independence, with higher taxes, more imposed duties, etc. For Mansur, imperial solidarity trumps nationalist separatism. Like Sultan Abdülhamid II, Mansur advocates for a broader, Ottoman and even pan-Islamic approach to reform and progress, as opposed to the particular, nationalism-/patriotism-driven approach. That is why Mansur left Algeria to come to Istanbul in the first place, to focus his efforts on the imperial and not the local level. When a relative from Algeria suggests that Mansur was interested in personal gain and bribery, Mansur is indignant. His telltale involuntary reaction – the 'electric current' – manifests itself again. 'For the others maybe! But for the Mansurs never!'[8]

Importantly Mansur is engaged in a broader educational campaign than even that taking place across the Ottoman lands. This is evidenced by his work and correspondence with Muslims in the Russian Empire (Kashgar and the Caucasus) and India, inviting them to come to Istanbul for educational purposes. For Mansur, 'the force that will effect the unity of Islam is not the sword but education.'[9] Mansur is remarkably bullish on the empire's future once modern education is harnessed to his pan-Islamic agenda. Within fifty years, he insists, the Muslims will be the envy of the world and 'the future is ours.' 'The only thing missing is education.'[10] Mansur even says that sometimes he thinks that the strong presence of missionary schools in the empire's lands – to which he had reacted with shock in the novel's opening scene – is now something that even makes him happy because they serve as a reminder of the importance of learning and a spur to the empire's efforts. Once again, it is clear that Mansur's plans for spreading education target not only the subjects of the Ottoman Empire but also contain provision for attracting Muslims from across the world.

Vast as his hero's agenda is, Mizancı Murad must somehow make it play out within the confines of the unfamiliar genre of the novel. The reader senses his struggling to balance the personal and the political. So great is Mansur's dedication to his mission that he continually forswears marriage throughout most of the novel. This disavowal produces disappointment in the marriage-eligible women who occupy important positions in the novel, namely, his cousins Sabiha, Fatma and Zehra. The romantic aspects of the novel are further complicated by the fact that Zehra and Mansur had a difficult and often antagonistic relationship as children in their native Algeria. But Zehra, who moved to Istanbul while Mansur was studying in France, and Mansur are clearly destined for each other. Both are depicted as headstrong and independent but also supremely dedicated to their religion and empire. Both are highly disapproving of signs of moral laxity around them, such as when on separate occasions both hero and heroine object strenuously to such 'scandalous' behaviour as public flirtation between the sexes. And both exhibit the same kind of high-minded, idealistic pride that almost keeps them apart. Thanks to a plot twist late in the novel that sees Mansur gallantly dash off in the middle of a thunder-and-lightning storm in an attempt to prevent Zehra from catching a cold, only to be knocked unconscious by a falling branch, Zehra and Mansur are brought together to profess their undying love. In Mansur's case, his profession of love for Zehra, which he had previously confided to his diary, is rather mixed up with his allegiance to religion and state,[11] demonstrating the difficulties inherent in being both an uncompromising, policy-driven hero and a love object. Fortunately for Mansur, Zehra is equally willing to mix personal affairs with imperial exigencies; when Mansur regains consciousness, Zehra is there by his side, telling him 'You will live, Mansur. You will live for me, for the country and for your ideas.'[12] After many delays – and no little sloganeering – the plot has brought the happy, high-minded, patriotic, model Ottoman couple together at last. While not exactly equals, Zehra and Mansur are perhaps equally dedicated to the empire and its progress.

Throughout the novel a useful foil to Mansur's nearly all-conquering character is provided in the form of Raşid, the brother of Mansur's uncle Salih's second wife. When he first appears in the novel, his colours are flagged for the reader through what Mansur considers to be outrageously immoral behaviour when he tries to pass notes to women in other carriages. He later takes a stance in favour of what Mansur considers to be reckless support for Algerian rebels against the French. But Raşid's essentially evil character is fully revealed when he launches a plot to steal Salih's inheritance. As if to be sure of leaving no doubt as to his evil character, Raşid's methods encompass not only threats and devious machinations but also a dagger attack, poisoning and arson. Luckily for the novel's righteous characters, Mansur is alive to Raşid's designs and plays the twin role of zealous defender and detective, especially in investigating the poisoning and in confronting the villainous Raşid as he burns Salih's historic mansion to the ground. Evil is perpetrated, the novel seems to be saying, but justice will prevail through men such as Mansur who manage to bend their individual desiderata to the service of the greater good. In them the individualism of the West is sublimated to the ideal of the modern Ottomans and their empire.

The novel's final, epistolary section again emphasizes the wide-ranging, internationalist dimension of Mansur's cause. Having married Zehra, the protagonist volunteers to fight in the Russo-Turkish war of 1877–8 (thus bringing the novel somewhat uncomfortably into the regnal period of Sultan Abdülhamid II). Mansur being Mansur, he cannot refrain from levelling the same kind of impolitic criticisms at his military superiors in the field that he did at the civilian grandees when serving in the Foreign Ministry. Now, amidst the carnage of that brutal war, his interventions attract a less lenient reaction and Mansur is soon punished by being transferred away from the Balkan front to Syria and even accused of serving as a Russian spy! While others plead his case back in Istanbul he falls ill in Damascus and, alas, the physician, unable to heal himself, moves to the Sudanese desert for his health. His final letter to Zehra makes arrangements for her and their infant son in the case of his death but reserves the last lines to support the life and reign of the sultan, who is in Mansur's view the sole force capable of revivifying the Ottoman state and the Caliphate. Through Mansur's final plea, Mizancı Murad emphasizes the gradualist approach of Sultan Abülhamid II and encourages his readers to support the palace in troubled times.

Turfanda mı yoksa Turfa mı? does not conclude in a happy-ever-after kind of way. Mansur's premature death casts a tragic pall against which the final paragraphs attempt, somewhat lamely, to offer a remedy in the form of patriotic appeal to the Ottoman imperial cause. In the end Mizancı Murad settles the tussle between personal and political – and with the internal contradictions he loaded onto Mansur's character – by emphasizing the political message over the personal one. It is as if, having wrestled with the constraints of this deeply political novel for over four hundred pages, the author decides that even the stoutest of fictional protagonists was in the end simply too virtuous, too high-minded to survive the ignominious tests to which he was put by the late Ottoman predicament. Mansur's fierce resolve and his electric current fade away in distant Sudan, far from his adopted and beloved empire and its capital. And, oh yes, far from his wife and child, too.

Notes

1 Mehmed Mizancı Murad. *Turfanda mı yoksa Turfa mı?*, p.30/31. Page numbers refer first to the Ottoman original (Istanbul, 1308AH) and secondly to the Latinized/'purified' version of Osman Sevim (Istanbul, 2012).
2 Ibid., p.74/62.
3 Ibid., pp.80–1/67.
4 Ibid., p.29/28.
5 Ibid., p.314/164.
6 Ibid., pp.202/155–6.
7 Ibid., p.200/154.
8 Ibid., p.209/160.
9 Ibid., p.212/163.
10 Ibid., p.214/164.
11 Ibid., pp.231/176–7.
12 Ibid., p.386/289.

8

Inconvertible romance: Piety, community and the politically disruptive force of love in *Akabi Hikayesi*

Neveser Köker

Muslim, Christian, Israelite, you are all subjects of the same emperor, sons of the same father.

Rıza Pasha, Address to the leaders of Greek, Armenian, and Jewish communities of Western Anatolia, 1839[1]

All individuals who are under the subjection of the Ottoman State are called 'Ottoman' regardless of their religion or sect without exception, and the status of Ottoman is created and granted according to conditions decreed by laws.

Kanun-u Esasi, 1876[2]

In the first three quarters of the nineteenth century, there was a gradual shift in how the Ottoman Empire codified its subjects' relationship to the state. In turn, a growing number of these subjects formulated the political stakes of their identities and affective attachments as they started making more frequent claims to political power and agency. The first epigraph, drawn from an Ottoman bureaucrat's speech from the beginning of the Tanzimat Era, references equality of subjects using a distinctly familial and paternalistic language. In doing so, it showcases the space of the family, and specifically the paternal relations it captures, as a proxy for politics. The second epigraph, drawn from the first and only constitution of the empire, highlights the equality of subjects before the law. The gradual transition from monarcho-imperial structures and institutions to national-imperial ones affected the conditions of articulation for political belonging during the Tanzimat Era. Hence, the *Kanun-u Esasi* – a document that is often read as the culmination of Tanzimat bureaucrats' and intellectuals' efforts to rearticulate the foundational terms of Ottoman subjecthood – does not replicate Rıza Pasha's paternalist language. However, this does not mean that the Tanzimat Era erased the overlap between familial and political articulations of community. On the contrary, the gradual transformation of 'fraternal subjects' into 'subjects equal before the law' seems to have solidified and stratified the identity-based distinctions between 'self' and 'other', expanding the overlap between the linguistic and discursive fields of political, familial and religious belonging.

Through a historically contextualized reading of Hovsep Vartan Pasha's *Akabi Hikayesi* [Akabi's Story] (1851),[3] a short novel written by an Ottoman Armenian bureaucrat, this chapter examines the paradoxical shift in the articulation of political belonging. Throughout the chapter, I build a two-fold argument: first, I suggest that the shifting languages of political belonging in the Tanzimat Era are best understood through the lens of modalities. In linguistics and semiotics, modality designates the ethical and epistemic possibilities of a given utterance. I use the term to refer to the grammatical and lexical frameworks which were used to define who can, who may, and who must (and consequently, who cannot, may not, and must not) be 'Ottoman'. Modalities of political belonging are the fields in which geographic, religious, ethnic and cultural differences are transformed into political ones. They also contain potential ways of being or becoming members of the political community even when they clearly structure one type of affective attachment over another.[4]

Second, I argue that the term 'conversion' best captures the modality of political belonging in the Tanzimat Era. Conversion, experienced from the perspective of the converter (and not the convert), imagines the self as politically and morally superior and seeks to recast the other in that image. It also has a deep-seated mistrust of the other's capacity to transform correctly. *Akabi Hikayesi* captures the affective, socio-cultural and political challenges of the era's simultaneous cultivation of politico-moral hierarchy and mistrust of individual transformation. Specifically, the tragedy of the novel's otherwise mundane plot of romance between an Armenian Apostolic young woman and an Armenian Catholic young man seems predicated on the inconvertibility of their religious identities and of their romantic attachment. As Vartan Pasha depicts the life-worlds[5] of two distinct ethno-religious communities, he sets up a story that suggests that romantic love encourages a kind of individuality that is often in opposition to a strong sense of community, whether it be religious or political. As such, romantic love is always potentially threatening to a communal existence. This threatening potential of romantic love contrasts with the imperatives of conversion as a modality of belonging, which require a zealous belief in the righteousness of one's own community and an ongoing desire to bring outsiders into that community.

In what follows, I first give a brief overview of the theoretical and historical framework of the paper. I then discuss why the shifting dynamics of political belonging in the Tanzimat Era are best understood through a perhaps counterintuitive turn to a fictional genre, the novel. I highlight the ways in which political community building and reading practices came to be intertwined during the Tanzimat Era. It is also in this section that I offer a gloss of Chateaubriand's *Atala*,[6] one of the most frequently read texts in the Ottoman Empire in the second half of the nineteenth century. This text has a central place in *Akabi Hikayesi*, and I argue that it is a precursor to the kinds of familial, religious, and romantic impasses that overlap in Vartan Pasha's novel. Finally, I turn to the text of *Akabi Hikayesi* itself and discuss the ways in which it narrates the threateningly individualistic potential of romantic love. I conclude with a few remarks on the limits on conversion as a modality of political belonging.

Theoretical framework and brief history of conversion in the Tanzimat Era

Throughout this chapter, I use 'conversion as a modality of political belonging' to describe what I see as the primary logic of intelligibility of political belonging in the Ottoman Empire between 1839 and 1876. Experienced and understood through the lens of the converter (and not the potential convert), this modality of political belonging is premised on an ardent belief that membership in a political community, whether it be a nation, an empire or both, is the ultimate righteous state of communal existence. While this belief suggests that there ought to be a clear boundary between those who are included in the political community and those who are excluded from it, it paradoxically casts the relationship between 'self' and 'other' as continuous and referential to a universal ideal of human understanding. Conversion as a modality of political belonging places self and other on a spectrum of difference. It also allows the community to envision a moment of transformation that will enable them to address one another, overcoming the trappings of linguistic and cultural difference. Anchored in the belief that the location of the self is the universal ideal, the 'spectrum' of conversion is a highly hierarchical one in which only the location of the self could be just and righteous.

While conversions from Judaism or Christianity to Islam had always been commonplace, and in some cases entirely necessary for physical, social or political survival in the Ottoman Empire's seven-centuries-long existence, the reverse was forbidden by law, and by imperial edicts.[7] More critically, with the start of Tanzimat reforms in 1839, the Ottoman centre had become invested in clearly identifying and regulating the different religious communities within the empire. On the one hand, these reforms aimed at guaranteeing the safety, integrity and property of all subjects of the empire, regardless of their religion. On the other hand, such reforms required a tightly organized and centralized state apparatus that could enforce these guarantees. These reforms thus led to an increase in the Ottoman state's efforts to identify and to stabilize the various ethno-confessional communities to which its subjects belonged. In a political order that was dependent upon the self-administration of religious 'nations' (*millet*), such efforts meant that the rights of an Ottoman subject depended on the religious community to which they belonged more than ever.[8]

It was during these same decades that led up to the adoption of the Ottoman constitution that new, ostensibly 'Western' genres of texts, ranging from charters limiting the absolute authority of the Sultan to novels, were repeatedly refashioned for Ottoman sensibilities. While such generic adaptation was not new,[9] the speed with which such adaptations flourished was unparalleled.[10] This suggests that in this period, 'being an Ottoman' was less a juridical-political status than a perpetually shifting state of becoming that was guided by a quest for political belonging.[11] In the next section, I turn to the literary-historical aspects of this moment to further illustrate the stakes of conversion as modality of political belonging.

Reading and conversion: constitutions, novels and Chateaubriand's *Atala*

There are two genres of texts that are historically and conceptually linked to the emergence of the 'imagined political community' that is the nation:[12] constitutions and novels.[13] While the former can be a productive site for understanding the institutional arrangements that regulate the relationship between state and society[14] as well as the juridical principles that animate the interaction between religion and politics, the latter is a richer site for understanding the affective dimensions of religious and political belonging.[15] Unlike the constitution, the novel is formally, functionally and substantively paradoxical. On the one hand, reading a novel is the quintessential form of individualistic and solitary consumption that is closely linked to capitalist modes of production. On the other hand, the stories that are told in and through each novel can offer 'the individual a more conscious and selective pattern of social life to replace the more diffuse, and as it were involuntary, social cohesions.'[16] Functionally and formally, the novel encourages a kind of introspective individuality that is compatible with mass consumption. Substantively, however, it offers an imaginative landscape that is simultaneously individual and communal.

In the three and a half decades that led to the adoption of the first Ottoman constitution, the Ottoman reading public grew substantially. Translated novels (often, but not exclusively, translated from French into the various languages of the empire) quickly gained popularity among Ottoman readers from all ethnic and religious communities.[17] Given the low rates of industrialization, the limited scope of what can be called an Ottoman bourgeoisie, and the state-centric spread of literacy, it is difficult to suggest that the novel's popularity in the Ottoman Empire was one of the consequences of the empire's integration into global markets. For Jale Parla, the popularity of the genre was made possible by the paternalist reformism of Tanzimat reformers. This popularity was reflective of a conservative Islamic epistemology that sought to adapt to a world that came to be dominated by European ways of living and being without losing too much of its religious and cultural 'essence'.[18] The appeal of this new literary genre seems to transgress not just geographic borders but ethno-confessional ones as well. In fact, the earliest local example of the genre, *Akabi Hikayesi*, was written in vernacular Turkish in Armenian script by an Ottoman Armenian bureaucrat.[19]

Given the trans-ethnic and trans-religious popularity of the genre in the Ottoman Empire, it is difficult to think of the genre's adoption as an illustration of the eclectic yet Islamic modernization efforts of Ottoman Muslim elites. Here, I want to consider an alternative explanation for the growing popularity of the genre during the Tanzimat Era by turning to the staging of the first encounter between Akabi and Hagop, the two protagonists of *Akabi Hikayesi*. The story is set in Istanbul in 1846–7. Akabi, a young woman from an Armenian Apostolic family, and Hagop, a young man from an Armenian Catholic family, fall in love the first time they see each other. When Akabi gets up to greet Hagop, Chateaubriand's *Atala* falls out of her fur coat. Hagop asks:

> 'Efendim,[20] could you tell me what is this book you have with you?'
> 'Atala.'
> 'It is a book that I have enjoyed very much, and such a sad story.'
> 'Indeed, I have yet to finish it, but I am very happy that I have started it.'
> 'Surely, you must have felt compassion for Chactas' state in your heart?'
> Akabi's cheeks blushed when she heard this question, and she could only muster 'yes, it is beautifully written.' They understood their mutual fluency in French[21] and started a long conversation on French literature.[22]

Akabi and Hagop's romance starts with a discussion of the French romantic author Chateaubriand's *Atala*. *Atala* is a novella that tells the tragic love story of Chactas and Atala, two Native Americans who meet by chance. Chactas becomes the prisoner of a rival tribe. He is saved by Atala, a Native American young woman whose 'smile was heavenly.'[23] Although Chactas is under duress as a prisoner of war, he remarks on her beauty, and Atala responds by asking 'Are you Christian?'[24] Chactas is taken aback, but his response is striking. 'I told her that I never betrayed the Spirits of my home.'[25] Chactas initially thinks of conversion to Christianity as a betrayal of the essence of his community.

As they try to run away from Chactas' tormentors, they get caught in a terrible thunderstorm in the middle of the woods. They are saved by a missionary priest who offers to marry them by converting Chactas into Christianity. However, Atala's mother had told Atala that she had promised God that her daughter would remain a virgin if she were born healthy. Atala decides to poison herself to avoid betraying her mother and her religion, even though she is in love with Chactas. Right before she dies, she learns that such promises are not absolute in Christianity. Chactas, 'maddened by heartache' promises Atala to 'one day adopt the Christian faith.'²⁶ The story is told in the form of a dialogue between René 'the European'²⁷ who is in an 'unhappy exile, without even the slightest reminder of the bones of his fathers,'²⁸ and Chactas, 'son of Outalissi the Natchez,'²⁹ whom the Great Spirit 'wanted to civilize (I don't know for what purpose).'³⁰

In this novella, the reader finds recurring motifs of sadness and suffering. The causes of such sadness and suffering alternate between the imperfect conversion of Atala, the rootlessness of René, and the tragic (self-)betrayal of Chactas, who 'like all men, had bought virtue through misfortune.'³¹ Chateaubriand's reflection on the human condition, its fragility and tragedy regularly refers the reader back to the compassion of (Catholic) Christianity. The moral of the story is to emphasize not only human beings' universal and primordial need for religious belief and religious community, but the superiority of its Catholic–Christian variant in assuaging the suffering of mankind.

As a genre, the novel creates a space in which authors can narrate stories of individual suffering while reproducing a strong sense of religio-political community. Even in translation, or perhaps because the genre was in translation, it gave Ottoman readers (and later authors) the power to imagine a lifeworld that anchored them as individual members of a multilingual and multiethnic empire without undermining their communitarian attachments. The popularity of the genre was connected to its ability to centre around a communal self. In the next section, I offer a close reading of *Akabi Hikayesi* to examine the ways in which Vartan Pasha's version of the 'communal self' interweaves religious, familial and political authority.

Inconvertible romance: Piety, community and the disruptive force of love and desire

Akabi Hikayesi, like Atala, reimagines the dangers of straying from one's own family, religious community, and socioeconomic class³² through the plot of tragic love. In the ideological order of the Tanzimat Era, it was not possible to imagine loving outside one's religious community *and* without obedience to one's own family. To be more precise, in the late Ottoman context, the household became a locus of religious, familial and civil-political authority. While the imperial household had been such a locus since the early eighteenth century, non-dynastic households were not considered to be in the same political-cultural realm as the imperial palace. As the Ottoman state became increasingly preoccupied with creating an overarching category of 'Ottomanness' for its subjects, the location of religious, civil and political authority became more dissipated. The impossibility of imagining cross-confessional, cross-ethnic or cross-religious love emanated from this dissipation.

The tragic impossibility of cross-confessional, cross-ethnic, cross-religious romance starts with the transformation of the non-dynastic Ottoman household. Throughout the novel, priests from the Armenian Apostolic and Armenian Catholic churches move in and out of the households of the two patriarchs, Bagdasar and Viçen. For instance, when the Catholic priest, M. Fasidyan, questions Viçen's hasty decision to disown his son Hagop for loving 'an Armenian girl', their exchange revolves around Hagop's obedience to his father. Viçen repeatedly claims that his son is no longer under his sovereignty (tr. *hükmümden çıkmış*) and M. Fasidyan pressures him to forgive this one transgression. 'We must call on him and advise him with kindness.'[33] While the priest insists on caution, kindness and ruse, the father insists on punishment because he sees his son's transgression as an act of absolute disobedience. If one were to change the names in the dialogue and block out the narrative that precedes it, this exchange can easily be read as a reflection on the two common ways of reinforcing political authority (cunning and coercion). Interestingly, however, the dialogue takes place in a 'private' living room, between an urban merchant and his priest, and it is about how to stop his son from marrying outside his faith and community.

Cross-confessional romance also highlights individual political predispositions that are not compatible with the hierarchical communal selves that are being imagined in the Tanzimat Era. As Akabi and Hagop's relationship develops, they realize that they both share a disdain of aristocracy and value education. Their love is as much an intellectual and political attraction as it is a romantic one.[34] Right before Hagop's family discovers their son's relationship with Akabi, Akabi herself declares that 'only a tyrant would separate two people who love each other; sadly tyranny is never missing from the face of this earth.'[35] Hagop's response once again points to a tragedy: 'Akabi, no man or human power can separate us from now on since the emotions of our souls that have brought together our hearts were given to us by the rightful one; they are not *matters of human judgment or human will.*'³⁶ The way romantic love is formulated by the two lovers directly confronts and negates parental as well as ecclesiastic authority. It establishes a direct connection between individual souls and God. Romantic love transforms piety from a communal experience into a binary one, defying the communal logic of conversion.

When families and family priests learn about Akabi and Hagop's relationship, they channel all their will to put an end to it. They confiscate letters Akabi sends Hagop while Hagop worries that Akabi might have fallen out of love with him. It is at this juncture that the intergenerational aspects of the story are introduced, adding first a layer of intrigue, then a layer of tragedy to the plot. The older, sickly neighbour who had become a confidante and a friend to Akabi reveals to her that she is her mother, Anna. Anna had fallen in love with Bogos, a Catholic Armenian, who was a friend of her father's despite the differences in their age and sect. Bogos proposes to elope by sending a letter to Anna with a mutual friend. They meet in the middle of the night and head over to Monsieur de Longville's house. Monsieur de Longville offers them housing and protection. Shortly thereafter, the Armenian patriarch orders the expulsion of all Catholic Armenians from Istanbul. Accused of being a French spy, Bogos flees to London two months before Akabi is born. Akabi's uncle, Anna's brother Bagdasar, the man who has raised Akabi, is complicit in Bogos' exile and Anna's ensuing misery and exclusion from the Apostolic community.³⁷

Bagdasar's character and specifically his cruelty towards Anna and Akabi capture both the disruptive potential of romantic love and its tragic impossibility. Defying one's religious community in the name of romantic love does not simply break the bonds of one religious community for another's. It breaks all communal bonds, including familial ones between brother and sister, and father and daughter. As such, it strips away the bonds that intimately and socially connect individuals to one another. When Akabi defies Bagdasar's orders to write Hagop a letter denying her love for him, Bagdasar declares forcefully: 'Then, I will drag your dead mother's body out of her grave and throw it to the dogs!'³⁸ Reminiscent of Creon in Antigone, Bagdasar is willing to take away his own sister's burial rites to protect the boundaries of his religious community and to show Akabi that she needs to obey authority.

Unlike Antigone, Akabi deceives Bagdasar into thinking she has obeyed him, but she pays the price of such deception with her own life. One of her final sentences captures the inconvertibility of romantic love: 'Ah Hagop Agha, would our relatives ever want the happiness of anyone who does not share their opinions and interpretations?' Hagop dies twenty-one days after Akabi, and he dies of sorrow. What creates and preserves communities is a shared set of conventions and rules of interpretation. Romantic love causes individuals to become introspective, to value their own emotions over such rules and conventions. As such, it categorically cannot be channelled into the logic of conversion, lovers cannot belong anywhere and those who cannot belong cannot survive.

Although its precursor *Atala* reads like a romanticized defence of Catholic Christianity as a religio-political project, *Akabi Hikayesi*'s lessons about the Armenian Apostolic and the Armenian Catholic visions of religio-political life remains much more ambivalent. This ambivalence relates to the limits of thinking about political belonging through the lens of conversion, namely the way it focuses on an imagined self when the very construction of that self remains intimately connected to an imagined other.

Conclusion: Imperial survival and the limits of conversion as modality of political belonging

Akabi Hikayesi was written and circulated at a time when the Ottoman state is trying to learn how to survive in a changing global order. This is also a time in which the structures of monarchical–imperial rule and the ideologies that hold them in place no longer work as well as they used to. Hence, Ottoman elites and the growing reading public are in search of a new identity, one that can accommodate the dissipation of imperial power. It is here that the logic of conversion becomes apparent. As a modality of political belonging, conversion emphasizes a communal sense of self, which it regards as the most exalted form of existence.

Along with this exaltation of communitarian selves, there is also scepticism of the corrupting effects of the communal others that remain outside the scope of conversion. In *Akabi Hikayesi*, these are presented as emerging Ottoman urban consumption and leisure habits that directly mirror those of Europeans. Vartan Pasha's depictions of affluent Armenian homes include thinly veiled critiques of the new habit of decorating these domestic spaces with paintings of scenes from the European artistic and philosophic canon. For him, this habit arose out of a need to demonstrate a socio-cultural superiority that is entirely unearned. The books are never read, the paintings are never examined closely. They act as foreign decorative objects that serve to demonstrate a family's wealth and status through a superficial affinity with European culture.

Somewhat ironically expressed within the confines of a transnational genre that originally emerged in Britain and France,[39] these critiques suggest that whatever its ethno-religious shades may be, the new Ottoman subjectivity that was emerging during Tanzimat also entailed reimagining the 'West' as simultaneously and paradoxically the location of 'advanced science and knowledge'[40] and 'frivolous consumption.' Behind this paradox is an acute awareness of changing global power dynamics. Conversion as a modality of political belonging does not capture the cultural dimensions of these dynamics. As the Ottoman Empire increasingly became embroiled in battles of survival, Ottomans of various ethno-religious backgrounds started contesting the value of European cultural imports precisely because it was both materially impossible and ethically undesirable for new Ottoman subjects to wholeheartedly adopt the habits of frivolous consumption and leisure embodied by European cultures.

Archival Collections Consulted

Archives Nationales, Site Pierrefitte-Sur-Seine, France
    Fonds/Cotes: F/19/6246; F/19/6240A

Archives d'Œuvres Pontificales Missionaires, Lyon, France
    Fonds Lyon : Dossiers E/15.i ; E/20.p
    Fonds Paris : Cote E/1 ; E/2 ; E/15.2 ; E/20.2 ; E/23

Notes

1 'Musulmans, chrétiens, israélites, vous êtes tous les sujets d'un même empereur, les enfants d'un même père.' See Edouard Engelhardt, *La Turquie et Le Tanzimat* (Paris: A. Cotillon et Cie, 1882), vol.1, p.69. All translations from French are mine unless otherwise noted.

2 'Devlet-i Osmaniye tabîyetinde bulunan efradın cümlesine herhangi din ve mezhepten olur ise bilâ istisna Osmanlı tabir olunur ve Osmanlı sıfatı kanunen muayyen olan ahvale göre istihsal ve izae edilir.' 1876 Kanun-i Esasisi: http://www.anayasa.gen.tr/1876ke.htm. All translations from Turkish are mine unless otherwise noted.

3 Vartan Pasha, *Akabi Hikâyesi: Ilk Türkçe Roman* (Istanbul: Eren Yayincilik, 1991).

4 Some of the sources I draw on for this definition are Quentin Skinner, 'On Performing and Explaining Linguistic Actions,' *The Philosophical Quarterly* XXI.82 (1971), pp.1–21; Quentin Skinner, *Visions of Politics: Volume 1: Regarding Method* (Cambridge, 2002); Roland Barthes, *Image-Music-Text* (New York, 1977); Eve Sweetser, *From Etymology to Pragmatics: Metaphorical and Cultural Aspects of Semantic Structure* (Cambridge, 1990); F.R. Palmer, *Mood and modality* (Cambridge, 2001); Rod Girle, *Possible Worlds* (Chesham: Acumen, 2003); Bob Hale and Avi Hoffman, *Modality: Metaphysics, Logic, and Epistemology* (Oxford, 2010); Sino Knuuttila, *Modern Modalities: Studies of the History of Modal Theories from Medieval Nominalism to Logical Positivism* (Dordrecht, 1988); Elizabeth Leiss and Werner Abraham, *Modes of Modality: Modality, Typology, and Universal Grammar* (Amsterdam, 2014).

5 Here, I am drawing on the concept of *Lebenswelt* that Habermas outlines in Jürgen Habermas, *The Theory of Communicative Action*, Vol 2, *Lifeworld and System: A Critique of Functionalist Reason*, (Boston, 1987).

6 François-René Chateaubriand, *Atala* (Paris, 18??). The edition I am working with appears to be the third edition but there is no year specified anywhere in the book. The preface dates the first edition as 1800. See ibid., p.3 and p.9. All references are to this edition, and all translations from French are mine.

7 For detailed histories of conversion practices in the Ottoman Empire, see Marc Baer, *Honored by the Glory of Islam: Conversion and Conquest in Ottoman Europe* (Oxford University Press, USA, 2011) and *The Dönme: Jewish Converts, Muslim Revolutionaries, and Secular Turks* (Palo Alto, 2010); Selim Deringil, *Conversion and Apostasy in the Late Ottoman Empire* (Cambridge, 2012). I will discuss conversions to Islam later in this section.

8 See Ussama Makdisi, *The Culture of Sectarianism: Community, History, and Violence in Nineteenth-Century Ottoman Lebanon* (Berkeley, CA, 2000). Also see James C. Scott, *Seeing like a State: How Certain Schemes to Improve the Human Condition Have Failed* (New Haven, CT, 1999).

9 Hatice Aynur et. al., *Metnin Halleri: Osmanlı'da telif, tercüme, ve şerh* (Istanbul, 2014).

10 Johann Strauss, 'Who Read What in the Ottoman Empire (19th–20th centuries)?' *Middle Eastern Literatures* 6.1 (2003), pp.39–76.

11 I am borrowing Hans-Lukas Kieser's terminology. See Hans-Lukas Kieser, *A Quest for Belonging: Anatolia Beyond Empire and Nation (19th–21st Centuries)* (Istanbul, 2007).
12 Here, I am drawing on Benedict Anderson's definition of 'nation' as a political community that is imagined as inherently 'limited and sovereign'. See Benedict Anderson, *Imagined Communities* (London, 2006), p.6.
13 Nancy Armstrong, *How Novels Think* (New York, 2006); Dorothy J. Hale (ed.), *The Novel: An Anthology of Criticism and Theory 1900–2000* (Malden, MA, 2006); Franco Moretti, *The Novel. Vol. 1: History, Geography, and Culture* (Princeton, NJ, 2006); Mary Helen McMurran, *The Spread of Novels: Translation and Prose Fiction in the Eighteenth Century* (Princeton, NJ, 2009).
14 See for example Pascal Firges (ed.), *Well-Connected Domains: Towards an Entangled Ottoman History* (Leiden, 2014) and Kelly Grotke and Marcus Prutsce (eds), *Constitutionalism, Legitimacy, and Power: Nineteenth Century Experiences* (Oxford, 2014).
15 It is important to emphasize that I see these two genres not as mutually exclusive, but mutually reinforcing textual forms.
16 Michael McKeon, *Theory of the Novel: A Historical Approach* (Baltimore, 2000), p.435. For a detailed exploration of the paradoxical ways in which public, private, and intimate spaces are constructed in novels, and the reflection of these constructions onto subjectivity, see ibid., pp.435–586.
17 Strauss, 'Who Read What in the Ottoman Empire', pp.51–2.
18 Jale Parla, *Babalar ve Oğullar: Tanzimat Romanının Epistemolojik Temelleri* (Istanbul, 1990).
19 See Andreas Tietze's introduction in *Akabi Hikâyesi*, p.10.
20 'My master.' It is used as a gender-neutral form of polite address, much like 'monsieur' or 'madame' in French. Hagop addresses Akabi here.
21 Since Atala wasn't translated into Armenian until 1858 and into Ottoman Turkish until 1872, Akabi must be carrying a copy of the French original. Etienne Charrière carefully tracks the translations of novels and novellas like *Atala*. He writes that the first translation into Armenian appeared in the periodical Masis in 1858. See Etienne Charriere, '"We Must Ourselves Write About Ourselves:" The Trans-Communal Rise of the Novel in the Late Ottoman Empire'. PhD Dissertation, University of Michigan, 2016.
22 Vartan Pasha, *Akabi Hikâyesi*, p.58.
23 Chateaubriand, *Atala*, p.26.
24 Ibid., p.26
25 Ibid., p.26
26 Ibid., p.76.

27 Ibid., p.83.
28 Ibid., p.91.
29 Ibid., p.83.
30 Ibid., p.22.
31 Ibid., p.20.
32 It should be noted that the term 'class' is somewhat anachronistically used here. It is meant to capture the differences in financial and cultural capital, and not necessarily different positions in the capitalist mode of production. For a compelling discussion of the emergence of capitalist production in the Ottoman Empire, see Çağlar Keyder, *State and Class in Turkey: A Study in Capitalist Development* (London, 1987).
33 Vartan Pasha, *Akabi Hikâyesi*, pp.89–90.
34 See Murat Cankara, 'Reading *Akabi*, (Re-)Writing History: On the Questions of Currency and Interpretation of Armeno-Turkish Fiction', in Evangelia Balta (ed.), *Cultural Encounters in the Turkish Speaking Communities of the Late Ottoman Empire* (Istanbul, 2014), pp.53–75 for a more detailed discussion of the overtly political dimensions of Hagop and Akabi's love.
35 Vartan Pasha, *Akabi Hikâyesi*, p.76.
36 Ibid., p.77.
37 There are echoes of the Ottoman Armenian dragoman Ignatius Mouradgea d'Ohsson's life story in Bogos' story. It seems that being forced to live in exile after being accused of being a French spy was not just a sad biographical detail. It was also a tragic trope that marked the dangers of straying too far away from one's own community, or of becoming too close to a community of (European) foreigners.
38 Ibid., p.142.
39 Margaret Cohen and Carolyn Dever, *The Literary Channel: The Inter-National Invention of the Novel* (Princeton, 2009).
40 Vartan Pasha, *Akabi Hikâyesi*, p.7.

9

The late Ottoman novel as social laboratory: Celal Nuri and the 'woman question'

Ayşe Polat

Celal Nuri [İleri] (1882–1938), a social and political commentator, wrote prolifically in numerous genres and topics; but most strongly on issues of social change and reform. He also wrote novels, particularly during the First World War years – five of his six novels were published between 1916 and 1919.[1] These novels provide a rich manifestation of post-First World War society through the eyes of a famous late Ottoman intellectual. They are mirrors into society as well as pedagogical tools aimed at its redesigning. Celal Nuri's deliberate selection of the novel as a medium exemplifies his creative experimentation with the genre in order to articulate and implement his vision for the remedy of the present, the post-First World War social ills.

In this essay I examine two novels by Celal Nuri: *Apocalyptic Times* (*Ahir Zaman*) and *The Prostitute Merchant (Tacire-i Facire)*. The two short novels were published as feuilletons in his newspapers *The Future (Ati)* and *Forward (İleri)* between 6 November 1918 and 17 March 1919, and 29 November 1919 and 31 December 1919, respectively. In the former he narrates the affairs of a young man with a number of Muslim married women in Istanbul, and in the latter he recounts the life story of a female prostitute in Rome. In both novels, Celal Nuri explored issues surrounding women, marriage, family formation, gender, sexuality and social morality in post-First World War society.

Apocalyptic Times and *The Prostitute Merchant* engage with the 'woman question,' widely conceived. Celal Nuri makes this project explicit by entitling the intellectual preface to the latter novel '*mesele-i nisaiyye*,' the Ottoman Turkish expression for the 'woman question.' The 'woman question' was a phrase first coined in Europe in the eighteenth century and became widespread in other parts of the world by the nineteenth century, including the Ottoman Empire. The 'woman question' was neither merely about women, nor was it comprised of one single question.[2] Rather, it encapsulated various intellectual, cultural and political disputations on the nature of women, their attributes, social status and roles, and less directly but no less significantly, about society, juxtaposed with perspectives on a remodelling of social institutions, particularly issues of family structure, economy and the law.

The two novels were not the first pieces Celal Nuri penned on women and society. In 1913 Celal Nuri published a collection of essays, *Our Women (Kadınlarımız)*.[3] It is entitled *Our Women* because the essays on the one hand cover women, sexuality, marriage and family types across human history, exploring cultural norms and perspectives in different societies and civilizations. On the other hand, it is titled *Our Women* because it specifically refers to the contemporary problems of Muslim Turkish women. Celal Nuri, similar to many other nineteenth- and twentieth-century Muslim reformists, articulated his views on veiling and polygamy. He proposed a re-understanding of these Islamic precepts, asserting that polygamy and women's lack of right to issue a divorce, rather than strengthening the institution of marriage, actually weakened Muslim marriages and families – one main factor behind Muslims' social decline.

Celal Nuri's engagement with the 'woman question' is different in his intellectual essays than it appears in his novels both due to the nature of the literary forms and Celal Nuri's skilful usage of different literary techniques, as well as due to the outcomes of the historical context. I will unpack first the latter and then explain the former in the second section of this article.

First World War was an important milestone for continuing the achievements of pre-war women's rights movements (as in, for instance, increasing women's public visibility and enrolment in workforces), and at the same time, for leading to significant setbacks and the reaffirmation of gender roles (as in the case of identifying men with soldiering and leadership in post-war nation-building, while identifying women with household tasks and motherhood).[4] Celal Nuri follows these contradictory impulses, arguing that women proved that they could perform any job, even the 'manly' tasks during war years, but that now, with the resumption of peace, it was time for them to go back to their main duty – 'motherhood' – in order to save and 'elevate the nation.'[5] While Celal

Nuri emphasizes women's household roles in rebuilding state and society in his intellectual newspaper essays, in his novels he draws attention to the socio-economic and human consequences of First World War, underlining a number of gendered social issues about women and families.

Apocalyptic Times and *The Prostitute Merchant* satirize characters that benefit from war and post-war conditions such as the war profiteers; and seek to generate readers' sympathy for those that pay the costs of the war at higher stakes, such as prostitutes (in *The Prostitute Merchant*) and the married women that lost their husbands, families, and wealth *(in Apocalyptic Times)*. The two novels also discuss ideas current in intellectual and political debates, such as comparing advantages of capitalism and socialism to those of conservatism and liberalism. All these subthemes about First World War and its aftermath are interwoven into the novels' plots, but they lie behind the primary issues that Celal Nuri sought to address: women, their plights and the erosion of family.

In the two novels, Celal Nuri focuses on the ways in which the war deepened and made more extensive, visible and harder to ignore, a number of social matters concerning women. The novels address gender norms and values about sexual morality, implicitly asserting that society's ways of thinking about women's sexuality, prostitution, or marital and free sex need to be revisited. He argues that the easy labelling of certain acts as immoral no longer suffices in the face of present grim social realities. A reorganization of social institutions, especially regarding family and morality, is essential in order to regenerate society and social order.

Celal Nuri does not juxtapose the 'woman question' and social morality merely in the post-war Ottoman society; he emphasizes it as encapsulating the similarities and connections between different societies in the aftermath of the war. The 'woman question' remains 'the most enduring problem of the time,' he explained, for those in the 'East' as well as in the 'West.'[6] In the preface to *The Prostitute Merchant*, Celal Nuri draws attention to the shared experiences of the war by explicitly drawing parallels between post-war Rome and post-war Istanbul.[7] He first refers to the contemporary political scene, stating that in the aftermath of First World War, Istanbul was under the occupation of the Allied forces. He then compares his exile in Rome to that of the Sultan Cem, the son of Sultan Mehmed II, the conqueror of Constantinople. Both were sent to

Rome by force by the Ottoman regime, but the latter, Celal Nuri proposed, at least experienced the glory of the Ottoman Empire and met his true love in Rome. In an overt juxtaposition to Sultan Cem's experiences of Rome and Istanbul, Celal Nuri experienced the painful death throes of the Ottoman Empire and visited a Rome flooded by miserable prostitute women.

Celal Nuri does not further elaborate on the political outcomes of First World War; he quickly moves to illustrating the deep fissures of the social fabric in both Rome and Istanbul. The 'woman question' prevails in both contexts as a major social problem. Celal Nuri implicitly suggests that the histories of Istanbul and Rome were connected since, in the aftermath of First World War, similar to other belligerent countries, the two cities were struck by war losses: from lost and wounded generations to increased poverty, shortage of basic goods, and human trafficking, including prostitution and spread of sexual diseases. Celal Nuri introduces these isues in the subplots of his novels, implicitly weaving them into a discussion of the larger 'woman question.'

He underlines that Rome was in desperate conditions – even though Italy was on the winning side of war. All he could see was 'prostitutes,' and 'their deep sorrows.'[8] He regrets that Rome only offered 'stories of the prostitute women,' in contrast to its glorious past – the city that was once home to the glorious baths of Caracalla (where 'women would display their splendid bodies') and the 'capital of Pomponia.' In the juxtaposition of past and present prostitution, Celal Nuri implies that the problem was not prostitution *per se*. In the past Rome witnessed women's freedom and agency in sex and sexuality, whereas now women were among the weakest and most vulnerable strata of society, having no control over their wealth, well-being or even their bodies. They do not choose prostitution but are forced into it and then labelled 'dishonoured' by society – the recurring theme that he emphasizes and unpacks throughout the plot of *The Prostitute Merchant*. Yet, Celal Nuri also contends that the married women of Istanbul were in no better condition than the prostitute women of Rome. This is evident in his portrayal of the former in *Apocalyptic Times*. Written several months apart, both novels affirm the difficulties women experienced particularly under war and post-war circumstances.

In both *Apocalyptic Times* and *The Prostitute Merchant*, Celal Nuri interweaves the main narrative around the woman characters in the novels.

Even though in the former the protagonist is a man, Ecmel Bey, his narrative is subsidized to different women whose relationships with Ecmel are narrated. In *The Prostitute Merchant* the predominant plot of the novel is the prostitute woman Sonya; the men she meets have only minor roles. In both novels Celal Nuri elaborates on prostitution through the main characters. Ecmel Bey is a flirtatious, debauchee man that feels overwhelmed by Istanbulite women's love and sexual passions for him. He considers using a 'face cover' to avoid the gazes of women in Istanbul who compete with each other 'to get on the ferry just to see him;' and feels like a 'prostitute,' wondering if 'he is just for breeding' in the hands of the women.[9] Celal Nuri's naming of a male character *Ecmel*, 'the most beautiful,' by using the term prostitute *(fahişe)* to denote a male, and by describing Ecmel's inclination to 'veil', provocatively inverts traditional gender assumptions, and problematizes women's agency in prostitution. Reading the two novels in retrospect, it becomes even more obvious that by stating that Ecmel *feels like a prostitute*, whereas Sonya *is a prostitute*, Celal Nuri highlights the gender bias embedded in cultural conceptions of prostitution. Ecmel Bey only *feels* exhausted by the overdose of sex – it is a personal problem on his part; whereas Sonya's prostitution is a social problem – she is labelled as a prostitute by society and considered 'dishonoured, or unchaste,' moral claims which she helplessly rejects.

The novel *Apocalyptic Times* derives its title not from the male protagonist but the women he has affairs with; from the fragility of the institution of marriage in the context of post-war poverty, dearth of men and family norms in transition. *Apocalyptic Times* is explicitly stated in the novel to denote contemporary circumstances that rendered Muslim women incapable of finding their suitable marital equivalents and forming productive marriages. As a result, their families remained fragile, unhealthy and vulnerable to dissolution.

Celal Nuri draws attention to class differences, underlining that contemporary conditions affect women of different strata differently; however, the end result is the same: unhappy or failed marriages, broken families – rips in the social fabric. For the women of the middle or upper middle classes, as marriage patterns change it becomes harder for them to find suitable partners. Celal Nuri illustrates this by way of Sena Hanım, who came from a respected family and was educated in Ottoman and European literary cultures. The family wealth diminished and Sena eventually was forced to accept a war profiteer's marriage proposal that he sought largely to clear his name as a war profiteer and take advantage of her family's reputation. In this example, Sena, valued in the pre-war marriage market, was vastly undervalued in the post-war context. As Sena's grandmother explained, her education, good manners and breeding could not compete with the 'time-server girls' that were not bound by traditional marriage procedures and could flirt and hang out with young boys. The latter type was 'easy to marry and equally easy to divorce'.[10]

Women of lower social classes also had new challenges. They could not protect their families or attract viable husbands either. In an implicit reference to the increased sex and human traffic during and after the First World War years, Celal Nuri described how foreign women found themselves transported to Istanbul and introduced into cheap entertainment venues. On the one hand these women's lives were torn apart; on the other hand, they also participated in the destruction of the local, Istanbulite women who fought desperately to keep their husbands' and their families' meagre wealth from being spent on them. Even though Celal Nuri voices through the Istanbulite women that the 'end of times' had come, when 'a Muslim woman or girl does not have any rights, not even equal to those of a whore',[11] he also tries to explain to his readers that it is always women who pay the price of the weakening of social mores and institutions – whether it is the unfortunate foreign non-Muslim women brought to and sold in Istanbul, or the poor Muslim women of Istanbul trying to save their families during desperate times. The same holds true for the women in Rome and other post-war societies.

Apocalyptic Times describes the realities of women's lives, and invites readers to empathize with the full implications of the 'woman question.' Celal Nuri also provides a solution, hinting at possible ways of repelling this impending apocalypse: unless institutions regarding women and sexuality are fundamentally changed, he insists, the political end of times of the Ottoman Empire will be accompanied by social and familial collapse. In the subsequent novel, *The Prostitute Merchant*, Celal Nuri challenges his readers' assumptions that prostitute women are liable for seducing men, breaking other women's marriages or willfully offering sex for money. With every single detail implanted into the narrative in *The Prostitute Merchant*, Celal Nuri incites readers' empathy with prostitute women who unwillingly perform the job merely to survive. In so doing, he forces his readers to reexamine cultural norms about honour, chastity and the ethics of sexuality.

Sonya, the prostitute protagonist of *The Prostitute Merchant*, 'sells her body,' 'takes her chastity to the market,' and turns into 'the merchant of a dissolute woman.'[12] Again the title of the novel is ironic, underlining that Sonya had no option other than using her 'beauty and youth' to survive as a young girl completely on her own.[13] She lost her father, was sexually assaulted by her mother's lover and betrayed by her beloved who brought her to a foreign city supposedly to save her but in fact abandoned her in a hotel room after making love with her for a couple of days. Sonya saw death as the only way out but after her suicide attempt failed she took shelter in the hotel maid's advice to sell her physical beauty. As she later reflects: '*The law even permits killing, if it is out of necessity. Did I have any other option but to submit my body?*'[14]

The novel recounts the rest of Sonya's story as a totally exhausted woman who never likes what she does nor seeks to take advantage of it. She does not seduce rich men; but rather always dreams of what she has lost forever; marrying her beloved and having a happy marriage with her children. Even though Sonya questions fate, God and her lover for pushing her life in this direction, she is most troubled by the cultural norms and values that consider a prostitute woman unchaste or dishonoured. Celal Nuri, through Sonya's monologues, voices a reassessment of conceptions of honour, shame, or morality:

> Why did you [honour] not come to save me when Ivan cruelly left me and killed the purity of my life? If I were to dream of you, I would remain hungry, thirsty, with no place to stay, and with no one around during the most grievous moments.[15]

In the two narratives of married women of Istanbul and the prostitute women of Rome, which read like universal stories of women's suffering, Celal Nuri implies the connected histories and shared conceptions of the East and the West, the European and the Ottoman, the traditional and the modern. The theatres of First World War and its aftermath revealed the problems in each binary as well as across them. As a reformist, Celal Nuri sought refuge in novels as public discourses of the present circumstances and imagined solutions in the face of frustrating traditions and modernities. The solution to the apocalyptic social dissolution experienced by post-war societies lay in reforming family structure and reestablishing a new social order. It was essential to rethink the Ottoman modern.

For Celal Nuri, rethinking the Ottoman modern entailed going so far as to professionalize prostitution. The late Ottoman regulations on prostitution date back to around the last quarter of the mid-nineteenth century. However, via the novel, Celal Nuri tried to create a more widespread perceptional change in people's minds. There is a clear shift in the last published episode of *The Prostitute Merchant*. Celal Nuri suddenly changes the main character: Sonya is initially described as, a naïve young woman who neither likes prostitution nor even makes a lot of money out of it. Later in the novel, however, Sonya becomes a rationalist actor who actively defends the opening of a school of prostitution for girls, and supports training them in 'the art of whoredom.'[16] Prior to this last instalment of the novel, there is also a married woman character who puts forward the idea of sexual libertarianism. She likens marriage to a prison, defends the choice of both men and women to enjoy the freedom to be with whomever they want.[17] Defenders of the same perspective appear in *Apocalpytic Times* as well. Celal Nuri's choice of having this character in these last episodes enabled him to air this contemporary viewpoint as well as to discuss the advantages and disadvantages of both limited and unlimited sex. In contrast to critiques that led to the censorship of *Apocalpytic Times*, Celal Nuri's aim was not to support and propagate extramarital affairs or reject the institutions of morality and marriage. Rather, he used these discussions as a technique in the novel to expose readers to multiple perspectives and to allow them to recognize the 'extreme' ends of each alternative. Celal Nuri's ideal was to encourage happy, well-matched marriages, but if prostitution was an unavoidable social reality, then, he contended, it was better to professionalize it.

Theorizing and practising the novel

In a 1917 essay, Celal Nuri compared the novel as a genre with other literary forms and proposed that novels can enable 'people to feel, to think, and thereby to reach a higher stage of maturity.' He stated that 'the common herd (*avam*) cannot grasp big issues in an abstract form,' nor can they 'digest' them.[18] The novel, unlike classical Ottoman poetry in which the rhyme is essential, can use its content to express such 'big issues.' In this way, he continues, 'ordinary people can be made to swallow any emotional, intellectual, incorporeal, or high and material need and necessity first and foremost through novels and fairy tales'.[19]

While he gives examples from other contemporary Ottoman novels and appreciates their authors' success in nurturing patriotic, nationalist sentiments among the Ottoman public, Celal Nuri's focus was in engaging the public in complex matters about cultural norms and practices about sexuality, marriage, family, prostitution and gender. He considered it urgent to cultivate a new social morality that enhanced citizenship, redefined attitudes and values about women (who after all comprised half of the population), reassessed women's needs and strengthened the family. Like other proponents of the 'woman question,' Celal Nuri believed that the family was the microcosm of society, the most basic unit that would either promote or hinder modernity and socio-economic progress.

He deployed the novel to these ends and took advantage of a number of features of fictional prose to offer his prescriptions for society. The novel provided Celal Nuri with a public space to engage in an open-ended discussion without explicit argumentation; it rendered his pen more free than intellectual essays' systematic, complete examination of a topic; it enabled him to reach out to readers' affective capacities and to emotionally persuade and prepare them for new conceptions; it promoted a less didactic but more bottom-up, engaged pedagogical connection with readers, permitting the examination of multiple views and positions on difficult, controversial social matters, allowing for the problematization of prevailing dichotomies and binaries of modernity. It permitted the refashioning of the Ottoman, Turkish modern.

Celal Nuri's intended audience was broader in the novels than in his intellectual essays. He had in mind a general readership, not necessarily intellectuals or highly educated classes, but one that could understand what he was seeking to convey through plots involving everyday characters and situations. He imagined that many readers would be able to empathize with the female characters of *Apocalyptic Times* who feared losing their husbands to easily attainable women. Celal Nuri deliberately deployed novels in order to drag readers to his intended conclusions by skilfully taking advantage of fictional prose's capability to create empathy and make readers understand the point or argument driven by implicit suggestions. This strategy is evident in the different techniques Celal Nuri employs in intellectual prose and fiction, respectively.

In *Our Women*, Celal Nuri wrote in a semi-scientific style. He quoted other intellectuals' ideas, referred to scientific perspectives of anthropology, sociology and physiology. The book was written as a collection of intellectual essays, and pursued a systematic flow of ideas, arguments and statements, substantiated through examples given from human civilization. However, in *The Prostitute Merchant* and *Apocalyptic Times*, Celal Nuri provided his readers with concrete, contemporary, 'non-scientific' examples that a general readership could easily identify with and understand. He did not offer arguments, but subtly implanted them into the text. Assertions were scattered through the fictional text in one or two sentences, in contrast to the intellectual essays' long, systematized statements or defences of a particular viewpoint.

To give one example, Celal Nuri wrote in *Our Women* about how conceptions of honour, privacy, love and sexuality have evolved in human history. Like an anthropologist, he cited lifestyles of different tribes and nations, and pointed to the historical and cultural specificity of these concepts, explicitly calling for them to be redressed according to the needs of the contemporary age. In *The Prostitute Merchant*, Celal Nuri proffered the same message – that honour is a relative term whose meaning changes over time and across societies. However, the explicit statement is hidden in the novel's text and is voiced only in one of the monologues of the protagonist. Addressing honour, Sonya denounces it as a 'relative, conjectural, imaginary truth,' asserting that it was not even clear 'who invented' it.[20] The entire plot of the novel hints at the constructed nature of honour, but this is done obliquely, for general public consumption, not directly in conversation with other intellectuals, as he did in his essays.

Furthermore, Celal Nuri voices this idea only pages after provoking readers' emotive capacities, particularly empathy. He enables his readers to empathize with Sonya and build into her fictional life story the elements that could draw them to the conclusion that cultural preconception of prostitute women as immoral and dishonourable is wrong. The novel, by way of concrete, day-to-day characters, introduces and illustrates these ideas, seeking to persuade readers gradually by evoking their emotions rather than direct argumentation. The difference between scientific and intellectual argumentation versus everyday experiential and emotional suggestion is evident in the novels and Celal Nuri's newspaper advice columns, too. Shortly before publishing *Apocalyptic Times*, Celal Nuri penned a woman's advice column in a newspaper, entitled *In the Company of A Lady (Hanımefendinin Musahabesi)* under a female pen name, Afife Fikret. Compared to the the more scientific and intellectual tone of *Our Women*, the newspaper advice column engages more directly with readers, advising women about their family and marriage problems. However, compared to *Apocalyptic Times* it is still more didactic, intellectual and idea-driven.

In both the newspaper advice column and the novel, Celal Nuri shares the same fundamental idea: that well-formed marriages and strong families are vital for individual and social well-being. However, in the former, he supports this idea by teaching and explicitly offering to his readers the 'true' understanding of current intellectual thoughts and ideologies; for instance by unequivocally refuting the perspective that feminism is against marriage and childbearing.[21] In *Apocalyptic Times* he alludes to these intellectual trends (e.g. feminism, conservatism, liberalism); but they appear only in the background. He does not take a direct intellectual engagement with them. Rather, he deploys them to show his readers the spectrum of ideas and stances, to provide a menu of possible viewpoints. Even though he guides and directs readers to the 'truth' through activating their empathy and other emotive capacities, the novel is intended to make readers come to their own conclusions.

To this end, that is to show the multiple views, positions and ideas on numerous topics in concrete and condensed ways to readers, Celal Nuri took advantage of the binaries existing in the Tanzimat novels and also created new ones. Through the interplay of these binaries, he disclosed the complexities of matters about women, gender, morality, social change or modernization. However, his pedagogy in the novel was to offer evasive and hidden answers, preparing readers for certain deductions and conclusions, but not offering them clear-cut answers and solutions. It is through the comparative posing of binaries and dichotomous views that Celal Nuri effectively builds concealed arguments and implicit suggestions into his novelistic texts.

Celal Nuri used the novel as what the editors of the present volume have called 'a motor and site of translation' in their introduction. The Tanzimat novel's famous *alaturka* versus *alafranga* typologies, that is those representing traditional Ottoman versus Westernized modern customs and lifestyles, frequently appear in Celal Nuri's *Apocalyptic Times*. Like other Tanzimat novelists, Celal Nuri does not simply borrow from foreign European novels – his version of the modern is not an imitative one. Rather, he engages in a multi-directional conversation, problematizing binaries of East and West in order to reformulate and reimagine the Ottoman modern.

Unlike in Ahmet Midhat's 1875 novel *Felatun Bey and Rakım Efendi*, the spectrum of possibilities was even broader in the post-First World War years. Celal Nuri did not take sides with any of the binaries on absolute terms. Rather he believed in and used novels to convince the rest of society, the literate citizens of the collapsing empire and emerging Turkish nation-state, to rebuild their state and society by assessing and evaluating the terms of each dichotomy according to current conditions and the particular context. This explains Celal Nuri's seemingly contradictory statements about the vehemence of building Turkish feminism at the same time as he argues that Turkish women's primary duty is that of motherhood, or his emphasis on the significance of rebuilding family on strong grounds, yet his support for professionalizing prostitution and his recognition of women's sexual needs despite his discouragement of the unlimited pursuit of sex.

Nonetheless, I am not asserting that Celal Nuri was an absolute relativist who believed that any choice was equally valid. On the contrary, Celal Nuri was a universalist in the sense that he believed in universal premises and social realities. He evoked his universals in the novels. For instance; he proposed that necessity exempted one from being legally or morally accountable for what one does; that agency and free choice conveyed responsibility and virtue; that women have throughout history been generally among the less powerful, persistently subjugated to the desires and enslavement of the more powerful; that social norms vary for men and women; and that family and morality are pivotal social institutions.

Celal Nuri remained committed to the novel as a medium that provided him with unique ways to expose the social ills exacerbated by First World War and the burdens of profound socio-political transition. He has been accused, in a cartoon in a contemporary newspaper, of writing serialized novels simply to sell them and in some sense his novels might be evaluated as 'cheap fiction.'[22] However, regardless of their literary quality, Celal Nuri creatively experimented with the novel as a genre to convey to readers his ideas and to promote a change in their ways of thinking. Novels were central motors of change – his audience both subjects and objects of the construction of the new Ottoman modern.

Notes

1 For a list and brief summary of his stories and novels, see Recep Duymaz, 'Celal Nuri İleri ve Ati gazetesi'. PhD dissertation, Marmara University, 1991, pp.93–111.
2 Lucy Delap, 'The "Woman Question" and the Origin of Feminism' in Gareth S. Jones and Gregory Claeys, *The Cambridge History of Nineteenth-Century Political Thought* (Cambridge, 2011).
3 Celal Nuri, *Kadınlarımız* (Istanbul, 1331 [1913]).
4 Susan R. Grayzel, *Women's Identities at War: Gender, Motherhood, and Politics in Britain and France during the First World War* (Chapel Hill, NC, 1999), p.11. See also Susan R. Grayzel, *Women and the First World War* (New York, 2002).
5 Afife Fikret [Celal Nuri], 'Hanımefendinin Musahabesi', *Ati*, 21 Mart 1334 [21 March 1918], p.2; Ibid., 6 Kanun-i Sani 1334 [6 January 1918], p. 1; Ibid., 2 Kanun-i Sani 1334 [2 January 1918], p.1.
6 Celal Nuri, 'İleri'nin Tefrikası: 1, Tacire-i Facire, Sultan Cem'e Hemdem', *İleri*, 29 Teşrin-i Sani 1335 [29 November 1919].
7 Ibid.
8 Ibid.
9 See Mustafa Kurt, *Celal Nuri İleri'nin Romanları: Perviz–Ölmeyen–Merhume–Ahir Zaman* (Ankara, 2012), pp.255–98.
10 Ibid., p.215.
11 Ibid., p.283.
12 Celal Nuri, 'İleri'nin Tefrikası: 10, Tacire-i Facire', *İleri*, 12 Kanun-i Evvel 1335 [12 December 1919].
13 Celal Nuri, 'İleri'nin Tefrikası: 6, Tacire-i Facire', *İleri*, 4 Kanun-i Evvel 1335 [4 December 1919].
14 Celal Nuri, 'İleri'nin Tefrikası: 10, Tacire-i Facire', *İleri*, 12 Kanun-i Evvel 1335 [12 December 1919].
15 Celal Nuri, 'İleri'nin Tefrikası: 11, Tacire-i Facire', *İleri*, 14 Kanun-i Evvel 1335 [14 December 1919].
16 Celal Nuri, 'İleri'nin Tefrikası: 23, Tacire-i Facire'. *İleri*, 31 Kanun-i Evvel 1335 [31 December 1919].

17 Celal Nuri 'İleri'nin Tefrikası: 20, Tacire-i Facire', *İleri*, 26 Kanun-i Evvel 1335 [26 December 1919]; Celal Nuri, 'İleri'nin tefrikası: 21, Tacire-I Facire', *İleri*, 27 Kanun-i Evvel 1335 [27 December 1919].

18 Celal Nuri, 'Mütalaanın Lezzeti, Zevki', in *Harbden Sonra Türkleri Yükseltelim* (Istanbul, 1917), p.68.

19 Ibid.

20 Celal Nuri, 'İleri'nin Tefrikası: 11, Tacire-i Facire', *İleri*, 14 Kanun-i Evvel 1335 [14 December 1919]; Celal Nuri, 'İleri'nin Tefrikası: 23, Tacire-i Facire', *İleri*, 31 Kanun-i Evvel 1335 [31 December 1919].

21 Afife Fikret [Celal Nuri], 'Hanımefendinin Musahabesi', *Ati*, 16 Kanun-i Sani 1334 [16 January 1918], p.1.

22 *Ayine*, 1 Teşrinisani 1337 [1 November 1921].

10

Ottoman Babel: Language, cosmopolitanism and the novel in the long Tanzimat period

Ali Bolcakan

In general terms, comparative studies and specifically the discipline of comparative literature performs readings across different boundaries, namely, linguistic (comparing works written in different languages, Italian and German for example), national (comparing works, that may or may not be in the same language, from two different nation states) and disciplinary (linking literature with other forms of art and/or recruiting the methodological tools of other disciplines), and thus problematizing one or more of these boundaries. Yet the Ottoman Empire of the nineteenth century, especially the Tanzimat era, immediately presents a problem about how to delineate linguistic and cultural boundaries and national borders at a time when these borders were very porous and constantly in flux. First of all, what does 'Ottoman novel,' mean? Is it literature written in *the* Ottoman or in *an* Ottoman language; is it literature by an Ottoman subject within or outside of the actual borders of the empire or merely a work composed within the actual borders of the Ottoman Empire? Depending on one's answer to either of these questions, entire languages and their literary outputs are either included or excluded from the Ottoman corpus. The tensions that revolve around the multiplicity of languages, scripts and also original works, translations and adaptations we see in the late Ottoman Empire necessarily and unavoidably complicate our understanding of the period but they also force us to re-evaluate how to classify and codify literature and ascribe them a place within a particular literary historiography.

Tanzimat novels are marked by the momentous changes a non-European Empire was undertaking: they are not only the consequence of modernization but also always a response and reaction to the changing sentiments and to the changes that were being implemented. My goal in this chapter is to situate the Tanzimat novel against the backdrop of contemporary scholarship about translation studies, Ottoman cosmopolitanism, imperialism, and (post-)colonialism, and to argue two major points: first, that the scope of the Tanzimat novel should be rethought to include novels that were composed in non-Ottoman Turkish languages of the empire; and second, to convincingly achieve the uncoupling of the literary historiography of the Tanzimat period from that of the Turkish Republic's.

A productive comparative example would be the case of the Austro-Hungarian Empire. The empire's multilingual composition, especially that of Prague, has been the subject of excellent contemporary scholarship. Scott Spector's *Prague Territories*,[1] Judson's *Guardians of the Nation*[2] and Yasemin Yıldız's *Beyond the Mother Tongue* all problematize the notions of the term 'mother tongue'; multilingualism and competition between languages within a singular political body; and what it means to belong to the said body depending on the usage of a certain language. As Yıldız notes, 'for the multilingualism of the empire increasingly shifted from being constituted by subjects with diverse multilingual competences to a multilingualism constituted by the side-by-side existence of a series of monolingual communities.'[3] In their works, Spector, Judson and Yıldız demonstrate that it was language that ultimately determined in the last instance the place and role of a community in the larger society, how a predominantly Czech speaking majority and a German speaking bourgeoisie, primarily Jewish, were at odds with each other.

Even a brief comparison of the constantly changing linguistic frontiers of the Habsburg Empire can further complicate considerations of the political, social, and cultural composition of the Ottoman Empire. Certainly it demonstrates that divided loyalties concerning language are decidedly not unique to the Ottoman case. But what makes the monolingual paradigm at work in this case significant in itself and valuable for other contexts, is that it is one of the few examples in which the issue of multiple co-existing diglossia, and extreme linguistic reinventions in the case of Modern Greek and Turkish, in the form of standardization and purification, coalesce in a non-colonial and/or a non-post-colonial setting.

When tracing these throughout the course of the transformation of the late Ottoman Empire during the Tanzimat it becomes evident that the Ottoman novel is inextricably bound to discussions of the political, social, religious, cultural and linguistic senses of belonging of different communities of the Empire. We have examples of communities, which used a language that didn't correspond to their supposed national/ethno-religious mother tongue and used a script which also might not correspond to the traditional usage of that specific language. But we also see fragmentation within any given language as well. In his seminal essay for the field, 'Who Read What in the Ottoman Empire (19th–20th Centuries),' Johann Strauss emphasizes the pluralistic aspect of the Ottoman Empire as a society which was divided by religion, language and script, but also, and more importantly, that religion, language and script did not necessarily overlap, saying 'in particular, literatures which do not fit the nationalist paradigm, such as that of the Turkish speaking Greek-Orthodox (Karamanlı) or the Turcophone Armenians, fall between two stools. Generally, they are not regarded either by Turkish or by Greek and Armenian scholars as part of their literary heritage, and have been studied only by specialists.'[4]

The fragmentation of languages along this axis and the literary output inscribed by these kinds of nationalist sentiments are surrounded by negotiations concerning tradition, conservatism and secularism. For the creation of an idealized community/nation a language with mythical prowess and purity is necessary.[5] In this sense, language reforms are linked to an idealized sense of community whose cement is language, but the efforts of purification always come at the expense of the construction of another community whose language is deemed harmful and/or backward and must be rejected. Any reconsiderations of the Tanzimat novel would always have to be careful to show that these subsequent destructive discursive practices weren't in circulation during that period. Broadly, in this context there are two main tensions: first, we see negotiations about choosing the best language for publication in order for any written text to reach the most populous audience possible or to reorientate a community in a specific way. Second, there were intracommunal tensions that arose between classical and vernacular languages. This problem of diglossia caused divisions and brought about discussion of tradition and religiosity/divinity through which some of these languages resisted change. The nineteenth century was marked by clashes between the vernacular and classical forms of a language, precisely because proponents of the classical forms attributed to them an inherent divinity. In this context, at the beginning of the early nineteenth century, we see a change in the discursive practices that link language and script to a sense of a new kind of national belonging. In the continued negotiations and debates concerning Greek diglossia happening in the Ottoman Empire, i.e. outside of the borders of the independent Greek state, and the role of Armenian Catholic Mekhitarist literary productions in both Armenian and Turkish languages, we see them cutting across transnational, transcommunal and intracommunal boundaries. For example, Boghos Levon Zekiyan notes that Mekhitarist comedies utilized multiple languages and reflected the particular pronunciations of Ottoman Empires. Metin And also notes that Armenian theatre in the Ottoman Empire was vital for the development of a modern Turkish vernacular later on.[6] So for example, while a religious authority was firmly rooted in the classical form, it was also forced to utilize the exact vernacular forms to reach a broader audience within and outside of its community to promulgate its social, political, cultural and/or religious 'gospel.'

The Ottoman Empire contained a multitude of communities with different languages and without a strict hierarchy governing these languages and their use. Yet in the nineteenth century, the creative ways in which European works of literary prose, poetry and theatre were translated and also appropriated/rewritten demonstrate the crucial roles translation has played in brokering translational and multilingual encounters. Censorship, financial constraints, market demands, sensibilities of different ethno-religious communities and social and economic classes meant that foreign works were translated/adapted/rewritten differently depending on the intended audience and the political circumstances. The repeated translations and adaptations of any single work in the different languages of the empire, not only the most widespread ones such as Arabic, Armenian, Greek and Turkish with the corresponding prevalent scripts, but also hybrid forms such as Karamanlidika and Armeno-Turkish, show that the space of language and the agents within weren't yet fixed. But the circulation of new modern political ideas created a literary space in which different communities experimented with new modes of writing and collaborated with and competed against each other.

When cosmopolitanism stands in for a medley of languages and cultures in any given place, with an emphasis on cohabitation of different communities and securing the rights of minorities, it still does not prescribe any sort of interaction. And if these communities did indeed interact with rather than avoid each other, it is also unclear what kind of interaction between these communities cosmopolitanism would have entailed. It can be either an exchange that is based on genuine care, concern, curiosity for one's 'neighbours,' or 'compatriots' or it can be built on a form of wariness (which does not have to be synonymous with hate, but rather an inverted version of 'concern'), that is predicated on the recognition of the difference and a desire to sustain it as a safety mechanism; or it can be an unstable combination of the two. But the Gülhane Decree signals, for the first time, the empire's willingness to treat its subjects as equals and guarantees the life, honour and property of its inhabitants. But this didn't mean that Ottoman society became a de-facto cosmopolitan society. Robbins and Horta, in their introduction to *Cosmopolitanisms* – one of many recent examples of considerations of the empire in a cosmopolitan framework – posit that '[i]n its association with secularism in the political sense, however, cosmopolitanism can also be taken to indicate zones and practices of peaceful coexistence, as between [...] Muslims, Christians, and Jews under the Ottoman Empire, without any necessary recourse to a universal, transfaith theory of humanity like that posited by monotheism and by the European Enlightenment.'[7] Furthermore, in the same volume Thomas Bender argues that 'the Ottomans supported pluralism and toleration. Tolerance is a considerable virtue, but if it is cosmopolitanism, it is cosmopolitanism lite, as it does not demand self-reflexivity.'[8]

When the term cosmopolitanism is invoked to describe an actual space, it is used to refer to a specific community and/or communities with multiple – sometimes competing and sometimes multi-layered – local allegiances, obligations, and loyalties. In this sense, it seems that when used to describe a particular historical space, cosmopolitanism is being mistakenly used for conditions of heterogeneity, ethno-masquerade and does not mean much more than (possibly peaceful but also precarious) segregated coexistence of different linguistic, religious and ethnic communities and less about a well-integrated pluralistic society. Thus, it is not clear how a truly cosmopolitan space would and should work, and also whether it would be a desirable condition for all the parties dwelling in it. How can there be a peaceful, harmonious space where members of different communities live together but have no affinities, no senses of belonging and do not feel a particular responsibility and local allegiance to each other. It is precisely this clash of interests that is brewing in the Tanzimat novel and it is in this sense that the Ottoman Empire and the novels of the Tanzimat Period offer a fantastically different vantage point to the underpinnings of a system of world literature.

It is this difficulty, these questions of compatibility, tolerance, pluralism and coexistence put forth by cosmopolitanism, that is crucial for '[invoking] untranslatability as a deflationary gesture toward the expansionism and gargantuan scale of world-literary endeavors,'[9] as Emily Apter notes, which makes this project a viable alternative for tracking the dissemination of modernity. I argue that Constantinople/Istanbul can function, not merely as the unstable periphery of a stable Europe, but as a radically different but equally valid example of how nation states, and by extension national literatures, are formed.

It was because of this issue of untranslatability within the national literary framework that non-Ottoman Turkish works written in Arabic script were until very recently considered to be part of the Ottoman canon. In his writings on the Armeno-Turkish novel and Turkish literary historiography, Laurent Mignon notes that from eighteenth century up to the 1950s more than 2,000 works were written in Turkish but with the Armenian alphabet. Conservative and nationalist Turkish literary historiographies dictated until recently that the first Turkish novel was written by a Muslim Ottoman subject in the Arabic script. Of course, Ottoman literary historiography becomes more complex when the first Turkish novel, *Akabi Hikayesi*, turns out to be written by a Catholic Armenian, Hovsep Vartanyan, also known as Vartan Pasha (1851–1879); was a subject of the Ottoman Empire; is written in Turkish but with Armenian letters; and is about the clashes between the Armenian communities of religious denominations, namely Catholic and Armenian Orthodox.

There has been ample discussion about the exclusion of novels produced by minority writers. Johann Strauss notes that 'given the central position of translations and translated literature in the Middle East in general and in the Ottoman context in particular, one would have expected [translations of European novels by Greek-Ottomans into primarily Greek] to have had a much greater impact. However, works by non-Muslims always seem to have had a somewhat different reception and their position in the annals of Turkish literature is therefore precarious' (247). Laurent Mignon emphasizes the importance of Armeno-Turkish, and adds works like Hovsep Balıkçıyan's *Karnig, Gülunya ve Dikran'ın Dehşetli Vefatli Hikayesi* (1863), Hovsep Marush's

Bir Sefil Zevce (1868) and Vichen Tilkiyan's *Gülunya Yahut Kendi Görünmeyerek Herkesi Gören Kız* (1868) to the list of works that appeared before the first Turkish novels printed with Arabic letters, *Taaşşuk-u Tal'at ve Fitnat* (1872). In this excellent essay on the canon formation, the emphasis is decidedly on Turkish literature and the Turkish canon and not on their Ottoman counterparts. There is also Greek Ottoman Evangelinos Misailidis' Karamanli novel *Temaşa-i Dünya ve Cefakar-ü Cefakeş* [*Theatrum Mundi, and Tyrants and Tyranized* (1871–2)], which is a rewriting of the Greek novel *O Polypathis* [*The Man of Many Sufferings*] by Grigorios Paleologos, also born as an Ottoman subject in Constantinople in 1794, which further complicates the timeline.[10] Additional novels by non-Muslims from the Tanzimat era will perhaps be discovered. But taking stock here I would like to posit that rethinking Ottoman literature of the Tanzimat Period even in light of the full inclusion of Armenian, Greek and Jewish novels coming primarily from the Western part of the Empire, Constantinople, Smyrna, Salonica etc., would constitute only a part of the total Ottoman literary production.

I would like to first suggest that as a program for re-evaluating the Tanzimat period, the literary historiography of the period should be uncoupled from that of the Turkish Republic's so as to be able to divert attention to social dynamics, political movements, ideologies, and geographical spaces which can be directly traced to the Turkish Republic. C. Ceyhun Arslan, in his article 'Canons as Reservoirs: The Ottoman Ocean in Ziya Pasha's Harabat and Reframing the History of Comparative Literature,' analyses Ziya Pasha's anthology, *Harabat*, and observes that while Ziya Pasha characterized Ottoman language 'as an "ocean" that encompasses Arabic, Persian, and Turkish "streams"' this oceanic feeling didn't extend to other languages 'such as Armenian or Kurdish, did not shape the cultural reservoir that the elite Ottoman men of letters identified with.' But by which mechanisms can someone be counted among the elite Ottoman men of letters, and also, when and where?

For a true re-conceptualization of Ottoman literature all considerations related to national canon formations should be discarded. I would argue that it would be a difficult endeavour to understand and also to overcome the hitherto overlooked novels and their writers by solely focusing on the criteria, mechanisms and historical figures that created the conditions of such systems of exclusion. In this respect, the lack of engagement with non-Turkish novels is suspect. It is paramount for a thorough analysis of Tanzimat novels to include non-Turkish language works.

Tzerents's historical novels (real name Hovsep Shishmanian, 1822–1888) *Thoros of Levon* (1877) and *The Birth Pangs of the 9th Century* (1879) are both set in the Middle Ages and deal with the Armenians' war against occupiers of different kinds. Another important example in Armenian would be Hagop Baronian's novel *Honourable Beggars* (1887), which is a satire of marriage in the nineteenth century Ottoman Empire and in that sense would complement İbrahim Şinasî's play *Şair Evlenmesi* [Marriage of a Poet], which is also considered one of the first Ottoman Turkish plays.

But a book of utmost importance for rethinking the Tanzimat novel is Aḥmad Fāris al-Shidyāq's (180?–1887) *Al-Sāq ʿalā l-sāq fī mā huwa al-Fāriyāq (Leg over Leg or the Turtle in the Tree concerning the Fāriyāq, What Manner of Creature Might He Be*, 1855), recognized and dubbed as 'the first great Arabic novel' by even mainstream accounts, e.g. in a namesake piece *New York Review Books* by Robin Creswell[11]. In her foreword to the English translation, Rebecca C. Johnson describes al-Shidyāq as the author of at least four published works of literary prose, ten linguistic studies of Arabic, Turkish, English, and French, over 20,000 lines of poetry, and at least four unpublished manuscripts (not to mention his many translations, journalistic and critical essays, or those works that have been lost). It's disheartening that al-Shidyāq is solely considered in the national framework of Arabic literature[12] even though he was born as an Ottoman subject in modern day Lebanon, spent 30 years in Constantinople (which coincides with the last two decades of the Tanzimat era) where he operated the first Arabic newspaper in Constantinople, operated a major printing house, which also published *Taaşşuk-u Tal'at ve Fitnat*,[13] was in the employ of the Sublime Porte as a translator, and died there.

Focusing on novels written in languages other than Turkish, brings forward other considerations, other figures, other urban centres, and forcibly stretches any considerations of an Ottoman cosmopolitanism. In *Farewell to Alexandria*, a Harry Tzalas describes Alexandria as a cosmopolitan city in the following way:

> Alexandria – the last great cosmopolitan center of the Mediterranean – is special, unique, because people of different nationalities and faiths lived there, people going about their ordinary, everyday lives. They lived side by side – Muslims, Copts, Nubians, Greeks, Italians, Armenians, Maltese,

Shamis, Lebanese, Jews, English, French, Spaniards, Germans, Austrians – they were all Alexandrians; together they made up the whole. They laid the foundations of the new Alexandria upon the remains of the ancient city.

Reading this passage (notwithstanding the lumping together of all Muslims under one category), it is unclear whether these communities interacted with each other 'as people [were] going about their ordinary, everyday lives.' And this precisely describes the ambiguity concerning the major cosmopolitan literary centres of the Tanzimat Period of the Ottoman Empire. Writing about Tanzimat-era Alexandria, al-Shidyāq describes the relationship between Turks and Arabs in this way:

> As for the city's men, the Turks boss the Arabs around like tyrants. The Arab is as much forbidden to look into the face of a Turk as he is into that of another man's wife. [. . . .] If the Turk sneezes, the Arab tells him, 'God have mercy on you!' If he clears his throat, he tells him, 'God protect you!' If he blows his nose, he tells him, 'God guard you!' And if he trips, the other trips along with him out of respect and says, 'May God right you and not us!'[14]

What sets apart this passage is the way al-Shidyāq openly criticizes, and satirizes, the relationship between the Arabs and the Turks, which is seldom this clear in Armeno-Turkish or Karamanli novels that were published in the Western parts of the Empire.

In the past decade there have been very important considerations of the Ottoman Empire vis-à-vis colonialism, imperialism and orientalism in the works of Özgür Türesay, Vangelis Kechriotis, Ussama Makdisi, Isa Blumi, and Herzog & Motika[15] and others. The Tanzimat period should be conceptualized in a much different way compared to the scholarship that focuses on the geopolitical nexus which later became Modern Turkey. Ussama Makdisi, for example, argues that the 'nineteenth-century Tanzimat reflected the birth of a distinctly modern Ottoman imperialism.' This meant formulating Arab provinces (Makdisi refers to them as 'Arab peripheries') as out-of-touch with the Western part of the empire and as such, backward, primitive and in need of the forced and total transformation that Ottoman modernity wanted to exert on them. In one of the most openly critical passages a few pages after the passage quoted above, al-Shidyāq openly questions the authority of the Turkish masters:

I have never been able to work out the reason for the sense of superiority felt by these Turks here with regard to the Arabs, when the Prophet (peace be upon him) was an Arab, the Qur'an was revealed in Arabic, and the imams, Rightly-guided Caliphs, and scholars of Islam were all Arabs. I think, though, that most Turks are unaware of these facts and believe that the Prophet (peace be upon him) used to say *şöyle böyle* ('thus and so') and *bakalım kapalım* ('let's see-bee') and

Ghaṭālıq chāp khay dilhā
    Ṭughālıq pāq yakh balhā
Ṣafālıq pāh khusht wa-kurd
    Faṣālıq hāp daraklahā
Dakhā zāwusht geldi nang
    Khudā shawizt qardlahā
Eshekler hem gibi va-llāh
    Qalāqiluhā balābiluhā

Never, I swear, was the language of the Prophet so, nor that of the Companions or the generation that followed them or the Rightly-guided Imams, God be pleased with them all unto the Day of Resurrection, amen and again amen!

In this passage al-Shidyāq is fearlessly exalting Arabic at the expense of Turkish: by emphasizing the fact that 'Rightly-guided Caliphs' were Arabs and spoke Arabic, he dismisses the power and position of the Ottoman Caliphs. Here the tension is between the supreme position of Arabic and all the native Arabic speakers and those, who while in power, naively believe that their unworthy language was ever uttered by those who were touched by divinity. This reaches its zenith with the gibberish poem, which is in a way an act of turning Ottoman Turkish on its head, Arabic with Turkish elements suffused in it: it's grotesque.

Forty years later, in another novel, one finds a different critique of a grotesque linguistic mixture and also the issue of translatability further problematized in Recaizade Mahmut Ekrem's *Araba Sevdası* (Carriage Affair, 1898).[16] In the novel, the protagonist, Bihruz Bey is a 'dandy'[17] who is completely out of touch with and alienated from his culture. Another character, Keşfi Bey, to the extent permitted by his father's power and position, was 'wandering in fancy Frankish style, reading French, looking for people to say "Bonjur! Bonsuvar! Vu zalle biyen?" [*sic*, mimicks Turkish pronunciation], mixing French words into Turkish conversations, carrying a novel under his arm and aspiring to wastefulness and debauchery, indebtedness and considering Turkish as a language without a literature and as rude and taking pride in being ignorant of this language' so as to be able to pull himself away from national ideals and in that regard had caught up to Bihruz.[18] But the main issue is the sense of inbetweenness of linguistic inadequacy that Bihruz is stuck in. Nurdan Gürbilek notes '[f]or Bihruz the Turkish language itself has become an uninspiring tongue incapable of expressing sublime feelings; thus the effort to speak of desire will always be hindered by the "inadequacy" ["lisan-ı Türkî'nin kifayetsizliğine hamlederek"[19]] of the Turkish language.'[20] Bihruz is certain of the fact that there is no *poesie* in Turkish and there can be no poets among Turks ['Türkçe'de poezi yoktur. Türklerde şair olamaz demiyor muydu?'[21]], because he had heard from people like himself that it is impossible to write poetry in Turkish ['Türklerde adam gibi şair yetişmediğini ve çünkü Türkçe'de şiir söylenemeyeceğini yine kendisi gibi alafranga beylerden işitmiş']. But Bihruz is obsessed with translation, and his lack of proficiency in both of his native and his preferred languages, respectively Turkish and French, always results in his inability to fully understand the source French texts that he is working with; and also his inability to successfully convey the meaning in translation subsequently reproduces the sense of inadequacy. As Parla notes 'semantic dilemmas, communication impasses and strategies that negate its own text' are at the crux of Bihruz Bey's relationship with language itself.

Today, comparative literary studies, with their emphasis on the concept of world literature – which itself is part of a broader socio-political trend towards being more inclusive of hitherto overlooked, ignored and even actively repressed and silenced peoples and their histories, languages and literatures – places a heavy emphasis on translation and re-evaluating national canons of literature. Yet trying to carve out a space for Ottoman literature is no easy task and produces faultlines when faced with epistemological and methodological problems that comparative literature is to an extent unfamiliar with. Following Vangelis Kechriotis' warnings, my intention is neither to argue that we should 'place the Ottoman Empire on a par with the major European colonial empires of the era, claiming in scholarship what the Ottomans themselves never managed to achieve in politics' nor to approach it 'from the point of view of the alleged subaltern, building on an old-fashioned perception of the Tanzimat centre–periphery debate and an understanding of the Turkish nature of the

Ottoman bureaucracy which reiterates similar perceptions inherited from Arab nationalism.' But by focusing on the debates surrounding (un)translatability, multilingualism and multiculturalism, it can be argued that the modernization, expansion and transformation of the Ottoman literary space of the Tanzimat Period is intertwined with the discussions of cultural and political belonging of the different communities of the empire and how they negotiated somehow contradicting ideologies of citizenship, cosmopolitanism, multilingualism and nationalism as modernization efforts introduced new sets of rights and ideas as well as new senses of belonging. In this sense, Ottoman Studies has much to contribute to comparative literary studies.

The Tanzimat novel has an inherent complexity that stems from the empire's multiple cultural centres and their multiethnic, multi-confessional and multilingual composition which do exhibit the complexities that contemporary scholarship usually can only trace transnationally. What Gayatri Spivak finds in contemporary, post-colonial Bengali fiction and names as 'planetarity' in her book, *Death of a Discipline,* to describe the blurring of boundaries between language, literature and geography is already present in the Ottoman Empire and becomes doubly important in the Tanzimat period. I believe that framed in this way, the discussion can be steered towards complexities on a metalinguistic level, veering away from the assumptions about the supposed inescapable pitfalls in Third World Literatures that the Ottoman novel is considered a part of, specifically regarding aspects of plot, style and content.

How can one effectively translate today and hope to convey the radical aspects of the kinds of works, like *Akabi Hikayesi*, that exist in multiple linguistic domains and sometimes do not belong to any kind of national canon other than as a footnote. Whether we are comparing a *karamanlidika* text to an Armeno-Turkish one, or works from the opposite ends of the spectrum of a language that grappled with diglossia, readers of these works are forced to re-evaluate the concept of linguistic borders and national literatures at every turn.

By using different currents within the same language and/or recruiting words and expressions from other languages that are in immediate contact with that respective language (and doing so without supplying any translations) these works also demand translation, and, at the same time, call attention to their specific mode of untranslatability. I argue that in the corpus of Ottoman novels, while the texts themselves are, to an extent, untranslatable – that is to say, the act of translation flattens both their linguistic aspects and the more encompassing and complex linguistic and political milieu they emerged from – they still call for and would benefit from translation. Here, I suggest that a reformulation of Walter Benjamin's well-known idea of translatability (*Übersetzbarkeit*) is necessary for properly analysing the significance of these works. In his monograph *Benjamin's Abilities*, Samuel Weber emphasizes the difference between translation and translatability on the basis of a 'structural possibility.' This *structural possibility* which is 'potentially "at work" even there where it seems factually not to have occurred' is what makes these works special and significant vis-à-vis their untranslatability. Regardless of their status as being difficult to translate, and the conditions of the capitalist book market that has little appetite for such works, examining the embedded challenges of the potential for translation of these works can present us with alternative ways of undertaking a comparative analysis that would complicate the goals and the disciplinary narrative of World Literature. The complexity of the circumstances in which Tanzimat novels were produced, published, circulated and consumed presents us with a mode of literature which circumvents the preconceived ways with which literary studies, even today, classifies, codifies languages and literary output, and ultimately ratifies national canons.

Notes

1 Spector, Scott, *Prague Territories: National Conflict and Cultural Innovation in Kafka's Fin de Siècle* (Berkeley, CA, 2000).
2 Pieter Judson, *Guardians of the Nation: Activists on the Language Frontiers of Imperial Austria* (Cambridge, MA, 2007).
3 Yasemin Yildiz, *Beyond the Mother Tongue: The Postmonolingual Condition* (New York, 2012), p.30.
4 Strauss, Johann. 'Who Read What in the Ottoman Empire (19th–20th Centuries)?', *Middle Eastern Literatures* 6 (1) 2003.
5 Burton Feldman and Robert D. Richardson, *The Rise of Modern Mythology, 1680–1860.* (Bloomington, IN, 1972); E.J. Hobsbawm, *Nations and Nationalism since 1780: Programme, Myth, Reality* (Cambridge, 1992); Andrew von Hendy, *The Modern Construction of Myth* (Bloomington, IN, 2002); Marc Nichanian,

Mourning Philology: Art and Religion at the Margins of the Ottoman Empire (New York, 2014); Marc Nichanian, *The Historiographic Perversion* (New York, 2009).
6. Metin And, *Tanzimat ve İstibdat Döneminde Türk Tiyatrosu (1839–1908)* (Ankara, 1972).
7. Bruce Robbins and Paulo Lemos Horta, 'Introduction' in Bruce Robbins, Paulo Lemos Horta, and Kwame Anthony Appiah (eds), *Cosmopolitanisms* (New York, 2017).
8. Thomas Bender, 'The Cosmopolitan Experience and Its Uses' in Robbins, Horta, and Appiah (eds), *Cosmopolitanisms*.
9. Emily Apter, *Against World Literature: On the Politics of Untranslatability* (New York, 2014), p.3.
10. For more information between the two novels and their relationship, see: Dimitris Tziovas 'Palaiologos's *O Polypathis*: Picaresque (Auto)biography as a National Romance' in Dimitris Tziovas, *The Other Self: Selfhood and Society in Modern Greek Fiction* (Lanham, 2003), pp.55–82.
11. https://www.nybooks.com/articles/2015/10/08/first-great-arabic-novel/
12. For more information see 'The Arabic Literary Language: the Nahda (and beyond)' in Jonathan Owens (ed.), *The Oxford Handbook of Arabic Linguistics* (Oxford, 2103), pp.472–94.
13. Geoffrey J. Roper, 'El Cevaib Matbaası ve 19. Yüzyılda Arapça Yazmaların Basımı ile Aktarımı' in Mehmet Fatih Uslu and Fatih Altuğ (eds), *Tanzimat ve Edebiyat: Osmanlı İstanbulu'nda Modern Edebi Kültür* (Istanbul, 2014) pp.439–54.
14. Aḥmad Fāris al-Shidyāq, *Leg over Leg: Volumes One and Two* (New York, 2015), p.211.
15. Ussama Makdisi, 'Ottoman Orientalism,' *American Historical Review* 107.3 (June 2002), pp.768–96; Thomas Kühn, 'Shaping and Reshaping Colonial Ottomanism: Contesting Boundaries of Difference and Integration in Ottoman Yemen', *Comparative Studies of South Asia, Africa and the Middle East* 27.2 (2007), p.318; Christoph Herzog and Raoul Motika, 'Orientalism alla turca: Late 19th–Early 20th Century Ottoman Voyages into the Muslim "Outback"', *Die Welt des Islams* 40.2 (July 2000), pp.139–95; Özgür Türesay, 'L'Empire ottoman sous le prisme des études postcoloniales. À propos d'un tournant historiographique récent', *Revue d'histoire moderne et contemporaine* 60.2 (2013), pp.127–45.
16. Recaizade Mahmut Ekrem, *Araba Sevdası* (Istanbul, 2014).
17. The issue of 'dandyism' that is parodied in *Araba Sevdası* has been amply analysed: Nurdan Gürbilek, 'Dandies and Originals: Authenticity, Belatedness, and the Turkish Novel', *The South Atlantic Quarterly* 102.2 (2003), pp.599–628; Nurdan Gürbilek, *Kötü Çocuk Türk* (Istanbul, 2011); Korhan Mühürcüoğlu, 'The Alla Franca Dandy; Modernity and the Novel in the Late 19th-Century Ottoman

Empire,' *British Journal of Middle Eastern Studies*, September 4, 2018, pp.1–21; Jale Parla, *Babalar ve Oğullar: Tanzimat Romanının Epistemolojik Temelleri* (Istanbul, 1990).
18 Recaizade Mahmut Ekrem, *Araba Sevdası*, p.210.
19 Ibid., p.111.
20 Gürbilek, 'Dandies and Originals', pp.620–1.
21 Recaizade Mahmut Ekrem, *Araba Sevdası*, p.112.

11

Translating communities: Reading foreign fiction across communal boundaries in the Tanzimat period

Etienne E. Charrière

For the contemporary scholar familiar with what some still insist on calling the 'Western canon,' investigating the translation of Western European novels in the late Ottoman period is a somewhat disconcerting experience. If it were possible to visit a library collecting all the novels translated from French, English or German into Ottoman Turkish, as well as in the languages of the largest non-Muslim groups of the Empire (Greek, Armenian, or Ladino), there is no doubt that, while perusing its contents, one would recognize many familiar works. Yet, one would also be compelled to notice some puzzling absences, as well as the massive presence of obscure, long-forgotten works enjoying there a peculiar prominence, entirely disproportionate to the position they occupy in modern literary historiography. If we imagine that the volumes of this hypothetical library of Ottoman translations were placed on its bookshelves by order of publication, the visitor would then be left with the nagging impression that, when Ottoman literati endeavoured to translate Western European novels into the main literary languages of the Empire, they did so at random, with a clear lack of coherence and without any organizing principle.

In his 1949 *History of Nineteenth-Century Turkish Literature*, poet, novelist, and literary critic Ahmet Hamdi Tanpınar speaks precisely to this dimension of 'randomness' in late Ottoman translation trends, writing that '[...] all the gains in favor of the great interest that existed for foreign languages and literatures were to a large extent accidental in the absence of any serious help from the official educational institutions.'[1] According to Tanpınar, this 'fortuitous' (*tesadüfi*) character of literary translation during the Tanzimat period was therefore due to the fact that, in spite of the great appetite of the reading public for foreign literature, the translation of imported literary works was primarily the result of private initiatives rather than the product of a concerted, systematic effort akin to what the Translation Chamber (*Tercüme Odası*) established by the Porte in 1832 was able to achieve with the translation of scientific, political, and legal works from Western Europe, or to what the Translation Bureau of the Ministry of Education would do for the promotion of world literature in Turkey during the Republican era. For a mid-twentieth-century *esthète* like Tanpınar, the corpus of nineteenth-century Ottoman translations of Western literature was therefore an incomplete one and the lack of 'institutions of planning'[2] able to organize translation activities resulted in the victory of popular taste over considerations of pure literary merit:

> The best evidence of the fortuitousness that we mentioned earlier is the fact that, among these first translations, very few were of the type of novels that we would consider truly major works today. As a matter of fact, neither Cervantes, nor Balzac, nor Stendhal, nor Dickens were translated (*nakledilmemişlerdir*) into Turkish during that period ... This state of affairs was the natural consequence of the absence of educational or cultural institutions able to regulate our intellectual and literary relations with the West. Therefore, young people entering the life of letters started by publishing what would help them learn French – for most of them would learn French or improve their skills through translation – and would then translate (*naklediyordu*) the work that would be read the most by the public (*halkın en çok okuyacağı eseri.*)[3]

Although implicitly used by Tanpınar as evidence of a form of peripheral aesthetic 'belatedness,' such a trope – which consists in approaching the corpus of nineteenth-century translations through the prism of its lacunae and in listing 'missing' canonical authors – finds an echo in the work of scholars interested in nineteenth-century reading practices in Western Europe itself. Book historian Martin Lyons indicates for instance that '[a] history of nineteenth-century French literary culture based on authors such as Stendhal, Balzac, Flaubert, and Zola would be of little use to a social historian (...) Thus, a more representative selection of novelists read in France during the nineteenth century would include Walter Scott, Pigault-Lebrun, Sue, Dumas, Erckmann-Chatrian and

Jules Verne.'4 Indeed, one of the most powerful – and deleterious – effects of the various processes of literary canonization rests in their capacity to create the fiction of their own permanence and endurance through time. Even after cultural and literary studies have long cast doubt on the validity of the very concept of canon, even after the mechanisms of canon formation have long been the object of intense critical scrutiny, the idea retains enough of its pernicious force to assert, in many different ways, both its stability in the future and its immutability in the past. It is only through a persistent and detailed inquiry into the evolution of reading (and translating) practices within a given literary system that processes of canon formation can be exposed as what they are, a series of eminently performative acts, contingent upon the fluctuations of, among other factors, taste and ideology.

In the present chapter, I am interested in problematizing the notion present in Tanpınar (and in much of the scholarship on late Ottoman literary translation) according to which the selection of foreign works – and in particular of foreign novels – slated for translation into Turkish during the Tanzimat era happened 'at random' and I challenge the idea that the absence of what Tanpınar calls 'truly major works' in the repertoire of foreign works of fiction translated during the period bore the mark of an aesthetic 'disconnect' between the Ottoman reading public and its Western European counterpart. Shifting away from an exclusive focus on translations of foreign prose fiction into Ottoman Turkish, I first examine the dominant trends in the translation of Western novels in another of the Empire's literary languages, Greek, the language in which an important number of foreign works – although not all them – were first translated in the Ottoman Empire and I show how these trends, far from pointing to a 'disconnect', in fact largely mirrored developments in the realm of novel publishing in Western Europe itself. In addition to showing how attuned the Ottoman market for fiction was to its Western European counterpart, I also highlight the *internal* coherence of the Tanzimat-era translation landscape, underlining the ways in which the practice of translation cut across linguistic and communal boundaries within the Empire, an element which allows me to deploy the concept of 'transcommunal translational community' to describe the collective engagement of various religious and linguistic groups with literary fiction imported from Western Europe. Finally, I argue for a re-evaluation of the theoretical frameworks traditionally used for the study of Tanzimat-era translations of foreign novels, as well as for a more comprehensive and comparative analysis of literary translation during the period, one taking into account the coexistence of various literary communities, including non-Muslim and non-Turcophone ones, within the border of the Empire, and the numerous ways in which their respective engagement with literary translation intersected.

An examination of the very large corpus of nineteenth-century Greek translations of Western European (and predominantly French) novels published during the long Tanzimat period provides a telling example of the sharp contrast that can exist between modern expectations of what such a corpus could have – or *should* have – included and the reality of the translation choices, the editorial practices and the reading habits of the Greek community in the late Ottoman Empire. While one might expect highly canonical Western European prose writers of the nineteenth century to have enjoyed a particularly rich reception on the Greek Ottoman literary scene, a look at bibliographies and catalogues of Greek translations of foreign literature during the period indicates, on the contrary, that it was a profoundly different roster of European novelists that was imported, translated and consumed by Greeks living in the Ottoman Empire during the nineteenth century. The diffusion of the Western – and in particular French – novel and its acclimatization to the cultural environment of the late Ottoman Empire through translation therefore appears to have resulted in the formation of a sort of parallel canon of the Western novel, one that seemingly overlapped only very partially with the canon as it solidified at its source in the West.

In the second half of the nineteenth century, in a context where the cultural domination of not only Western literature, but much more specifically of the French novel, was extremely strong, the Greek Ottoman reading public acquired, through the mediation of a variety of agents such as translators and publishers, a particularly intense appetite for authors who, with only a few exceptions, have since fallen into obscurity both in their native market and in the spaces that once massively imported them. Instead of Balzac, Stendhal, Flaubert or Zola, Greek Ottomans mostly translated and consumed the works of Alexandre Dumas, Jules Verne, Eugène Sue (among the names still familiar to French readers), as well as those of Xavier de Montépin, Emile Richebourg, Jules Mary, Pierre-Alexis Ponson du Terrail, or Paul Féval (all more or less forgotten today). The prominence of these authors on the Greek Ottoman literary scene was not only due to the number of their novels translated into Greek but was also a question of sheer volume: the propensity of French authors of popular fiction to produce enormously long works – often with the help of one or more ghost writers, as is well-documented in the case of Alexandre Dumas – resulted in the publication of multi-volume novels in translation, often numbering one thousand pages or more in total, even when translators proceeded to extensive cuts. The extreme prolixity of these translated works often presented a sharp contrast with the relative brevity of original Greek-language novels published during the same period in the Ottoman Empire, which very rarely extended over more than a few hundred pages at most. These elements underline that, in the tension that existed during the nineteenth century between a traditional canon based on aesthetic merit only and a popular, market-based 'counter-canon,' the Greek Ottoman public massively opted for the latter, thus highlighting the absolute contingency – and, in a sense, the untranslatability – of the various mechanisms which, in Western Europe, ascribed value to literary products.

With only a few isolated works of foreign literature translated into Greek during the first decades of the nineteenth century, the Greek Ottoman translation scene only truly started to develop at the beginning of the 1840s.[5] Although it took place in the wake of the proclamation of the Gülhane Decree of 1839, which inaugurated the period know as the Tanzimat era, the rapid increase in the number of foreign literary works published in Greek in the Ottoman Empire was also a reflection of a major shift at play in translation trends across the Greek-speaking world at large, both in the Greek communities of the Ottoman Empire and in the newly established independent Greek state. While, until then, the vast majority of foreign novels translated into Greek had been works originally written in Western European languages several decades before their publication in Greek – either in the early to mid-eighteenth century such as Fénelon's *Adventures of Telemachus* (1699) and Defoe's *Robinson Crusoe* (1740), or in the early Romantic period such as Germaine de Staël's *Corinne* (1807) – most of the foreign works of fiction translated into Greek after 1845 were significantly more recent and, in many cases, works by living authors, such as Eugène Sue, Alexandre Dumas or George Sand. Greek Ottoman translators, particularly those active in Izmir, made a major contribution to this shift and, in 1845 alone, four major recent French novels (Sand's *Lélia*, 1833; Dumas's *Count of Monte Cristo*, 1844–5; Sue's *Mysteries of Paris*, 1842–3; and *The Wandering Jew*, 1844) were published in Greek translation in the Empire.

Interestingly, this turn to contemporary fiction, so clearly perceptible in the Greek Ottoman case, was not limited to that particular community but, on the contrary, mirrored similar evolution that had recently taken place in the publishing field of Western Europe. An analysis of nineteenth-century French bestseller lists indicates for instance a progressive – and increasingly massive – turn of the reading public towards works of contemporary fiction, at the expense of older, more canonical works which had dominated the market in the first half of the century.[6] Until 1825, the works that dominated the French bestseller lists were almost exclusively composed by authors who died before the French Revolution (Molière, Racine, La Fontaine, Perrault, Fénelon, Rousseau, Voltaire) or shortly thereafter but, in any case, before 1800 (Florian, Barthélémy). In parallel, popular authors of the seventeenth century (Molière, Racine, La Fontaine, Perrault) remained, for over a century after their death, very largely present on the publishing market in the first quarter of the nineteenth century, selling more copies than any living author – and more even than many equally canonical names of the French seventeenth century. Overall, the French book market remained, for most of the first half of the nineteenth century, largely shaped by a conception of reading as a morally beneficial and edifying activity, rather than as a leisurely one.

First serialized in the *Journal des débats* between June 1842 and October 1843 and published in book form shortly thereafter, Eugène Sue's *Mysteries of Paris* carved a new space for contemporary fiction in the French literary field of the nineteenth century. If the overnight, smashing success of the work has acquired somewhat of a mythical dimension and the images of thousands of avid readers anxiously awaiting to find out what fate – or the author – had in store for the novel's colourful and relatable characters have been somewhat romanticized in the historiography of nineteenth-century French prose, the sales numbers of the *Mysteries of Paris*, of Sue's subsequent novel *The Wandering Jew*, or of Alexandre Dumas's *Count of Monte Cristo* and *Three Musketeers* (both published in 1844 and translated into Greek in the Ottoman Empire relatively shortly thereafter) confirm the extent to which the publication of these works constituted an important shift in the French book market, just like it did, almost at the exact same time, in its Greek and, more specifically, Greek Ottoman counterpart.

Thus, far from being a purely local event, entirely disconnected from the mutations of the publishing world in Western Europe, the Greek (and Greek Ottoman) *translational shift* of the mid-1840s almost exactly mirrored the French *editorial shift* that culminated with the massive sales of novels by Sue and Dumas starting only a few years earlier. In both cases, a specific area of the cultural sphere at large (the book market as a whole in the case of France, the market for translated literature in the case of the Greek-speaking world) experienced a rapid mutation that led to the influx, on a massive scale, of works pertaining to a specific type of literature (contemporary prose fiction, both original and translated). There is no doubt that, in both cases, such a shift was ultimately the result of deep social, economic and cultural changes beyond the literary field itself; yet, it is important to note that this relatively abrupt reorientation of the publishing industry was precipitated by the unprecedented success of a select few works – original in the French case, translated in the Greek one – which happened to be largely the same ones (primarily Eugène Sue and Alexandre Dumas) in both contexts.

In the Greek Ottoman case – which, as I will show, exhibited traits that would later also characterize translation activities in other languages of the Empire – the 1840s shift was both a temporal and an aesthetic one. The overall turn to contemporary fiction and the progressive reduction of the gap between original publication and translation into Greek signalled a dramatic acceleration of the literary exchanges between Western Europe and the Greek Ottoman community. Looking at these exchanges from the vantage point of literary translation (and in particular from that of prose fiction), I argue – going against the grain of accounts that emphasize the presumed belatedness of the late Ottoman literary field vis-à-vis Western modernity – that *rapidity*, such as that with which foreign novels reached the Greek reading public of the Empire world after their original publication, was in fact a defining characteristic of the literary commerce of Tanzimat-era literary circles with Western Europe. While there existed of course exceptions to this pattern, the fact that, in the second half of the century, certain foreign novels were translated into Greek very shortly after – or even, in a few particularly striking cases, such as Xavier de Montépin *Bread Seller* (*La Porteuse de Pain*,1884) *before* – their original publication in book form in France is, I believe, indicative of how the notion that the Ottoman literary scene 'caught up' with the literature produced in Western Europe only slowly and belatedly, deserves to be recontextualized and significantly amended.

As I have noted before, this alignment, rather than disconnect, of the Greek Ottoman market for translated foreign fiction with the publishing trends of Western Europe coexisted with an additional movement towards synchronicity, this time *internal* to the Empire. Indeed, the shift towards the translation of contemporary foreign fiction that I have described in the Greek Ottoman case was not specific to that community but similarly affected all of the main literatures of the Ottoman Empire to some degree during the second half of the nineteenth century. In Armenian letters, a similar shift took place starting in the 1860s and although it happened somewhat more gradually than on the Greek Ottoman market, the evolution of translation practices was no less perceptible. Before the 1860s, all of the French novels translated into Armenian had been works originally published between the late seventeenth century and the early nineteenth century, at the very least fifty years before their first Armenian translation: Fénelon's *Telemachus* (1699), Voltaire's *Zadig* (1747) and *Micromegas* (1752), or Chateaubriand's *Atala* (1801). The landscape started to change relatively abruptly in 1863 – as it had in 1845 in the Greek case – when three French novels all originally published after 1829 – two of them by authors still alive in the 1860s – were translated into Armenian.[7] Quite tellingly, two out of three were works that had also been translated into Greek during the shift of the mid-1840s: Mérimée's *Colomba* (1840) and Sue's *Mysteries of Paris* (1842–3). Two other important works in the first group of contemporary French novels translated into Greek in the milestone year of 1845 (Dumas's *Monte Cristo* in 1866 and Sue's *Wandering Jew* in 1867) circulated in Armenian translation slightly later in the 1860s. During the same decade, Hugo's *Les Misérables* (published in French in 1862) also circulated in Armenian translation, which constituted the first instance of a foreign novel being translated into Western Armenian less than a decade after its original publication. The interval between the time of the original publication in French and the time of the first translation into Armenian would continue to decrease steadily from the mid-1870s onwards, starting with the novels of Jules Verne

– such as, for instance, *Around the World in Eighty Days*, published in French in 1873 and in Armenian in 1875 already, or *Matthias Sandorf*, published in French in 1885 and translated the same year into Armenian. By the end of the century, the vast majority of novels translated into Armenian and published in the Ottoman Empire had been published less than a decade earlier in the original.

In the case of Arabic-scripted Ottoman Turkish, the early 1870s were the moment when translators decidedly turned to contemporary fiction and concentrated their efforts on works imported from France. Dumas's *Count of Monte Cristo* (1844–6) appeared in Ottoman Turkish translation in 1872 and Verne's *Around the World in Eighty Days* was translated in 1875, only two years after its original publication in France, as had been the case for the Armenian translation of the same novel. The Ottoman Turkish case was, however, somewhat idiosyncratic in that literary translation *tout court* – or at least the translation of foreign novels – had only begun about a decade earlier in the late 1850s and early 1860s. As a result, the (extremely abridged) translation of Hugo's *Les Misérables* by Münif Pasha (published in 1862, the same year as the source text) appeared only three years after the very first book-length translation of a foreign novel into Ottoman Turkish, Fénelon's *Telemachus*, translated in 1859 by Yusuf Kamil Pasha and *before* the first translations of eighteenth-century novels such as Defoe's *Robinson Crusoe* (1719, translated in 1862), Swift's *Gulliver's Travels* (1726, translated 1872) or Rousseau's *Emile* (1762, translated 1870). As a result, the shift towards contemporary fiction was much less dramatic than in the Greek or Armenian cases, as both novels from the eighteenth century and contemporary works by living authors were all translated around the same time, although the balance ultimately shifted in favour of the second group in the 1880s and most new translations published in the last two decades of the nineteenth century were of contemporary novels.

Ottoman Turkish translations of foreign novels printed in the Armenian script started to appear before Arabic-scripted Ottoman Turkish translations. Consequently, the turn towards contemporary fiction was perhaps more noticeable in this particular corpus than in the rest of Ottoman Turkish translations. The first foreign novels to be translated in the early 1850s were Lesage's *The Lame Devil*, (translated 1853) and Chateaubriand's *The Last Abencerage* (1826, translated 1860). Eighteenth-century novels – for instance

Voltaire's *Micromégas* (1752, translated 1869) or Defoe's *Robinson Crusoe* (1719, translated 1879) – would occasionally continue to be translated into Armenian-scripted Ottoman Turkish until the late 1870s, sometimes before their first translation into Arabic-scripted Ottoman Turkish. However, these older titles would rapidly give way to more recent – and even very contemporary – novels starting in the late 1850s already, with the Armeno-Turkish translation of Sue's *Mysteries of Paris* (1842–3) in 1858, and continuing from the 1860s and 1870s onwards with works by, among many others, Montépin's *Plaster Girls* (1855, translated 1863) and Verne's *Adventures of Captain Hatteras* (1866, translated 1877).

By far the smallest with less than 20 publications before 1900, the corpus of Greek-scripted Ottoman Turkish (*karamanlidika*) translations of foreign novels nevertheless presented strikingly similar patterns. Although two novels (Heliodorus' *Aethiopica* and Defoe's *Robinson Crusoe*) had been published in Greek-scripted Ottoman Turkish in the early 1850s, the bulk of *karamanlidika* translation activities was to take place in the last two decades of the century, which saw, on average, the publication of one new translated work per year until the mid-1890s. This second phase of *karamanlidika* translations of foreign novels started with Dumas's *Count of Monte Cristo* (translated 1882) and included authors and works also translated in other languages of the Ottoman Empire during the same period. All of these translations were of French texts originally published after 1840 – with the exception of Fénelon's *Telemachus*, published somewhat late in *karamanlidika* (1887) – and included novels by a small roster of authors, primarily Eugène Sue with three works but not, strangely, *The Mysteries of Paris* or *The Wandering Jew*, and Xavier de Montépin (with six translations, a third of all *karamanlidika* translations of foreign novels).

Finally, the case of Ladino translations of foreign novels was somewhat idiosyncratic in that the corpus, relatively small until the early twentieth century, included a few works not translated into other languages of the Ottoman Empire and chosen for their Jewish themes, such as, for instance, a historical novel dealing with Iberian Jews in the Middle Ages by German rabbi Ludwig Philippson (*Hispania and Jerusalem*, 1848; translated 1887) or Theodor Hertzl's utopian novel *Altneuland* (1902; translated 1908). In addition, it would be exaggerated to speak of a translational shift towards contemporary fiction in the Sephardic case in that pre-nineteenth-century fiction had almost not been translated at all into Ladino when the first translations of novels started to appear in the mid-1870s. However, when a few translators primarily based in Istanbul started to import foreign novels on a more regular basis in the 1880s, the works they selected were, as was the case for the other communities, almost exclusively modern and contemporary French novels and, as for Ottoman Turkish translations, the most popular authors until the end of the century were Eugène Sue and Xavier de Montépin. Further attesting to the integration of Sephardic translation activities into the broader, transcommunal Ottoman publishing landscape, some of these translated novels were printed, in the *rashi* script, using Greek- or Armenian-owned presses.

Despite the fact that the translation of foreign novels did not start at the exact same time in all of the literary communities of the late Ottoman Empire, translation trends in each of them did eventually become aligned and the focus on contemporary fiction, mostly imported from France, was general by the 1880s. Thus, a novel like Xavier de Montépin's *Simone et Marie*, published in France in 1883, had circulated in Istanbul in no fewer than six different translations (Greek, Armenian, Ottoman Turkish – one Arabic-scripted, one Greek-scripted and one Armenian-scripted – and Ladino) by 1890. It is therefore possible to say that, in the last decades of the nineteenth century, the various groups that composed the fragmented late Ottoman literary landscape were at least united as to the practice of literary translation and formed together what I would like to call a 'transcommunal translational community', a community of practice cutting across linguistic and communal boundaries and collectively engaged in the translation of contemporary fiction from Western Europe.

While their appetite for imported texts united the various communities of nineteenth-century Constantinople to the point that it is possible to speak of one common, multilingual market for translated literature rather than of three discrete, monolingual markets, the degree of saturation that resulted from an exclusive focus on Western – and mostly French – works ultimately precluded the creation of an intercommunal literary consciousness that could have led to a more active engagement of each community with the cultural production of their direct neighbours. In fact, in the few spaces of literary sociability that existed at times across the many ethnic, linguistic and religious divides, the West remained the exterior point of reference in all attempts at creating an intercommunal cultural conversation: for instance, the few traces that can be found, in the Ottoman press of the second half of the century, of a dialogue, conducted in Turkish, between Greek and Armenian literati are entirely focused on a discussion of the qualities and characteristics of the contemporary French novel and bear no mention of any form of novelistic production in either Greek or Armenian.

Additionally, it is worth noting that, during the long Tanzimat period when the translation of foreign – and primarily French – novels reached quasi-industrial proportions in all of the main literary languages of the Empire, an extremely small number of novels written and published locally in one of these same languages was translated into other Ottoman languages. If we exclude instances of *transcription* rather than *translation*, as in the case of Ottoman Turkish novels published both in the Arabic and Greek or Armenian scripts, the most salient – and among the only – such examples of transcommunal translation of novels hailing from inside the Empire rather than from Western Europe include Evangelinos Misailidis' *Temaşa-i Dünya ve Cefakar-u Cefakeş* (*Theatrum Mundi, and Tyrants and Tyrannised,* 1871–2), an adaptation of a Greek novel (Gregorios Paleologos' *Polypathis,* 1839, itself based on Lesage's *Gil Blas*), as well as Turkish and Greek translations of Yervant Odian's Armenian-language novels in the 1910s.

It would be tempting to only see this element – namely the saturation of a 'peripheral' publishing market, such as that of the Ottoman Empire during the long Tanzimat period, with works imported from the West and the resulting cultural disassociation of the different literary communities of the Empire from their most direct local interlocutors – as a symptom of the unequal exchanges across the global literary realm. Yet by looking not only at what was translated in the nineteenth century but also at *how* translation was performed, I argue that it is possible to identify a narrow space of autonomy vis-à-vis the domination of imported models emanating from Western Europe which lies within the texts themselves, and in the distance, sometimes limited but more often than not rather important, between novels originally published in the West and their translations in the Ottoman Empire. Indeed, the critical evaluation of nineteenth-century 'peripheral' translations of foreign novels can never be dominated by an assumption of faithfulness but should rather strive to identify and analyse the many divergences between originals and translations. In the present case, such an approach can overturn the narratives of absolute literary dependency of the Ottoman Empire during the long Tanzimat and highlight instead the agency of Ottoman translators by bringing to light the various instances where they distanced themselves from the foreign material with which they were working. These frequent differences range from the censoring of certain passages, sometimes lengthy, to direct interventions of the translator into the storyline, sometimes addressing the reader to comment upon and/or explain elements of the setting or of the plot, sometimes interpolating entire passages of their own creation, thus creating hybrid works, partly translated and partly original, partly foreign and partly local, which blurred the boundaries of what constitutes, in the modern definition of these concepts, literary translation on the one hand, and original creation on the other.

Rather than describing, as scholarship has often done, the work of Tanzimat-era Ottoman translators negatively, and instead of framing the lacunae in their translations primarily as the tangible marks of a supposed deficiency of their translational skills or of the linguistic means at their disposal, their engagement with foreign works of contemporary prose fiction can be mostly defined as a form of critical reading, as an active process of selection aimed at correcting what the translators perceived as the weaknesses of the source material. As such, these decisions enacted by the translators can be interpreted as a form of active and conscious intervention in the very economy of the original work.

In making such a suggestion, I question the lexicon developed in translation studies to account for the de-formations that take place during the translation of a text from one language to another. In *L'épreuve de l'étranger* (The Trial of the Foreign, 1984), an otherwise important and highly influential work – whose only limitation lies perhaps in the fact that it purports to develop universally applicable tools for the study of literary translation, but remains itself entirely focused in transnational cultural exchanges between Western European literatures and is grounded in the study of highly canonical works – Antoine Berman offered a list of the 'tendencies' pertaining to the 'system of deformation' at play in 'any operation of translation.'[8] For most of these, Berman uses a terminology that insists on an idea of deficiency and connotes translation strategies negatively: 'qualitative impoverishment' (*appauvrissement qualitatif*), 'quantitative impoverishment' (*appauvrissement quantitatif*), 'destruction of rhythms' (*destruction des rhythmes*), 'destruction of underlying networks of signification' (*destructions des réseaux signifiants sous-jacents*), 'destruction of vernacular terms or their exoticization' (*destruction des termes vernaculaires ou leur exotisation*), 'erasure of linguistic superpositions' (*effacement des superpositions de langues*), 'functioning of inedequate literary horizons' (*fonctionnement d'horizons littéraires inadéquats*).

Undoubtedly, it would be easy to locate multiple examples that would seem to fit Berman's categories in translations of foreign novels published in Ottoman Turkish, Greek, Armenian or Ladino during the long Tanzimat period. At first glance, such instances would appear to confirm Tanpınar's idea of 'randomness,' not only in terms of the selection of materials to be translated but also in terms of the very praxis of translation. However, the negative connotations of the terms used by Berman tend to frame translation only in terms of their supposed shortcomings. In that regard, their use would generate, in the textual and cultural analysis of nineteenth-century translations of Western European popular fiction in a 'peripheral' space like the late Ottoman Empire, an impression of deficiency that mirrors traditionally negative accounts such as the one proposed by Tanpınar, which saw this corpus as an incomplete one, marked by the absence of canonical works.

In an essay on the work of Ottoman novelist Ahmet Midhat as a translator of foreign novels, Cemal Demircioğlu[9] lists the various terms employed by the author in several paratextual notations to describe his approach to translation. These terms – which, beyond *terceme* ('translation'), include *iktibas* ('quotation'), *nazire* ('imitation'), *muhavere* ('conversation'), *nakl* ('transposition'), or *hulâsa* ('summary') – have the great advantage, compared to Berman's categories, of shifting the focus to the agency of the translator.[10] I conclude in suggesting that this terminology, specific to the late Ottoman context, could be fruitfully used in an analysis of the translation techniques set in motion by Ottoman translators belonging to different yet intersecting communities when they endeavoured to import the Western novel and acclimatize it to the context in which they lived. The adoption of such a framework would not only help resituate the late Ottoman praxis of literary translation within the immediate cultural surroundings in which it developed in the nineteenth century; in addition, by reappraising the work of late Ottoman translators as a form of active and critical engagement with foreign literature, it would allow us to fully account for the importance of translation as a site of initial experimentation with prose fiction that played a crucial role in later processes of domestication of the novel in the literary economy of the long Tanzimat.

Notes

1 '[...] ecnebî dil ve edebiyatlarına karşı büyuk alâkaya, resmî öğretim müesseselerinin hiç bir ciddî yardımı dokunmaması yüzünden bütün kazançlar âdeta tesadüfîdir.' Ahmet M.Tanpınar, *XIX. Asır Türk Edebiyatı Tarihi* (Istanbul, 1956), p.263.
2 Şehnaz Tahir Gürçağlar, *The Politics and Poetics of Translation in Turkey, 1923- 1960* (Amsterdam – New York, 2008), p.73.
3 'Bu ilk tercümeler arasında, roman nevinin bugün hakikaten büyük tanıdığımız nümunelerinin pek az bulunması da yukarıda bahsettiğimiz tesadüfîliğin en iyi delilidir. Filhakika ne Cervantes, ne Balzac, ne Stendhal, ne Dickens bu devirde Türkçeye nakledilmemişlerdir [...] Bu keyfiyet yukarıda bahsettiğimiz, garpla fikir ve edebiyat münasebetlerimizi tanzım edecek öğretim ve kültür kurullarının yokluğunun tabiî neticesidir. Böylece, yazı hayatına giren gençler Fransızca öğrenmelerine yardım eden kitabı – çünkü çoğu tercüme yoluyla Fransızcayı öğreniyor, yahut ilerletiyordu – neşretmekle işe başlıyor ve ondan sonra da halkın en çok okuyacağı eseri naklediyordu.' Tanpınar, *XIX. Asır Türk Edebiyatı Tarihi*, p.264.
4 Martin Lyons, *Le Triomphe du Livre: une histoire sociologique de la lecture dans la France du XIXe siècle* (Paris, 1987), p.77. My translation from the original French.
5 For a more detailed account of Greek Ottoman translation trends, see Etienne Charrière, 'Borrowed Texts : Translation and the Rise of the Ottoman-Greek Novel in the Nineteenth Century', *Syn-Thèses* 6 (2013), pp.12–26, and Etienne Charrière, '"We Must Ourselves Write About Ourselves:" The Trans-Communal Rise of the Novel in the Late Ottoman Empire.' PhD Dissertation, University of Michigan, 2016.
6 See, for instance, the tables compiled by Martin Lyons (Lyons, *Le Triomphe du Livre*, pp.76–104), which cross-reference data from the national French bibliography (*Bibliographie de la France*) with nineteenth-century printers' reports in the French National Archives and which I use here.
7 For all (Western) Armenian translations of foreign novels, see entries in the bibliography of James Etmekjian, *The French Influence on the Western Armenian Renaissance, 1843–1915* (New York, 1964), p.273–82.

8 Antoine Berman, *L'épreuve de l'étranger* (Paris, 1984), p.296. I translate Berman's terms myself rather than relying on the existing English translations of his work.
9 See Cemal Demircioğlu, 'From Discourse to Practice: Rethinking "Translation" (Terceme) and Related Practices of Text Production.' PhD Dissertation, Bogaziçi University, 2005.
10 See also Özen Nergis Dolcerocca's contribution to the present volume, p. 200.

12

The Tanzimat period and its diverse cultures of translation: Towards new thinking in comparative literature

Özen Nergis Dolcerocca

The nineteenth-century Ottoman poet Tevfik Fikret describes Ahmet Midhat, the most prolific author and translator of the era, as 'nothing but a big mouth,'[1] referring to Midhat's excessive indulgence of appetite, not only in his eating and drinking, but also in his writing habits. Ahmet Hamdi Tanpınar in his *19th Century Turkish Literature* seems to agree with Fikret and refers to Midhat's literary activity as immoderate *konsomasyon* (consumption):

> In Ahmet Midhat, one should not look for any dominant influence of a literary tradition, conscious inspiration drawn from works in a tradition, not even their classification or assessment. For this giant *konsomasyon* device, Cervantes and Octave Feuillet are in the same category as Victor Hugo, Xavier de Montépin and Eugène Sue. So much so that Emile Zola could be sacrificed for Paul de Kock. Flaubert could be utterly trivialized. A novel based on such an evaluation system would of course be nothing more than a long friendly conversation crowded with various cases in point.[2]

Tanpınar continues his characterization of Midhat as an impetuous and extravagant author, using the metaphor of a tipsy man who tells amusing tales to his friends at the dinner table. Midhat overindulges in low literature for entertainment and didactic purposes, paying no heed to distinctions between the two. Unlike some of his Victorian contemporaries, he playfully merges entertaining tales of seduction, adultery, forgery or murder with a strong moral tone. He adopts local popular storytelling practices of the *meddah* or *aşık*, and blends them with European romantic and realist methods without any premeditated structure or logic. With his highly formulaic and accessible stories, he speaks to a growing reading public, paying no heed to his critics who insist on distinguishing their literary standards from those of 'the man in the street.' His literary canon is based on a very different set of literary and cultural values in which conventional hierarchies between high and low art are entirely disregarded. There seems to be an assumed equivalency between Cervantes, who overturned traditional aesthetic paradigms and produced groundbreaking works, and Eugène Sue, the commercial French author who penned the most widely read novel of the nineteenth century, Les Mystères de Paris. Zola's naturalism is secondary to the risqué novels of Paul de Kock. In this disoriented system of literary standards, established literary notions such as originality and authorship, or translation and translator are disregarded if not entirely disdained.

A polarization between serious literature and popular fiction, and the complete division between intellectuals and masses, was of course emerging during the final decades of the nineteenth century on the Ottoman cultural scene. However, Fikret and Tanpınar's deprecation of Midhat was more than contempt for the increasingly commercialized literary scene. In Midhat's popular fiction, Fikret and Tanpınar saw the reflection of Sultan Abdülhamid's despotism: literature of entertainment emptied of any serious content, such as fundamental political, social and cultural problems under the *istibdat* (tyranny) period. While strict censorship prohibited any discussion of these matters in print, the sultan's elaborate spy system made sure that public conversations were limited to *sâye-i şâhane* (a common expression for royal or imperial protection). This is the period when the author and translator Teodor Kasap was exiled for speaking against the sultan, including his translation of Molière's *L'Avare* as Pinti Hamıd (Cheapskate Hamid). However, Midhat's almost wholly apolitical and personalized mass literature remained popular, and he stayed in the good graces of the Porte, until Abdülhamid's overthrow in 1908. Continuing with Fikret's metonym, we can say that Midhat's 'giant mouth' spoke volubly to (and in place of) the local people who were not allowed to open theirs.

Tanzimat literature thus evolved under political turmoil in the final century of the Empire, with conflicts between constitutional and absolute monarchy, rising nationalist movements and their repression, modernization efforts and conservative uprisings against infidel reformers. Midhat certainly had sycophantic tendencies in his professional life to propitiate the Porte. Yet, we may retain Fikret's characterization of Midhat not merely as criticism levelled against his commercialized work and political expediency, but as a metaphor for literary activity at large in the late Ottoman Empire. We can imagine reading, writing and translation practice in the Tanzimat era as one giant mouth: a mouth that speaks many tongues, among which are Turkish, Greek, Armenian, Arabic, Hebrew, Persian and Bulgarian, with an insatiable appetite for literature both from the West and the East, regardless of their quality or history. Much like the political situation the Empire found itself in, it produced, translated and read literature in pandemonium. In Tanzimat literature, epitomized in Midhat's work, we find carnivalesque and transgressive literary practices, including disregard for canon and literary standards, multilingual and cross-cultural printing and publishing, challenging notions of authorship and 'scandalous' understanding of translation.

The emerging idea (and ideal) of national literatures would soon obliterate the multiplicity and complexity of this particular period in world literary history. While Ottoman Turkish slowly evolved into modern Turkish, stripped of its Arabic and Persian elements, including the Arabic script, other languages spoken in the empire were also gradually assimilated by other nations. Those who were left outside of nation-state logic, such as the Turkish speaking Greek-Orthodox (*Karamanlı*) and the Turcophone Armenians, disappeared from literary history altogether. In view of its flexibility, diversity, elusiveness, and hence resistance to definition, Tanzimat literature remains unintelligible to nationalist paradigms and to the world literature model, to the extent that it relies on the former. It is only recently that scholars have revisited this unique moment in literary history, marked by linguistic and literary convergences, collaborations, intersections as well as conflicts between cultures within and outside the Ottoman Empire.[3] In this chapter, I would like to revisit the nineteenth-century Ottoman literary field as a complex multilingual literary system, and demonstrate the productive challenges it poses for the field of comparative literature and translation studies. Following the increased academic attention to world literature and transnational literary studies, scholars have been looking for new avenues to locate networks of circulations and translations beyond national borders. In this respect, the nineteenth century plays a significant role in the historiography of world literature as the age of global canonization of the European novel, following the footsteps of capitalist globalization. 'One and unequal,' Franco Moretti writes, 'with a core, and a periphery (and a semi-periphery) that are bound together in a relationship of growing inequality,' uncritically mapping literary exchange onto Braudel's world-systems analysis of economic history.[4] Tanzimat authors and translators, however, formed networks of dissemination and circulation that were incompatible with such centrer-periphery cartographies of world literature. They worked within regionally marked literary and translational concepts, practices and institutions within a heterogeneous cultural scene with its peculiar forms of exchange, hybridizations and tensions.

Yet, like many other non-European cultures that fail to be typecast as synchronic 'national' literatures, the late Ottoman literature has been largely entrusted to area studies. Although such philological and historical work remains invaluable, few of these have addressed the ethnic and linguistic complexity of the nineteenth-century literary scene. The world literature model in literary studies is yet to adapt to it and appropriate it, because locating and translating archetypal masterpieces of Tanzimat can prove extremely difficult. It resists global standards of readability and authentic local categories, and therefore fails to be systematically integrated into the world literary system. As Tanpınar sarcastically puts it, Tanzimat literature is an intemperate mouth that speaks, composes and consumes so uncontrollably that it eludes classification, evaluation and comparison. In Turkey, the past two decades have seen increased interest in Tanzimat literature with crucial work being done, particularly by young scholars. They have made literary texts available to contemporary readers of Turkish via transliteration, translation and *sadeleştirme* (intralingual translation from Ottoman to modern Turkish), as well as archival research, introducing works that have remained in the margins of literary history. Recent scholarship has also parted with the traditional study of Ottoman literature that has typically approached it either through national paradigms, that systematically conceals the context of cultural transfer in Ottoman literary history,[5] or with traditionalist bias in the study of classical works like Divan poetry, both of which have resulted in overlooking its multi-ethnic composition. Despite the recent local efforts to study Tanzimat literature in its complexity, the multilingual literary polysystem of the late Empire is yet to be embedded in questions that move the field of comparative literature today.

Due to its essentially transnational character, comparative literature has traditionally been attentive to problems of linguistic and cultural translation. Yet, despite this transnational character, the discipline remained entrenched in the inherently and almost exclusively European idea of humanism,[6] until the cultural turn and the age of theory. Questions regarding linguistic and cultural translation had revolved around a common genealogy, that is, European high culture. In the past three decades, we have seen various attempts to solve this crisis of the discipline: post-colonial criticism, radical theory, deconstruction, exilic consciousness, world literature, all of which in one way or another have tried to expand the geography of comparative literature, and critiqued the idea of the primacy of Europe and Eurocentric assumptions. National boundaries have been destabilized with the introduction of linguistic-based literatures, or '-phones,' such as Anglophone, Francophone, Hispanophone, et cetera; while the idea of world literature has become a globalizing force that circulates national literatures in translation. Theory, essentially French and German, has deflated the building blocks of European culture, and post-colonial thought has challenged its authority.

Most of these efforts of expansion to reach other cultures and national languages, however, have reproduced the Europe-centred humanities, only in forms that are more attentive to its 'others'. As many scholars of the Global South have argued, European literatures and languages still remain at the core of the project of comparison. None of these attempts renounce Europe entirely; instead, they become centrifugal forces that reach out to difference, by dispersing and decentring the field, while irresistibly revolving around the core of European philology. Simon Gikandi describes this crisis in comparative literature as that of 'sustain[ing] the idea of Europe as the organizing principle of comparison in a post-European age.'[7] Although it has become commonplace to elaborate on the discipline's Eurocentrism and to claim projects that challenge it, a new comparative literature that engages seriously with the languages and literatures of the global south has a long way to go.

In view of this call for a new vision of comparativity that approaches non-European literatures with 'linguistic rigor and historical savvy,'[8] as Spivak puts it, Tanzimat Literature constitutes a compelling case set in a culturally diversified multicultural empire, with its hegemonic language and localized vernaculars. A time of far-reaching transformations, the nineteenth century saw the democratization of the printing press and the concomitant formation of a reading public. The constitution of a contested literary field paints a highly complex picture, inhabited by multiple ethnic groups, producing literature mainly in Turkish, Greek, Armenian, Hebrew, Persian and Arabic. This of course did not mean that the ethnic language coincided with the written language used by the community: as Strauss demonstrates, Greek was the language of many educated Bulgarians and Rumanians (in fact, the first translation of the commercial hit *Paul et Virginie* was into Greek by a Bulgarian translator);[9] Jewish presses predominantly published in Judeo-Spanish, whereas French became the language of the community's upper class. While Istanbul was the centre of printing and publishing, books printed in the imperial cities of Salonika and Smyrna, as well as abroad in Cairo, Vienna, Venice, Leipzig and Amsterdam, were in circulation. We observe similar complexity in scripts: alphabet choice was not always determined by religious and ethnic belonging. For instance, the Turkophone reading public used Arabic, Greek and Armenian scripts. These cases I cite here are only a small representation of the literary activity in the late Ottoman Empire, of which this volume draws a more comprehensive picture. What I would like to emphasize here is the fact that languages are not identical to communities, nations, regions or religions. Even the lingua franca of the empire, Ottoman (*lisân-ı Osmâni*), lacks any hegemonic stability, due to its peculiar tri-lingual character in between Turkish, Arabic and Persian.[10] Writing and reading in the Ottoman Empire, therefore, have always been a comparative endeavour, from classical poetry derived from the Arabo-Persian tradition, to nineteenth-century literary activity largely shaped by its translational contact with the West.

What could then constitute a translational and comparative approach to Tanzimat literature? And most importantly, how could it help us expand and reshape the existing models and concepts in comparative literary and translation studies? The discipline is still largely structured by the national paradigm, in which multilingualism is laid out along the axis of national hegemonies and minority cultures. Yet, as the late Ottoman literary scene demonstrates, the multi-ethnic communities do not necessarily fit in a structure of marginality. We can hardly think of Armenian literature in this context as literature of a minority. In view of the populations that speak the major imperial languages Greek, Armenian, Arabic and Ladino, the notion of 'minority', as much as that of 'nation', is not only inadequate but also misleading and anachronistic. What appears to be minor in our contemporary institutional understanding 'might be powerful markers of territory, power, and cultural capital in their respective regions.'[11]

Let us consider some difficulties traditional comparatists face when they encounter the late Ottoman literary scene. This is the period when Ottoman intellectuals came into close contact with the West, due to increasing interest in the foreign, partly motivated by the political and economic conjuncture. Initially, literary translations from French were intended to serve as a source of innovation (*teceddüd*) for the Ottomans in order to accomplish cultural progress (*terâkki*).[12] Translation (*terceme*) was regarded as a means to an end. New genres were introduced in the literary scene – novel, Western style drama, modern poetry and short story – by translators, who also wrote 'originals' in these forms. Most of these were 'scandalous' translations, as far as our contemporary 'pretheoretical assumptions' go: sacrilegiously free translations, pseudo-translations, authorial counterfeits, summaries, adaptations, unfaithfully domesticated rewritings or outright forgeries.[13] Take Teodor Kasap's *Pinti Hamit*, for instance: it is a translation and adaptation of Molière's *L'Avare*, domesticated within the traditional *orta oyunu* genre, because Kasap believed that outright imitation of Western works would hinder the development of national theatre. Now, who is the actual author of *Pinti Hamit*? Is it an unfaithful translation, or an imitative original? When one considers our current presuppositions about translation, how would a traditional comparatist understand Kasap's play?

Classifying such cross-cultural domesticating practices within the Euro-taxonomy of literary studies as a belated work of modern theatre, or as an imitative copy of Western forms, is undoubtedly tempting. Yet, we must consider the diachronic structure of language and the history of translation in the Ottoman Empire, where cultural models were constantly being negotiated in the modernization process. One is reminded here of the task of comparison which, as Gikandi suggests, is to dislodge, question and revise the reigning ideologies of translation and to engage with the historicity of texts produced in the non-European languages. 'The challenge of comparative literature is how to rethink the role of translation as a diachronic practice in the multiplicity of languages, some hegemonic, others subaltern.'[14] The nineteenth-century Ottoman culture produced a multilingual heterodox literary scene, shaped by debates on how to reproduce and acknowledge the foreign in the constitution of a new Ottoman vernacular. Let us consider some of the specific variations of the concept of translation one might come across in these debates: translation (*terceme*), transfer/translation (*nakl*), adaptation (*tahvil*), borrowing/adaptation (*iktibâs*), study (*mutalâa/tedkîk*), modelling (*imtisâl*), emulation/response (*tanzîr*), importing (*idhâl*), commentary (*şerh*), annotation (*tahşiye/hâşiye*), taking (*ahz*), imitation (*taklîd*), summary (*hulâsa*), exegesis (*tefsîr*), comparison/stating (*beyân*) and authoring/original (*telîf*).[15] Even the meaning of 'original' varies from its modern counterpart, because an adaptation with enough domestication could be considered an original (*telif*). Many stories in Ahmet Midhat's collection *Letaif-i Rivayat* [Finest Stories] are considered in this category.[16] None of these translation modes seamlessly fit within prevalent yet unexamined Eurocentric conceptions of translation. This incomplete list shows that, in order to be able to engage with Tanzimat, and other cross-cultural concepts of translation, we need to go beyond ideas of transfer, fidelity, equivalence and even foreign as unproblematized categories.

The 'classics debate' of 1897, for instance, illustrates different conceptualizations of cultural identity with respect to Europe. In this heated debate on translation, which involved nine writers and thirty-three articles, we find the ongoing negotiation of the linguistic and cultural differences of the foreign, various translation types, the role of the translator and the question of domestication. We can also trace the transformation of the Ottoman understanding and practice of translation due to the introduction of Western conceptions of foreignness and difference; original and translation. Some of the main positions on translation of Western 'classics' in the debate is as follows: a. we should translate (*terceme*) European classics to promote innovation in literature but we should not 'imitate' (*taklid*) them, an argument everyone seems to agree on; b. we should imitate European literature by rewriting and conveying them according to the needs of the Ottoman culture; c. translation should serve a didactic purpose for the Ottoman reading public and translators need to be selective in their choice of originals, depending on the applicability of the foreign model to the Ottoman literary tradition; d. translation should serve the purpose of keeping up with Europe; e. translations can only convey the informative content of the classics; f. the Ottoman language is deficient in relation to the European languages (mainly French); g. we should not imitate them but examine and annotate them instead.[17] Although this is a highly condensed summary of the debate, it should clarify the role translation played in shaping the nineteenth-century Ottoman cultural system.

The question of the foreign, and the overwhelming lack of equality between the source and the receiving culture, lie at the very heart of Ottoman anxiety on translation. The negotiation with the linguistic and cultural difference of Europe begins with the very choice of texts for translation. One is here reminded of Tanpınar's reproach against Ahmet Midhat (and Teodor Kasap) for their haphazard selection of novels for translation, as a result of which early translations from European novels failed to include 'the great examples of the novel form.'[18] Instead of Cervantes, Balzac, Stendhal or Dickens, the early translations had a preference for popular fiction by Octave Feuillet, Eugène Sue, Georges Ohnet, Xavier de Montépin and Jules Verne. According to Tanpınar, this failure to select 'the true works of literature' (*asıl edebiyat*) results from 'the lack of educational and cultural institutions that would regulate (*tanzim*) our intellectual and literary contact (*münasebet*) with the West.'[19] The 'arbitrary' (*keyfi*) and 'accidental' (*tesadüfi*) nature of translation choices in the early stages of the Tanzimat period is thus regarded as a lack of literary standards and value systems.[20] Tanpınar's interpretation is partly a retrospective re-evaluation of nineteenth-century literary history, after this chaotic literary scene was disciplined into a unified national structure (i.e. Modern Turkish Literature), with comparable cultural entities in the West. The most illuminating part of his observation is the arbitrary and subjective selection of the translated text, because at some level all translations are selections, whether by personal preference, institutional choice or 'literary capital.'[21]

In late Ottoman translations and debates, we can observe the very *process* of such selections, which aim to establish values and institutions, and revisit the existing ones. The accidental and the arbitrary in the early translational encounter with the West is in fact a question of incommensurability with any canonical framework. What seems an uninformed or awkward choice of text for translation today, like the risqué novels of de Kock, is in fact part of a larger literary field that is in the process of negotiating hierarchies, forming canons and complicating standards in the domestic culture. Ahmet Midhat's following statement demonstrates such discursive strategies of translation:

> We are not in favour of literal translation. We read a sentence, a statement, or even a page in French and rewrite what we understand from it independently in Ottoman. That is why our translations appear to have been written originally in Ottoman. Let us try to translate Emile Augier's *L'Aventurière* in this way. But this work was not written in ordinary prose ... We pondered a great deal on how to translate a work written with such eloquence. Then we remembered the novel *Amiral Bing*, which we had written by way of translation.[22]

This extract is from his preface to *Nedamet mi? Heyhat* (Remorse? Alas!), which was serialized with the subtitle 'A Novel Borrowed from Emile Augier', and Ahmet Midhat cited as the author.[23] The preface was titled 'A Friendly Chat for the Preface,' quite in line with Tanpınar's characterization of him as an amicable babbler. He cites various translation practices he employs, in order to explain the status of the two works in question and shows that the domestication effect of rewriting in translation overwrites foreignness, and the translated text appears local (*re'sen Osmanlıca*). Yet, it seems that Augier's play retained unassimilable aspects of the source culture, reportedly its elevated poetic language. Midhat then decides to 'write it by way of translation,' just like he did in *Amiral Bing*, which is 'borrowed' from a popular play, *L'Amiral de l'Escadre bleue* by M. Paul Foucher. In order to inscribe them with domestic meaning, he converts them into novels (*romana tahvil ederek*). Curiously, Midhat lists his name as the author (*muharrir*) for the former and translator (*mütercim*) for the latter, although he reports that he has used the same techniques. He gives them new titles because he finds the French titles 'unworthy' (*liyakatsız*) of works of such eloquence. Among his other scandalous practices is his famous 'translation' of *Le Cid*, in the form of a summary, which is almost four times longer than Corneille's play.

Such idiosyncratic translation practices, which would likely be categorized as a self-confessed literary fraud today, were not uncommon in literary history, particularly when nineteenth-century popular fiction is concerned. We could even go back to late seventeenth-century France, following Antoine Berman's observations, where a renowned poet of the time wrote in strikingly similar terms to those of his late Ottoman counterparts: 'if there is any merit in translating [into French], it is perhaps only to perfect the original, if possible, to embellish it, to appropriate it, to give it a national air and, in some way, to naturalize this foreign plant.'[24] Lack of concern for fidelity could be part of a literary tradition, especially in those cultures that 'did not need to go through the law of the foreign to affirm its identity.'²⁵ This is certainly the case for the Ottoman culture: located in between Turkish, Persian and Arabic, Ottoman literary production perceived the last two as literary models, not in terms of their own belatedness, weakness or lack, but with intention to assimilate through imitative practice. It was not so much an opening of Ottoman culture to the foreign as revising and incorporating them into the domestic sphere. Part of Midhat's ideas on translation originate in this imperial understanding of literary imitation, which was a prominent practice before the nineteenth century. Ottoman poets 'borrowed' from these Islamic sources, in order to (re)write originals derived from the classic works of Arabic and Persian origin. Classic Ottoman poetry could be interpreted as a chain of creative imitation or responses, very much like *imitatio* in Latin poetry, a dynamic and fruitful process where the poet varies, praises, improves or exceeds the original.²⁶ Therefore, when confronted with the inevitability of cultural exchange with the West in the nineteenth century, many Ottoman intellectuals resorted to the strategies inherent in the 'Ottoman Interculture.'²⁷ Regarding Muallim Naci's attempts at imitating Western classics to create a domestic tragedy genre, for instance, Midhat points out the difficulty of writing a work comparable with those of Racine and Corneille. Yet, he adds, 'it is possible to imitate Voltaire's *Henriade* because it is a *şahnameh*.'²⁸ As long as the source text responds to or extends domestic conventions – in this case the Persian epic genre of the book of kings – it could be inscribed in the receiving literary system.

The Tanzimat tradition of creative imitation provided a point of entry for Western forms, but it soon became clear that the existing standards and practices had to be entirely revised and replaced with new conceptions from the source culture. Values and institutions at home gradually changed, favouring the ideas of transfer, fidelity and equivalence. Defenders of positivism and realist fiction, prominently Beşir Fuad and Halid Ziya, were committed to restoring and preserving the foreign, rather than to creative imitation, which, by then, was employed to catch up with the West or to compensate for domestic lack. By doing so, they developed an 'ethical' approach to translation that remains 'respectful of the source language and culture, open to their differences, and alert to its own linguistic refigurations.'²⁹ This ethical attitude of the *Servet-i Fünun* movement, precursors of literary modernism, was simultaneous with what Lawrence Venuti calls 'a political agenda.' They actively tried to 'set going processes of defamiliarization, canon reformation, ideological critique, and institutional change,[30] by displacing the linguistic and cultural differences of the foreign in translation, through a domestic difference. They thus allowed the foreign culture, specifically French realism in this case, to 'revise and develop domestic values and institutions'. While this view was adapted, and later revised for the national agenda, during the process of cultural transformation and centralization in the late Ottoman Empire through the early Republic of Turkey,[31] other modes of translation – some 'scandalous' and some 'unethical' – gradually moved to the margins of the literary field, in conformity with global literary standards.

For comparatists and the discipline's progressively enlarging explorations of the non-West, then, the problem of methodology arises in the contradiction between synchronic and diachronic approaches to translation. Once we engage with the historicity of translations produced during the Tanzimat period, it becomes evident that privileged paradigms of translation are overly limited. Attention to the Tanzimat would therefore be, as Spivak would put it, 'inconvenient and impractical' for a traditional comparatist.[32] The scale of literary and translational values change as we move from Europe to Asia, from nation to region, from one period to another, and from region to region. For instance, if we imposed the literary value system of India onto the Indian Ocean, or of imperial Istanbul onto its periphery Budapest, we would be committing 'epistemicide in relation to the concept of translation'.[33] There is enormous variation in translation models throughout the ages and across cultures. The Tanzimat case reminds us that we need to move scales each time we do a work of comparison, which would then save scholars of non-European literature from 'watering down conventions', or rendering works 'commensurable, transparent and consumable' to cater to the needs of the global literary system.[34] Perhaps in the light of what has been argued here, it might be time to invent a new way of studying cultural circulation and hybridization in multicultural empires that precede global capitalism, and that remain outside of colonial maps.

Notes

1 '*Yalnız koca bir fem/ Bir dağ gibi âdem*', cited in Ahmet Hamdi Tanpınar, *XIX. Asır Türk Edebiyatı Tarihi* (Istanbul, 2008), p.415.

2   Ibid.
3   See the case studies in Mehmet Fatih Uslu and Fatih Altuğ (eds.), *Tanzimat Ve Edebiyat: Osmanlı İstanbulu'nda Modern Edebi Kültür* (Istanbul, 2014).
4   Franco Moretti, 'Conjectures on World Literature', *New Left Review*, (2000), pp.54–68.
5   See Victoria R. Holbrook, 'Concealed Facts, Translation and the Turkish Literary Past', in Saliha Paker (ed.), *Translations: (Re)shaping of Literature and Culture* (Istanbul, 2002), pp.77–107.
6   I use the term humanism inflicted with European cultures, in line with Franz Fanon's critique of European humanism, and his call for an anti-racist humanism. See Frantz Fanon, *Peau Noire Masques Blancs* (Paris, 1982).
7   Simon Gikandi, 'Contested Grammars: Comparative Literature, Translation, and the Challenge of Locality', in Ali Behdad et al. (eds), *A Companion to Comparative Literature* (Hoboken, NJ, 2011).
8   Gayatri Chakravorty Spivak, *Death of a Discipline* (New York, 2003), p.5.
9   Johann Strauss, 'Who Read What in the Ottoman Empire (19th–20th centuries)?', *Middle Eastern Literatures*, 6:1, (2003), pp.39–76. See also Charrière, 'We Must Ourselves Write About Ourselves', *passim*.
10 See Paker, *Translations*.
11 Gikandi, 'Contested Grammars', p.265.
12 This view was prominent among leading authors such Kemal Paşazade Said and Ahmet Midhat, among others.
13 For the problem of Eurocentric pretheoretical assumptions about translation see Maria Tymoczko, *Enlarging Translation, Empowering Translators* (New York, 2010). For scandals of translation, see Lawrence Venuti, *The Scandals of Translation: Towards an Ethics of Difference* (London, 2006).
14 Gikandi, 'Contested Grammars', p.259.
15 See Cemal Demircioğlu's unpublished dissertation 'From Discourse to Practice: Rethinking "Translation" (Terceme) and Related Practices of Text Production', (Bogaziçi University, 2005) for an informative study on late Ottoman translation practices.
16 For an extensive study on the bibliography of Ahmet Midhat's work see Nüket Esen (ed.), *Ahmet Midhat Karı Koca Masalı ve Ahmet Midhat Bibliyografyası* (Istanbul, 1999).
17 For a detailed discussion of the debate, see Saliha Paker, 'Ottoman conceptions of translation and its practice: The 1897 "Classics debate" as a focus for examining change', in Theo Hermans (ed.), *Translating Others, Volume 2* (London, 2014), pp.325–48.

18 'Bu ilk tercümeler arasında, roman nev'inin bugün hakikaten büyük tanıdığımız numunelerinin pek az bulunması da yukarıda bahsettiğimiz tesadüfîliğin en iyi delilidir.'
19 Tanpınar, *XIX. Asır Türk Edebiyatı Tarihi*, pp.264–65.
20 See also Etienne Charrière's contribution to the present volume, p.178.
21 See Pascale Casanova, *The World Republic of Letters* (Cambridge, MA, 2004). According to the much contested and influential analysis of Casanova, literature produces a specific form of value, literary capital, which is a specific form of prestige national literatures accumulate, depending on centres of literary power.
22 Cited in Cemal Demircioğlu's dissertation, p.252: [. . .*biz terceme-i ayniyye taraftarı değiliz. Fransızca bir cümleyi, bir kelâmı hatta bir sahifeyi okuruz. Ne anlar isek onu müstakillen yani yeniden Osmanlıca yazarız. İşte bunun için bizim tercemelerimiz resen Osmanlıca yazılmış gibi olur. Haydi Emil Öjye'nin [in Turkish transcription] Serseri'sini de böyle terceme edelim. Fakat bu eser öyle âsar-ı adiyye-i mensureden değil. . . . Bu kadar itinalı eserin ne yolda tercemesi lâyık olacağı bizi bihakkın düşündürmeye başladı. Derken aklımıza vaktiyle terceme yollu yazmış olduğumuz 'Amiral Bing' romanı geldi.*
23 'Tefrika / Nedamet mi? Heyhat! / Emil Ujiye'den Muktebes Roman/ Muharriri Ahmed Midhat / Mukaddime Makamında bir Hasbihal.' Some issues of the novel, serialized in Tercuman-I Hakikat is digitized and could be accessed via Ozyegin University's tefrikalar collection. The library record has curiously catalogued Emile Augier as the author.
24 Cited in Antoine Berman, *The Experience of the Foreign: Culture and Translation in Romantic Germany* (Albany, NY, 1992), p.199.
25 Ibid, p.36.
26 See Walter G. Andrews, 'Starting Over Again: Some Suggestions for Rethinking Ottoman Divan Poetry in the Context of Translation and Transmission', in Saliha Paker (ed.). *Translations*, pp.15–40.
27 Saliha Paker, 'Translation as *Terceme* and *Nazire*: Culture-bound Concepts and their Implications for a Conceptual Framework for Research on Ottoman Translation History' Theo Hermans (ed.), *Crosscultural Transgressions, Research Models in Translation*, pp.120–43.
28 Cited in Cemal Demircioğlu's dissertation, p.158.
29 See Sandra Bermann's Introduction to Sandra Bermann and Michael Wood (eds.), *Nation, Language, and the Ethics of Translation* (Princeton, 2005), pp.1–10.
30 Lawrence Venuti, 'Translation, Community, Utopia', in Lawrence Venuti (ed.), *The Translation Studies Reader* (London, 2012), p.469.

31 For an informative study on the translation practices of the early republican Turkey, see Şehnaz Tahir Gürçağlar, *The Politics and Poetics of Translation in Turkey*, 1923–1960 (Amsterdam – New York, 2008).
32 Spivak, *Death of a Discipline*, p.10.
33 Maria Tymoczko, 'Cultural Hegemony and the Erosion of Translation Communities,' in A. Behdad et al. (eds), *A Companion to Comparative Literature*, p.166.
34 Gikandi, 'Contested Grammars', pp.260–1.

Bibliography

Ahmet Hikmet. 'Eslafta Dekadanlık ve Şeyh Galib'. *Servet-i Fünun* nr. 393 (22 September 1898).
Ahmet Midhat Efendi. 'Dekadanlar'. *Sabah* nr. 2680 (22 March 1897).
Ahmet Midhat Efendi. 'Klasikler ve Hüseyin Sabri'. *Tercüman-ı Hakikat* nr. 5912 (2 October 1897).
Ahmet Midhat Efendi. 'İcmal-i Edebisi Muharririne'. *Tercüman-ı Hakikat* nr. 6326 (5 December 1898).
Ahmet Midhat Efendi. *Letaif-i Rivayat*. Edited by Fazıl Gökçek and Sabahattin Çağın. Istanbul: Çağrı Yayınları, 2001.
Ahmet Midhat Efendi. *Fenni Bir Roman yahut Amerika Doktorları*. Edited by Nuri Sağlam and Fatih Andı. Ankara: Türk Dil Kurumu, 2003.
Ahmet Midhat Efendi. *Müşahedat*. Istanbul: Dergah Yayınları, 2013.
Ahmet Midhat Efendi. *Felâtun Bey and Râkım Efendi*. Translated by Melih Levi and Monica M. Ringer. Syracuse: Syracuse University Press, 2016.
Ahmet Rasim. *Şehir Mektupları*. Istanbul: İnkılap Yayınları, 2012.
And, Metin. *Tanzimat ve İstibdat Döneminde Türk Tiyatrosu (1839–1908)*. Ankara: Türkiye İş Bankası Kültür Yayınları, 1972.
Anderson, Benedict. *Imagined Communities*. London: Verso, 2006.
Andic, Fuat and Suphan Andic. *The Last of the Ottoman Grandees: The Life and the Political Testament of Âli Paşa*. Bibliotheca Ottomanica 2. Istanbul: Isis Press, 1996.
Andrews, Walter. *Poetry's Voice, Society's Song: Ottoman Lyric Poetry*. Seattle: University of Washington Press, 1985.
Andrews, Walter G. 'Starting Over Again: Some Suggestions for Rethinking Ottoman Divan Poetry in the Context of Translation and Transmission'. In Paker, Saliha (ed.). *Translations: (Re)shaping of Literature and Culture*. Istanbul: Bogaziçi University Press, 2002: 15–40.
Apter, Emily. *Against World Literature: On the Politics of Untranslatability*. New York: Verso, 2013.
Aracı, Emre. 'Naum Theatre: The Lost Opera House of Istanbul. Part I'. *Turkish Area Studies Review: Bulletin of the Turkish Area Study Group* 17 (2011).
Aytürk, İlker. 'Turkish Linguists Against the West: The Origins of Linguistic Nationalism in Atatürk's Turkey'. *Middle Eastern Studies* 40:6 (2004), 1–25.

Baer, Marc. *The Dönme: Jewish Converts, Muslim Revolutionaries, and Secular Turks.* Palo Alto: Stanford University Press, 2010.

Baer, Marc. *Honored by the Glory of Islam: Conversion and Conquest in Ottoman Europe.* Oxford: Oxford University Press, 2011.

Beecroft, Alexander. *An Ecology of World Literature: From Antiquity to the Present Day.* New York: Verso, 2015.

Benjamin, Walter. 'The Task of the Translator'. In *Selected Writings: Volume 1 (1913–1926)*, ed. Marcus Bullock and Michael W. Jennings. Cambridge, MA: The Belknap Press of Harvard University Press, 1996, 253–63.

Berkes, Niyazi. *The Development of Secularism in Turkey.* Montreal: McGill University Press, 1964.

Berman, Antoine. *L'épreuve de l'étranger.* Paris: Seuil, 1984.

Berman, Antoine. *The Experience of the Foreign.* Translated by S. Heyvaert. Albany, NY: SUNY Press, 1992.

Bermann, Sandra, and Michael Wood (eds). *Nation, Language and the Ethics of Translation.* Princeton: Princeton University Press, 2005.

Bernheimer, Charles. *Decadent Subjects: The Idea of Decadence in Art, Literature, Philosophy, and Culture of the Fin de Siècle in Europe.* Baltimore: The Johns Hopkins University Press, 2002.

Cankara, Murat 'Reading Akabi, (Re-)Writing History: On The Questions of Currency and Interpretation of Armeno-Turkish Fiction'. In Balta, E. and M. Ölmez (eds). *Cultural Encounters in the Turkish-Speaking Communities of the Late Ottoman Empire.* Istanbul: The Isis Press, 2014.

Casanova, Pascale. *The World Republic of Letters.* Translated by M. B. DeBevoise, Cambridge, MA: Harvard University Press, 2004.

Celal Nuri. *Kadınlarımız.* Istanbul: İctihad Matbaası, 1331 [1913].

Celal Nuri. *Harbden Sonra Türkleri Yükseltelim.* Istanbul: Cemiyet Kütüphanesi, 1917.

Cenap Şahabettin. 'Yeni Tabirat'. *Servet-i Fünun* nr. 330 (8 July 1897).

Cenap Şahabettin. 'Dekadizm Nedir?' *Servet-i Fünun* nr. 344 (14 October 1897).

Charle, Christophe. *Histoire sociale de la France au XIXe siècle.* Paris: Seuil, 1991.

Charrière, Etienne. 'Borrowed Texts : Translation and the Rise of the Ottoman-Greek Novel in the Nineteenth Century'. *Syn-Thèses* 6 (2013): 12–26.

Charrière, Etienne. '"We Must Ourselves Write About Ourselves:" The Trans-Communal Rise of the Novel in the Late Ottoman Empire'. PhD Dissertation. University of Michigan: 2016.

Chateaubriand, François-René. *Atala.* Paris: Gabriel Roux, 1801.

Clancy-Smith, Julia. *Rebel and Saint: Muslim Notables, Populist Protest, Colonial Encounters (Algeria and Tunisia, 1800–1904).* Berkeley and Los Angeles: University of California Press, 1994.

Clancy-Smith, Julia, and Frances Gouda (eds) *Domesticating the Empire: Race, Gender, and Family Life in French and Dutch Colonialism*. Charlottesville: University of Virginia Press, 1998.

Congrégation des Soeurs de Saint-Joseph de l'Apparition. *La Bienheureuse Emilie de Vialar: souvenirs et documents*. Oratorus Saint Léon, 1901.

Curtis, Sarah A. *Civilizing Habits: Women Missionaries and the Revival of French Empire*. Oxford: Oxford University Press, 2012.

Damrosch, David. *What is World Literature?* Princeton: Princeton University Press, 2003.

Delap, Lucy. 'The "Woman Question" and the Origins of Feminism'. In Jones, Gareth S., and Gregory Claeys. *The Cambridge History of Nineteenth-Century Political Thought*. Cambridge: Cambridge University Press, 2011.

Demircioğlu, Cemal. 'From Discourse to Practice: Rethinking "Translation" (Terceme) and Related Practices of Text Production'. PhD Dissertation, Bogaziçi University: 2005.

Demircioğlu, Cemal. 'Translating Europe: The Case of Ahmet Midhat as an Agent of Translation'. In Milton, John, and Paul Bandia (eds). *Agents of Translation*. Amsterdam – Philadelphia: John Benjamins, 2009.

Deringil, Selim. *Conversion and Apostasy in the Late Ottoman Empire*. Cambridge: Cambridge University Press, 2012.

Deringil, Selim. *The Well-Protected Domains: Ideology and the Legitimation of Power in the Ottoman Empire 1876–1909*. London – New York: I.B. Tauris, 2011.

Deringil, Selim. '"They Live in a State of Nomadism and Savagery": The Late Ottoman Empire and the Post-Colonial Debate'. *Comparative Studies in Society and History* 45, no. 2 (1 April 2003): 311–42.

Donzel-Verdeil, Chantal. *Les Jésuites de Syrie, 1830–1864: Une mission auprès des Chrétiens d'Orient au début des réformes ottomanes*. Lille: Atelier national de reproduction des thèses.

Durmaz, Recep. 'Celal Nuri İleri ve Ati gazetesi'. PhD dissertation, Marmara University, 1991.

Esen, Nüket (ed.). *Ahmet Midhat Karı Koca Masalı ve Ahmet Midhat Bibliyografyası*. Istanbul: Kaf Yayınları, 1999.

Essertel, Yannick. *L'aventure missionnaire lyonnaise, 1815–1962: De Pauline Jaricot À Jules Monchanin*. Paris: Cerf, 2001.

Etmekjian, James. *The French Influence on the Western Armenian Renaissance, 1843–1915*. New York: Twayne, 1964.

Ertürk, Nergis. *Grammatology and Literary Modernity in Turkey*. Oxford: Oxford University Press, 2011.

Evin, Ahmet Ö. *Origins and Development of the Turkish Novel*. Minneapolis: Bibliotheca Islamica, 1983.

Fanon, Frantz. *Peau noire, masques blancs.* Paris: Seuil, 1982.

Feldman, Burton, and Robert D. Richardson. *The Rise of Modern Mythology, 1680–1860.* Bloomington: Indiana University Press, 1972.

Finn, Robert. *The Early Turkish Novel: 1872–1900.* Istanbul: The Isis Press, 1984.

Fortna, Benjamin. 'Education and Autobiography at the End of the Ottoman Empire'. *Die Welt des Islams* 41/1 (2001): 1–31.

Fortna, Benjamin. *Learning to Read in the Late Ottoman Empire and the Early Turkish Republic.* London: Palgrave Macmillan, 2011.

Frangoudaki, Anna, and Çağlar Keyder (eds). *Ways to Modernity in Greece and Turkey: Encounters with Europe, 1850–1950.* London and New York: I.B. Tauris, 2007.

Gikandi, Simon. 'Contested Grammars: Comparative Literature, Translation, and the Challenge of Locality', in Behdad, Ali and D. Thomas (eds). *A Companion to Comparative Literature.* Hoboken, NJ: John Wiley & Sons, 2011.

Girle, Rod. *Possible Worlds.* Chesham: Acumen, 2003.

Göçek, Fatma Müge. *Rise of the Bourgeoisie, Demise of Empire: Ottoman Westernization and Social Change.* Oxford: Oxford University Press, 1996.

Gökalp, Ziya. *Turkish Nationalism and Western Civilization: Selected Essays of Ziya Gökalp.* Edited and Translated by Niyazi Berkes. Crows Nest: Allen & Unwin, 1959.

Grayzel, Susan R. *Women's Identities at War: Gender, Motherhood, and Politics in Britain and France during the First World War.* Chapel Hill: University of North Carolina Press, 1999.

Grayzel, Susan R. *Women and the First World War.* New York: Longman, 2002.

Gürbilek, Nurdan, 'Dandies and Originals: Authenticity, Belatedness, and the Turkish Novel'. *The South Atlantic Quarterly* 102, no. 2 (2003): 599–628.

Gürbilek, Nurdan. *Kötü Çocuk Türk.* Istanbul: Metis, 2011.

H. Nazım. 'Musahabe-i Edebiye 38'. *Servet-i Fünun* nr. 370 (14 April 1898).

Hale, Bob and Avi Hoffman. *Modality: Metaphysics, Logic, and Epistemology.* Oxford: Oxford University Press, 2010.

Hanioğlu, M. Şükrü. 'Blueprints for a Future Society: Late Ottoman Materialists on Science, Religion, and Art', in Özdalga, Elizabeth (ed.). *Late Ottoman Society: The Intellectual Legacy.* London: Routledge, 2005.

Hazareesingh, Sudhir. *From Subject to Citizen: The Second Empire and the Emergence of Modern French Democracy.* Princeton: Princeton University Press, 2014.

Hendy, Andrew von. *The Modern Construction of Myth.* Bloomington: Indiana University Press, 2002.

Herzog, Christoph and Raoul Motika. 'Orientalism alla turca: Late 19th/Early 20th Century Ottoman Voyages into the Muslim "Outback"'. *Die Welt des Islams* 40.2 (July 2000): 139–95.

Hobsbawm, E. J. *Nations and Nationalism since 1780: Programme, Myth, Reality.* Cambridge: Cambridge University Press, 1992.

Holbrook, Victoria. *The Unreadable Shores of Love: Turkish Modernity and Mystic Romance.* Austin: University of Texas Press, 1994.

Holbrook, Victoria. 'Concealed Facts, Translation and the Turkish Literary Past', in Paker, Saliha (ed.). *Translations: (Re)shaping of Literature and Culture.* Istanbul: Bogaziçi University Press, 2002: 77–107.

Hüseyin Cahit. *Kavgalarım.* Istanbul: Tanin Matbaası, 1910.

Imber, Colin. *The Ottoman Empire, 1300–1650: The Structure of Power.* New York: Palgrave Macmillan, 2002.

Jameson, Fredric, 'Third-World Literature in the Era of Multinational Capitalism'. *Social Text.* 15 (Autumn 1986), 65–88.

Jensen, Lamar. 'The Ottoman Turks in Sixteenth Century French Diplomacy'. *The Sixteenth Century Journal* 16.4 (December 1985): 451–70.

Judson, Pieter M. *Guardians of the Nation: Activists on the Language Frontiers of Imperial Austria.* Cambridge: Harvard University Press, 2007.

Kaplan, Ramazan. *Cumhuriyet Dönemi Türk Romanında Köy.* Ankara: Kültür ve Turizm Bakanlığı, 1988.

Kara, İsmail. *Din ile Modernleşme Arasında Çağdaş Türk Düşüncesinin Meseleleri.* Istanbul: Dergâh Yayınları, 2005.

Keyder, Çağlar. *State and Class in Turkey: A Study in Capitalist Development.* London: Verso, 1987.

Khoury, Philip S. *Urban Notables and Arab Nationalism: The Politics of Damascus 1860–1920.* Cambridge: Cambridge University Press, 2003.

Knuuttila, Sino. *Modern Modalities: Studies of the History of Modal Theories from Medieval Nominalism to Logical Positivism.* Dordrecht: Kluwer Academic Publishers, 1988.

Koçak, Orhan. '"Westernisation Against the West": Cultural Politics in the Early Turkish Republic'. In Kerslake, Celia, Kerem Öktem, and Philip Robins (eds). *Turkey's Engagement with Modernity: Conflict and Change in the Twentieth Century.* New York: Palgrave Macmillan, 2010.

Kühn, Thomas. 'Shaping and Reshaping Colonial Ottomanism: Contesting Boundaries of Difference and Integration in Ottoman Yemen'. *Comparative Studies of South Asia, Africa and the Middle East* 27.2 (2007): 315–31.

Kurt. *Celal Nuri İleri'nin Romanları (Perviz-Ölmeyen-Merhume-Ahir Zaman).* Ankara: Kurgan Edebiyat, 2012.

Langlois, Claude. 'Le Catholicisme au féminin / Women and Catholicism'. *Archives de Sciences Sociales Des Religions* 57. 1 (1984): 29–53.

Leiss, Elizabeth and Werner Abraham. *Modes of Modality: Modality, Typology, and Universal Grammar.* Amsterdam: John Benjamins Publishing Company, 2014.

Lewis, Reina. *Rethinking Orientalism: Women, Travel, and the Ottoman Harem.* 1st edition. New Brunswick, NJ: Rutgers University Press, 2004.

Lyons, Martin. *Le Triomphe du Livre: une histoire sociologique de la lecture dans la France du XIXe siècle.* Paris: Promodis, 1987.

Makdisi, Ussama. *The Culture of Sectarianism: Community, History, and Violence in Nineteenth-Century Ottoman Lebanon.* Berkeley: University of California Press, 2000.

Makdisi, Ussama. 'Ottoman Orientalism'. *American Historical Review* 107.3 (June 2002): 768–796.

Mardin, Şerif. *Türkiye'de Din ve Siyaset.* Istanbul: İletişim Yayınları, 1991.

Mehmed Mizancı Murad. *Turfanda mı yoksa Turfa mı?* Istanbul: Mahmud Bey Matbaası, 1308 [1891].

Mehmed Mizancı Murad. *Turfanda mı yoksa Turfa mı?* Istanbul: Bilge Kültür Sanat, 2012.

Moretti, Franco, 'Conjectures on World Literature'. *New Left Review* 1 (September–October 2000): 54–68.

Mühürcüoğlu, Korhan, 'The Alla Franca Dandy; Modernity and the Novel in the Late 19th-Century Ottoman Empire'. *British Journal of Middle Eastern Studies,* September 4, 2018 (online publication): 1–21.

Namık Kemal. *İntibah.* Istanbul: Özgür Yayınları, 2006.

Nichanian, Marc. *Mourning Philology: Art and Religion at the Margins of the Ottoman Empire.* Translated by G. M. Goshgarian and Jeff Fort. New York: Fordham University Press, 2014.

Nichanian, Marc. *The Historiographic Perversion.* Translated by Gil Anidjar. New York: Columbia University Press, 2009.

Œuvre Pontificale Missionaire de la Propagation de la Foi. *Annales de la Propagation de la Foi.* Paris: Librairie ecclésiastique de Poussielgue-Rusand, 1834–1920.

Œuvre Pontificale Missionaire de la Propagation de la Foi. *Les Missions Catholiques: Bulletin hebdomadaire de l'Oeuvre de la Propagation de la Foi.* Paris: Challamel, 1868–1964.

Owens, Jonathan (ed.). *The Oxford Handbook of Arabic Linguistics.* Oxford: Oxford University Press, 2018.

Paker, Saliha, 'Translation as *Terceme* and *Nazire*: Culture-Bound Concepts and Their Implications for a Conceptual Framework for Research on Ottoman Translation History'. In Hermans, Theo (ed.). *Crosscultural Transgressions, Research Models in Translation Studies. Volume II: Historical and Ideological Issues.* London: Routledge, 2002: 120–43.

Paker, Saliha. 'Ottoman Conceptions of Translation and Its Practice: The 1897 "Classics Debate" as a Focus for Examining Change' in Hermans, Theo (ed.). *Translating Others*. Vol. 2. London: Routledge, 2014: 325–48

Palmer, F. R. *Mood and Modality*. Cambridge: Cambridge University Press, 2001.

Parla, Jale. *Babalar ve Oğullar: Tanzimat Romanının Epistemolojik Temelleri*. Istanbul: İletişim Yayınları, 1990.

Pitts, Jennifer. 'Republicanism, Liberalism, and Empire in Post-Revolutionary France'. In Muthu, Sankar (ed.). *Empire and Modern Political Thought*. Cambridge: Cambridge University Press, 2012.

Pollock, Sheldon. 'Cosmopolitan and Vernacular in History'. *Public Culture* 12.3 (2000): 591–625.

Poston, L., *Islamic Daʻwah in the West: Muslim Missionary Activity and the Dynamics of Conversion to Islam*. Oxford: Oxford University Press, 1992.

Recaizade Mahmut Ekrem. *Araba Sevdası*. Istanbul: Özgür Yayınları, 2014.

Recaizade Mahmut Ekrem. *Araba Sevdası: Eleştirel Basım*. Istanbul: İletişim Yayınları, 2017.

Reşat Fevzi. 'Fecr-i Âtî Nasıl Bir Teşekküldü'. *Uyanış/Servet-i Fünun* (1930).

Ringer, Monica M. *Pious Citizens: Reforming Zoroastrianism in Iran and India*. Syracuse: Syracuse University Press, 2011.

Robbins, Bruce and Paulo Lemos Horta, and Kwame Anthony Appiah. *Cosmopolitanisms* (eds). New York: New York University Press, 2017.

Said, Edward W. *Orientalism*. New York: Vintage, 1979.

Schatkowski Schilcher, Linda. *Families in Politics: Damascene Factions and Estates of the 18th and 19th Centuries*. Stuttgart: F. Steiner Verlag, 1985.

Scott, James C. *Seeing like a State: How Certain Schemes to Improve the Human Condition Have Failed*. New Haven: Yale University Press, 1999.

al-Shidyāq, Aḥmad Fāris. *Leg over Leg*. Translated by Humphrey T. Davies. New York: New York University Press, 2015

Shissler, A. Holly. 'Haunting Ottoman Middle-class Sensibility: Ahmet Midhat Efendi's Gothic'. In Booth, Marilyn, and Claire Savina (eds). *Translation and Circulation in the Late Ottoman World*. Edinburgh: Edinburgh University Press, 2019.

Shissler, A. Holly. 'The Harem as the Seat of Middle-class Industry and Morality: The Fiction of Ahmet Midhat Efendi' in Booth, Marilyn, *Harem Histories: Envisioning Places and Living Spaces*. Durham: Duke University Press, 2010.

Skinner, Quentin. 'On Performing and Explaining Linguistic Actions'. *The Philosophical Quarterly* 21.82 (1971): 1.

Skinner, Quentin. *Visions of Politics: Volume 1: Regarding Method*. Cambridge: Cambridge University Press, 2007.

Sluglett, Peter. *The Urban Social History of the Middle East, 1750–1950*. Syracuse: Syracuse University Press, 2008.

Somel, Selçuk Akşin. *The Modernization of Public Education in the Ottoman Empire, 1839–1908: Islamization, Autocracy, and Discipline*. Leiden: Brill, 2001.

Spivak, Gayatri Chakravorty. *Death of a Discipline*. New York: Columbia University Press, 2003.

Spector, Scott. *Prague Territories: National Conflict and Cultural Innovation in Kafka's Fin de Siècle*. Berkeley: University of California Press, 2000.

Stone, Frank A. *The Rub of Cultures in Modern Turkey: Literary Views on Education*. Bloomington: Indiana University Publications, 1973.

Strauss, Johann. 'Who Read What in the Ottoman Empire (19th–20th Centuries)?' *Middle Eastern Literatures* 6.1 (2010): 39–76.

Süleyman Nesip. 'Dekadanlar'. *Tercüman-ı Hakikat* nr. 5740-5742 (23–25 April 1897).

Sweetser, Eve. *From Etymology to Pragmatics: Metaphorical and Cultural Aspects of Semantic Structure*. Cambridge: Cambridge University Press, 1990.

Tahir Gürçağlar, Şehnaz. *The Politics and Poetics of Translation in Turkey, 1923–1960*. Amsterdam – New York: Rodopi, 2008.

Tanpınar, Ahmet Hamdi. *XIX. Asır Türk Edebiyatı Tarihi*. Istanbul: İbrahim Horoz Basımevi, 1956.

Tanpınar, Ahmet Hamdi. *Edebiyat Üzerine Makaleler*. Istanbul: Dergah Yayınları, 1998.

Tepedelenlizade Hüseyin Kamil. 'Mehmet Celal Beyefendiye Cevap'. *Resimli Gazete* nr. 26 (May 6 1897).

Türesay, Özgür. 'L'Empire ottoman sous le prisme des études postcoloniales. À propos d'un tournant historiographique récent'. *Revue d'histoire moderne et contemporaine* 60.2 (2013): 127–45.

Tymoczko, Maria. *Enlarging Translation, Empowering Translators*. New York: Routledge, 2011.

Tymoczko, Maria. 'Cultural Hegemony and the Erosion of Translation Communities.' In Behdad, Ali and D. Thomas (eds). *A Companion to Comparative Literature*. Hoboken, NJ: John Wiley & Sons, 2011.

Tziovas, Dimitris. *The Other Self, Selfhood and Society in Modern Greek Fiction*. Lanham: Lexington Books, 2003. 55–82.

Uslu, Mehmet Fatih and Fatih Altuğ (eds). *Tanzimat ve Edebiyat: Osmanlı İstanbulu'nda Modern Edebi Kültür*. Istanbul: İş Bankası Yayınları, 2014.

Uşaklıgil, Halit Ziya. *Kırk Yıl*. Istanbul: Özgür Yayınları, 2008.

Uşaklıgil, Halit Ziya. *Mai ve Siyah*. Istanbul: Özgür Yayınları, 2008.

Uşaklıgil, Halit Ziya. *Hikâye*. Istanbul: Özgür Yayınları, 2012.

Uşaklıgil, Halit Ziya. *Sanata Dair*. Istanbul: Özgür Yayınları, 2014.

Uyanık, Seda. *Osmanlı Bilim Kurgusu: Fenni Edebiyat: Osmanlı-Türk Anlatılarında Bilime Yönelişin Mantığı ve Gelecek Tasarıları*. Istanbul: İletişim, 2013.

Vartan Paşa. Akabi Hikayesi: İlk Türkçe Roman (1851). Edited by Andreas Tietze. Istanbul: Eren Yayıncılık, 1991.

Venutti, Lawrence. *The Scandals of Translation: Towards an Ethics of Difference*. London: Routedge, 2006.

Venutti, Lawrence. 'Translation, Community, Utopia'. In Venuti, Lawrence (ed.). *The Translation Studies Reader*. London: Routledge, 2012.

White, Owen, and J. P. Daughton (eds). *In God's Empire: French Missionaries and the Modern World*. Oxford: Oxford University Press, 2012.

Wigen, Einar. 'Ottoman Concepts of Empire'. *Contributions to the History of Concepts* 8.1 (2013): 44–66.

Yalçınkaya, Alper M. *Learned Patriots: Debating Science, State, and Society in the Nineteenth-Century Ottoman Empire*. Chicago: The University of Chicago Press, 2015.

Yildiz, Yasemin. *Beyond the Mother Tongue: The Postmonolingual Condition*. New York: Fordham University Press, 2012.

Zilfi, Madeline C. *Women and Slavery in the Late Ottoman Empire*. Cambridge: Cambridge University Press, 2010.

Index

Abdülhamid II 2, 22, 118, 123, 126, 128, 130, 194
Abdülaziz 2, 22, 66
Abdülmecid 2, 22
Aethiopica, see Heliodorus
Ahmet Hikmet 28-9
Ahmet İhsan 23
Ahmet Midhat Efendi 5, 8, 9, 12, 23, 25, 26, 27, 28, 29, 193-4
   American Doctors 14, 103-15
   Amiral Bing 202
   Felatun Bey and Rakım Efendi 8, 11, 13, 37-51, 53-63, 67-8, 70-4, 78-82, 158
   Hayal ve Hakikat (*see also* Aliye, Fatma) 21
   Letaif-i Rivayat 14, 85-102, 200
   Müşahedat 29-30
   thoughts on language 19-21
   thoughts on translation 201-3
   Udolf Hısarı 86
Ahmet Rasim 27
Ahmet Reşit 24
Akabi Hikayesi, see Vartanyan, Hovsep
alafranga – alaturka 13, 37-8, 40, 42, 43, 53, 61, 157
Ali Pasha 2, 3, 66-82
Aliye, Fatma (*see also* Ahmet Midhat, *Hayal ve Hakikat*)
al-Shidyāq, Ahmad Faris 168-70
Altneuland, see Hertzl, Theodor
American Doctors, see Ahmet Midhat
Amiral Bing, see Ahmet Midhat
Apocalyptic Times, see Celal Nuri
Araba Sevdası, see Recaizade Mahmut Ekrem
Armenians 22, 23, 73, 80, 133-43, 163-73, 177-91, 193-204
Around the World in Eighty Days, see Verne, Jules
Atala, see Chateaubriand

Atay, Oğuz 32
Austro-Hungarian Empire 162
Avare, L', see Molière
Aventures de Télémaque, Les, see Fénelon, François
Aventures du capitaine Hattéras, Les, see Verne, Jules
Aventures du dernier Abencérage, Les, see Chateaubriand

Balıkçıyan, Hovsep 166-7
Balzac, Honoré de 178, 180, 201
Baronian, Hagop 168
Barthélémy, Jean-Jacques (abbé) 182
Bir Sefil Zevce, see Marush, Hovsep
Birth Pangs of the 9th Century, The, see Tzerents

Cahit, Hüseyin 19
Celal Nuri 15, 147-58
Cenap Şahabettin 27-9
Cervantes, Miguel de 178, 191, 193-4, 201
Chateaubriand, François-René de 137-9
'Classics Debate' 200-2
Colomba, see Mérimée, Prosper
Constitution of 1876 2
conversion (religious) 135-6
Corinne, ou L'Italie, see Staël, Germaine de
Corneille, Pierre 202-3
cosmopolitanism 164-6
Count of Monte Cristo, The, see Dumas, Alexandre

Daudet, Alphonse 86
Decadents' controversy 19-22, 28-9
Defoe, Daniel 181, 185-6
Diable boîteux, Le, see Lesage, Alain-René
Diglossia (linguistic) 163-4
Divan poetry 21, 22, 25, 42, 48-50, 196

Draper, John William 108
Dumas, Alexandre 87, 178, 180–6

Edebiyat-ı Cedide movement 30–3
Egypt 1, 118
Emile, see Rousseau, Jean-Jacques
Erckmann-Chatrian 178

Fatma Aliye 21
Fecr-i Ati movement 32
Felatun Bey and Rakım Efendi, see Ahmet Midhat
Fénelon, François 181–2, 184–6
Feuillet, Octave 193, 207
Féval, Paul 180
Filles de plâtre, Les, see Montépin, Xavier de
First World War 2, 16, 148–58
Flaubert, Gustave 178, 180, 193
Florian, Jean-Pierre Claris de 182

Gil Blas de Santillane, see Lesage, Alain-René
Gökalp, Ziya 31
Great Powers 1, 3, 127
Greek Ottomans 22, 177–91, 193–204
Gülhane Imperial Decree 2, 165, 181
Gulliver's Travels, see Swift, Jonathan
Gülunya Yahut Kendi Görünmeyerek Herkesi Gören Kız, see Tilkiyan, Vichen

Halit Ziya 23–4, 28–30, 32
Hatt-i Hümayun 2
Hayal ve Hakikat, see Fatma Aliye
Heliodorus 186
Hertzl, Theodor 186
Hikaye, see Halit Ziya
Hispania and Jerusalem, see Philippson, Ludwig
Honourable Beggars, see Baronian, Hagop
Hüseyin Cahit 19
Hugo, Victor 31, 193

İbrahim Şinasi 168
İntibah, see Namık Kemal
Iran 1

Jadid movement 1
Journal des débats 182

Kanun-u Esasi 133–4
karamanlidika (Greek-scripted Ottoman-Turkish) 163–4, 167, 169, 172, 186
Karnig, Gülunya ve Dikran'ın Dehşetli Vefatli Hikayesi, see Balıkçıyan, Hovsep
Kasap, Teodor 194, 199, 201
Kırık Hayatlar, see Halit Ziya
Kock, Paul de 193–4, 201

La Fontaine, Jean de 182
Ladino 177–91, 193–204
Le Figaro 106
Le secrétaire des amants 42
Leg over Leg, see al-Shidyāq, Ahmad Faris
Lélia, see Sand, George
Les Bourgraves, see Hugo, Victor
Lesage, Alain-René 185, 188
Letaif-i Rivayat, see Ahmet Midhat Efendi

Mai ve Siyah, see Halit Ziya
Matthias Sandorf, see Verne, Jules
Marush, Hovsep 166–7
Mary, Jules 180
Maupassant, Guy de 86
Mehmed II, Sultan 124, 149
Mekhitarists (religious order) 23, 164
mekteb, medrese schools 104
Mérimée, Prosper 184
Michon, Oscar 106
Micromégas, see Voltaire
Ministry of Public Education, Ottoman 22
Misailidis, Evangelinos 167, 188
Misérables, Les, see Hugo, Victor
Mizan (journal) 118
Mizanci Murad, Mehmed 15, 117–31
Molière 182, 194, 199
Montépin, Xavier de 180, 184, 186–7, 193, 201
Münif Pasha 185
Müşahedat, see Ahmet Midhat
Mysteries of Paris, The, see Sue, Eugène
Mysteries of Udolpho, see Radcliffe, Anne

al-*Nahda* 1
Namık Kemal 9, 26
Naum's Theatre 73
Nizam-i Cedid, Ottoman 2
Nuri, Celal, *see* Celal Nuri

Odian, Yervant 188
Ohnet, Georges 201
Ottoman constitution 2, 137
Our Women, see Celal Nuri

Painter, The, see Grigorios Paleologos
Paleologos, Grigorios 10, 167, 188
Perrault, Charles 182
Philippson, Ludwig 186
Pigault-Lebrun 178
Pinti Hamit, see Teodor Kasap
Ponson du Terrail, Pierre-Alexis 180
Prostitute Merchant, The, see Celal Nuri

Racine, Jean 182, 203
Radcliffe, Ann 86
Recaizade Mahmut Ekrem 21, 22, 23, 26, 38–44, 170, 172
René, see Chateaubriand
Reşat Fevzi 32
Richebourg, Emile 180
Riza Pasha 133–4
Robinson Crusoe, see Defoe, Daniel
Rousseau, Jean-Jacques 182, 185
rüşdiye 23
Russo-Turkish Wars 2, 130

Şair Evlenmesi, see İbrahim Şinasi
Sand, George 181–2
science fiction 105–6
Scott, Sir Walter 178
Selim III, Sultan 2
Şehir Mektupları, see Ahmet Rasim
Şemsettin Sami 9, 167–8
Servet-i Fünun (journal) 19–32, 203
Servet-i Fünun (journal) 12, 19–34
Şeyh Galib 29
Shishmanian, Hovsep 168
Simone et Marie, see Montépin, Xavier de
Şinasi, İbrahim 168
Staël, Germaine de 181
Stendhal 178, 180, 201
Sue, Eugène 87, 178, 180–4, 186–7, 193–4, 201
Süleyman Nesip 27
Sururi 20
Swift, Jonathan 185

Taaşşuk-u Tal'at ve Fitnat, see Şemsettin Sami
Talim-i Edebiyat, see Recaizade Mahmut Ekrem
Tanpınar, Ahmet Hamdi 30, 32, 126, 177–9, 190, 193–4, 196, 201–2
Tercüman-i Hakikat (journal) 85, 106
Tepedelenlizade Hüseyin Kamil 28
Tevfik Fikret 31, 193
Thoros of Levon, see Tzerents
Three Musketeers, The, see Dumas, Alexandre
Tilkiyan, Vichen 167
translation
  across Ottoman communities 188
  ethics of 69–71
  intralingual 196
  reform as 10, 54–5, 60–3
  as self-fashioning 38–43
  terminology of 189–90, 200
  untranslatability 28, 171–3
  of Western novels 87, 106, 110, 164, 177–87, 199
Turfanda mı yoksa Turfa mı?, see Mizancı Murad, Mehmed
Tutunamayanlar, see Atay, Oğuz 27
Tzerents 168

Udolf Hısarı, see Ahmet Midhat

Vartan Pasha, *see* Vartanyan, Hovsep
Vartanyan, Hovsep 9, 15, 134–43, 166, 172
Verlaine, Paul 26–7
Verne, Jules 106, 110, 179–80, 184–6, 201
Voltaire 182, 184, 186, 203

Wandering Jew, The, see Sue, Eugène

Young Turk Revolution 2, 194

Zadig, see Voltaire
Ziya Pasha 167
Zola, Emile 20, 26, 29, 178, 179, 193, 194

www.ingramcontent.com/pod-product-compliance
Lightning Source LLC
Chambersburg PA
CBHW072232290426
44111CB00012B/2062